Personal Finance
for Musicians

Other Books by Bobby Borg

Introduction to Music Publishing for Musicians: Business and Creative Perspectives for the New Music Industry (2021), by Bobby Borg and Michael Eames

Music Marketing for the DIY Musician: Creating and Executing a Plan of Attack on a Low Budget, second edition (2020), by Bobby Borg

Business Basics for Musicians: The Complete Handbook from Start to Success, second edition (2020), by Bobby Borg

Personal Finance for Musicians

Bobby Borg and Britt Hastey

ROWMAN & LITTLEFIELD
Lanham • Boulder • New York • London

Published by Rowman & Littlefield
An imprint of The Rowman & Littlefield Publishing Group, Inc.
4501 Forbes Boulevard, Suite 200, Lanham, Maryland 20706
www.rowman.com

86-90 Paul Street, London EC2A 4NE

Copyright © 2022 by Bobby Borg

All rights reserved. No part of this book may be reproduced in any form or by any electronic or mechanical means, including information storage and retrieval systems, without written permission from the publisher, except by a reviewer who may quote passages in a review.

British Library Cataloguing in Publication Information Available

Library of Congress Cataloging-in-Publication Data on File

ISBN 978-1-5381-6329-0 (cloth : alk. Paper)
ISBN 978-1-5381-6330-6 (pbk. : alk. Paper)
ISBN 978-1-5381-6331-3 (electronic)

Contents

Preface ix

Acknowledgments xi

PART 1. GETTING STARTED

1 So, What's Personal Finance All About? 2

2 Eleven Barriers to Personal Finance and
How to Overcome Them 10

PART 2. INCOME

3 Fifteen Types of Money that Independent Artists Can Make 18

4 Twenty Money-Making Ideas and Side Hustles for Musicians 28

PART 3. SAVINGS

5 Ten Tips for Spending Less and Saving More 38

PART 4. ACCOUNTING

6 Get Your Financial and Business Records in Order:
   Twenty-Four Tips — 48

7 Three Accounting Documents to Examine Your
   Financial Health — 57

PART 5. BANKING

8 Twenty-Four Reasons to Use a Bank — 66

9 Major Pros and Cons of Using an Online Bank — 76

PART 6. CREDIT AND DEBT

10 Ten Steps To Building "Rock" Solid Credit — 84

11 Monitor Your Credit Via Reports and Scores: Nine Steps — 90

12 Twenty Ways to Protect Yourself from Identity Theft
    and Fraud — 96

13 Ten Tips to Getting (and Staying) Out of Debt — 105

PART 7. RETIREMENT PLANNING

14 Twenty-Six Questions About Retirement
    Planning for Musicians — 114

15 The Seven Most Common Retirement Accounts
    (and Then Some) — 125

PART 8. INVESTING

16 One Hundred Finance and Investment Terms
    Musicians Should Know — 134

17	Seven-Point Checklist to Investing and Building Wealth	145
18	Nine Must-Know Quotes on Money, Investing, and More	156
19	Finding Experts to Provide Smart Financial Guidance: Ten Tips	165
20	Seven Investment Apps You Might Consider	173

PART 9. INSURANCE

21	Ten Types of Insurance You May Need in Your Twenties	180

PART 10. TAXES

22	Eleven Frequently Asked Questions about Filing Income Taxes	190
23	Six Steps to Organizing Your Tax Expense Receipts (and More)	199
24	How to Find a Tax Accountant to Do Your Returns: Ten Tips	206

PART 11. ESTATE ISSUES

25	Eight Ways to Prepare for the End (Depressing but Important)	214

PART 12. WRAP PARTY

26	Twelve Key Takeaways of Personal Finance for Musicians	224
Index		235
About the Authors		249

Preface

Many young musicians will admit they know little about personal finance. They have trouble budgeting their side-gig money earned from their part-time jobs, managing excessive credit card debt incurred from purchasing studio equipment they cannot afford, and trading on numerous investment apps that have them risking grandma's birthday card money.

Even worse, should they get lucky enough to blow up and experience career success, they typically go on spending sprees only to end up completely broke ten years later. You don't want this to happen to you, right? This is why a simple and easy-to-read personal finance book written specifically for musicians is so vital to building your career success and wealth.

Written by a thirty-year expert in the music business together with a twenty-five-year expert in personal finance and business management, *Personal Finance for Musicians* provides a brief overview of everything you should have learned in high school but didn't. Organized within the framework of twelve critical parts, you'll learn the very basics of:

1. *Getting Started:* To get you up to speed on personal finance
2. *Income:* To help you generate more money
3. *Savings:* To encourage you to save more and spend less
4. *Accounting:* To track finances more efficiently
5. *Banking:* To safeguard your money and utilize useful services
6. *Credit and Debt:* To build credibility and get out of debt
7. *Retirement Planning:* To build a "fuck you freedom fund" for the future

8. ***Investing:*** To make your money grow and build your fortune
9. ***Insurance:*** To cover your ass and your assets
10. ***Taxes:*** To reduce your tax liability to Uncle Sam
11. ***Estate Planning:*** To ensure your legacy continues successfully, and . . .
12. ***Wrap Party:*** To provide you with key takeaways for financial success

Each part includes actionable steps within short chapters that can be read in any order.

Composed in plain English with no jargon but often funny text, it's the perfect book for any musician who wants to get on the right track to financial health without feeling intimidated, or even worse—bored. We are extremely excited to be part of your financial journey. So, what do you say? Turn to any chapter or start from the beginning. Now, let's get this party started!

Note: Because everyone's personal financial situation differs, it is advised that you seek out a certified financial professional who can evaluate your individual situation and advise you appropriately. Just be sure to get recommendations from people you trust.

Acknowledgments

We would like to thank all of the students, clients, and educational institutions around the world who will read our work, watch our videos, and/or consult with us over the coming decades.

A big thanks to Michael Tan and all at Rowman & Littlefield for their dedication to this project.

Bobby would like to personally thank his father and mother, who set good examples of what responsible personal finance is all about, as well as the many legendary financial gurus who served as his inspiration.

Britt would like to personally thank his father and mother, who were also good examples of sound personal finance, his sister, and his girlfriend, for all of her support and understanding.

I

GETTING STARTED

The secret of getting ahead, is getting started.

—Mark Twain

1

So, What Is Personal Finance All About?

When many musicians think about personal finance they think about money.

While personal finance is indeed money-centric, there is more to it than meets the eye.

What follows is a brief overview of personal finance with hopes that we'll inspire you to learn more. This information can mean the difference between a bright future as a music artist and a dismal one, so pay close attention to every detail.

Are you ready to do this? Okay, let's rock!

1. INCOME

Perhaps the best way to start a discussion about personal finance is to talk about income and something called human capital—the economic value of an individual's abilities to earn money.

For most twenty-year-olds, the ability to generate a paycheck for fifty years at a stable job, invest it, and earn interest (on top of interest), will serve as one of the biggest factors toward achieving financial success than any one single investment.

But for musicians, who can easily risk twelve to fifteen years of their best income-generating years before making any substantial money (if they ever make any money at all), establishing alternate revenue streams while working toward "the big dream" is the needed course of action.

Whether it's writing for film and TV, recording other artists, or taking on other side hustles, you'll not only be more equipped to go the long haul but also able to pay your bills, build savings, and invest a little money too. It's not about falling back but, rather, hedging the risk of fame more wisely to ensure that you don't end up becoming a broke, couch-surfing thirty-five-year-old.

So, don't forget it, personal finance really does start with thinking practically about income and human capital. As Kanye West said, "Money isn't everything, but not having it is."

2. SAVINGS

While personal finance has a great deal to do with income and human capital, it's also about spending less and saving more. We're not talking about completely depriving yourself of having fun but, rather, adapting a more practical strategy for thinking about your hard-earned money.

Methods to cut back might include:

- cooking at home instead of going to fancy restaurants;
- chugging a few six packs in your studio with friends rather than ringing up a huge bar tab; or . . .
- re-directing a portion of your income directly into your investment accounts rather than cashing your checks and spending your money on every music festival known to man.

Look, it's not what you specifically cut back on, but the fact that you are trimming expenses and saving money wherever you can. It's just a matter of making small sacrifices and living more practically so that you can get your financial shit together and secure your future.

So, while your favorite artists like Jay-Z might sing about "Gucci this, and Prada that," know that he also frequently lectures and writes about financial responsibility. Make no mistake, savings is a huge part of what personal finance is all about.

3. ACCOUNTING

Dovetailing nicely with savings, accounting is yet another important part of personal finance.

As Snoop Dogg once rapped, "With my mind on my money and my money on my mind," accounting involves taking inventory of every dollar you have so you know where you stand.

There are three major accounting documents that you need to know about:

1. **Net Worth Statement:** A net worth statement presents a snapshot of your total wealth, which is essentially everything you own (like recording gear, guitars, and money in your savings), minus everything you owe (like school loans, credit card debt, and car loans). This information serves as the foundation for your entire financial plan and helps to determine what you must do to reach your objectives.
2. **Cash Flow Analysis:** A cash flow analysis tells you how much money you'll have available each month, which is basically calculated by taking all of the money you make (from doing studio sessions, teaching music lessons, playing gigs, etc.), and subtracting all that you spend (like monthly rent, groceries, and gas). Cash flow statements are important because they help you to determine whether you can fulfill your debt obligations. And finally . . .
3. **Personal Budget:** A personal budget presents a complete spending plan for every dollar, which is done by balancing your inflowing cash with outflowing cash. Monitoring a personal budget regularly is important since it helps you to stay on point with your spending habits.

So, as you can see, accounting is a major part of what personal finance is all about.

4. BANKING

Moving away from accounting, it's difficult to talk about finance without talking about banking.

While banks tend to have bad reputations for paying crappy interest rates on your money, or for charging huge fees for basic services, the truth is that banks provide a number of benefits:

1. When receiving money from an employer, you are typically going to get paid by check or direct deposit and then access it when you're out on the road through a national network of ATMs—which will require the use of a bank.

2. Should you ever get ahold of a lot of cash and want to keep it safe from the threat of theft and/or fire, you are typically going to keep it with an institution that can provide federal deposit insurance and a variety of "money making" investment products too, which again, are all things that big banks can offer you. And finally . . .
3. Should you need a line of credit via a credit card to purchase a new guitar, or need a personal loan to build your new recording studio, you'll likely utilize a bank.

Look, whether you like the reputation of banks or not, they are a big part of what personal finance is all about. What we touched on here is just the tip of what they have to offer.

5. CREDIT AND DEBT

Transitioning nicely from banks, no discussion on personal finance would be complete without a mention of credit and debt. There are essentially three areas of importance as follows:

1. **Building Credit:** Credit in general is short for the word credibility. Whether you are renting a new apartment, buying a car, or getting a mortgage, lenders are going to want to know that you can repay that debt on time. The more you use credit, the more credible to creditors you become.
2. **Managing Debt:** While using credit surely has its advantages, it also has its disadvantages. People have a tendency to assume too much debt and dig themselves into an endless hole of interest payments. So, a major part of personal finance is managing all of your debts so that you can get—and stay—completely debt free.
3. **Protecting Your Credit from Fraud:** Finally, personal finance is also about protecting your credit from fraudulent activity. The last thing you want is for people to use your credit to make illegal purchases and thus screw up your personal credit score. So, understanding credit monitoring organizations like TransUnion, Equifax, and Experian is also a very important part of personal finance.

6. RETIREMENT PLANNING

Now that you understand the importance of credit and debt, it's time to look into your future and briefly discuss retirement planning, since it serves an important part of personal finance.

While many musicians often confuse retirement to mean the thing that old people do when they are no longer able or willing to work, retirement is really about so much more.

Retirement is all about freedom—freedom from worrying about finances, freedom from taking gigs that you don't really want to play, and the freedom to start building that recording studio in your backyard that you always dreamed about.

Whatever retirement means to you, know that there are a number of "tax-advantaged" retirement accounts supported by our great country that incentivize you to save and invest in your future. Let's face it, it does no good to have a country full of helpless older folks, right?

While there are enough retirement accounts with crazy buzz words to make your head spin including IRAs, Roth IRAs, and 401(k)s, just remember that understanding the basics of these plans is a big part of personal finance.

So, as Kendrick Lamar sums it all up, "Invest in your future!" You'll be glad you did!

7. INVESTING

Moving on from retirement planning, investing is also crucial to personal finance in that it helps you to use the assets you have today to build a brighter life for tomorrow.

Next to retirement planning, buying a house, saving for college, getting an automobile, and vacationing rank as the biggest reasons why people invest their money to grow.

Types of investments include stocks, bonds, index funds, exchange traded funds, crypto currencies, options, gold, and more. While these investments are all different and a book chapter in and of themselves, just remember, for now, that the type of investments you choose depends on:

- **Goals:** What you want to achieve
- **Time Horizon:** How long you have to achieve your objectives, and . . .
- **Risk Tolerance:** Your ability to handle investment loss

Now, important investment strategies to increase your chances of success include:

- **Diversification:** Buying a variety of investments in different industries and geographic regions
- **Cost Avoidance:** Navigating around fees associated with money managers and certain funds, and . . .
- **Patience:** Hanging in for the long haul and not expecting to get rich overnight

So, as you can see, there is more to investing that meets the eye. Investing is not some game you play on a smart phone app. It involves your real, hard-earned money that you can't afford to just throw away in a few clicks.

So, if you really want to understand personal finance, it's extremely important that you study the basics of investing.

8. INSURANCE

A territory that many musicians would never think is an important part of personal finance is insurance. While many musicians just think of insurance as a bothersome monthly expense, it is really more like a life-saver that can save you millions.

Most people already have auto and medical insurance. But there's also rental, pet, and equipment insurance, which all musicians could use. There is also home, life, and long-term care insurance, too, which are things that you may need to consider down the road.

Not convinced insurance is for you? One night after a gig in New York City, I (this is Bobby) was crossing the street near my hotel and got hit by a truck. To make a long story short, without having medical and disability insurance, I would have had to pay hundreds of thousands in hospital bills, rehab, and mounting personal bills while I couldn't work. Said another way, because I shifted this unforeseen risk to an insurer, they assumed most of my responsibility.

It's not about being paranoid! We live in an uncertain world. And the good news about insurance is that it can take some of the worry away from knowing that if the shit hits the fan, you are not going to be fully responsible and robbed of all of your hard-earned music money.

9. TAXES

Since we briefly mentioned taxes in point six above when discussing retirement, it's time that we single them out here and mention their importance to the world of personal finance. As Benjamin Franklin once said, "Nothing is certain except death and taxes." And taxes are going to cost you!

While most people detest paying taxes, be clear that they help our world go round. Should you ever get hit by a truck when out on the road (like in our earlier story), your taxes will pay for the paramedics to show up. Your taxes also pay to pave the roads and bridges that you will use while on your nationwide concert tour, and so much more.

But taxes, especially income taxes, will cost the average person about 34 percent of their income (or $525,000) over the course of their lifetime. And can you imagine what you'll pay in taxes if you hit it big and make some really substantial money? This is nothing to sneeze at.

This is why a proper personal finance education will always include the importance of finding legal methods to reduce your tax liability. At the very least, this may include information on finding and hiring a great tax preparer who can guide you through the tax laws.

So, you see, taxes are a very complex part of personal finance and are certainly nothing that you should take lightly. Rapper NAS ended up owing the government more than six million dollars in back taxes due to years of improper tax filings. Don't let this happen to you, folks!

10. ESTATE PLANNING

Finally, our last topic is estate planning, which is also extremely important to the topic of personal finance. Estate planning is primarily about how your estate will transfer over after your death.

Estate planning includes things like:

- making a will to establish directions about how your assets will be distributed,
- establishing a trust to give a trustee the authority to hold and disburse assets over time, and
- setting up funeral arrangements to detail how your remains will be disposed of.

Though estate planning literally gives you the last and final word, many famous musicians fail to have proper estate plans.

Would you believe Prince died without a will? Yup, it's true. Minus a will, an estate typically flows to a spouse, or to the kids if there is no spouse, or relatives if there are no kids. So, after Prince's death, all types of characters came out of the woodwork demanding a piece of his estate. What a mess! You definitely do not want this to happen to your rock star fortune.

Sorry folks, no one likes to talk about the end, but as you already learned from Benjamin Franklin's quote above, the only other thing in life that is certain besides taxes, is death.

So, in closing, now that you have a better idea of what personal finance is all about, we hope you're inspired to dig deeper and learn so much more. While personal finance is not always exciting and sexy, it can mean the difference between your financial success and failure.

2

Eleven Barriers to Personal Finance and How to Overcome Them

Many young musicians are the first to admit that they are horrible with basic personal finance skills like balancing a monthly budget, building credit, or tracking personal expenses for taxes.

Even famous musicians—like Xzibit, Lil Kim, and NAS—admit that the serious financial problems they experienced may have been avoided if they handled their finances more wisely.

From not having access to personal finance education in schools, to thinking it is too time consuming or boring, below is a list of personal finance barriers that may relate to you.

Accepting what's holding you back and overcoming your personal issues will move you closer to creating a brighter future as a professional musician.

1. MY HIGH SCHOOL DIDN'T TEACH PERSONAL FINANCE

The first and biggest barrier to personal finance literacy for musicians is the fact that personal finance classes were not offered to them during their formative high school years.

Many schools don't have the specialized teachers needed to cover the subject or believe that it is important since it's not covered on the SAT and ACT standardized tests.

While we agree you may have been robbed of vital financial information, there is no reason you can't take advantage of the numerous resources that are currently available.

For instance, UCLA Extension offers a number of online classes in personal finance that you can take from any part of the world. These classes are taught by people who have worked in the field for many years and can offer you honest advice and feedback.

There are also a number of online blogs like Investopedia and NerdWallet that offer some very basic personal finance advice delivered in a concise and easy-to-understand style.

There are even online forums like Bogleheads where you can chat with people about personal finance.

As you see, there is plenty of information out there for you to start building your personal finance chops. Just be careful and choose resources referred by credible people—there are a lot of questionable sources out there, which can actually be more confusing than helpful.

2. I DON'T HAVE ANY MONEY TO MANAGE

Not having any money to invest in stocks, real estate, or other sophisticated things related to personal finance is yet another barrier to personal finance skills for musicians. They figure financial literacy can be put off till the day they hit it big.

But just remember that there is so much more to personal finance than investing money. Personal finance deals with things like:

1. Budgeting the pennies you have today so that you have more of them at the end of the month;
2. Understanding the difference between wants and needs so that you keep your spending in check while maintaining your credit; and
3. Filing your taxes correctly so that you don't pay more money to Uncle Sam than necessary.

So, yes, you may not have a lot of money right now to invest, but you can start learning personal finance basics today. This will help you better manage your day-to-day life and avoid stupid moves in the future as you establish your career and earn more money. Okay? Good!

3. I CAN JUST FAKE IT TILL I MAKE IT

Faking financial prowess until you one day make it as a successful musician is one of the most ridiculous excuses we've ever heard for financial illiteracy.

I (this is Bobby talking) once knew a model/actress whose philosophy about money was that if you act and live like you have a lot of money today, then the universe will provide you with a lot of money tomorrow. She called this the "fake it till you make it" philosophy.

While I agree with the power of positive affirmations, I should also add that my model/actress friend was $90,000 in credit card debt with Barney's of New York and one step away from bankruptcy. Let's just say that things didn't really end well for my model/actress friend.

Look, we totally get that in the music and entertainment business you have to present the look of grandeur to your fans to present a certain image (here you are dancing by the pool in front of the mansion, rapping on the cliffs of Malibu with your Hell-Cats doing doughnuts behind you, and sporting that new $7,000 purse from Louis Vuitton). So awesome!

But wake up, peeps! Truly smart and educated musicians aren't racking up credit card debt and spending themselves into bankruptcy. Instead, they use essential personal finance skills to live within their budgets by seeking out sponsorship deals, asking for loaner equipment from local businesses, and even asking the right people for special favors.

So "faking it till you make it" is not a substitute for financial literacy. There is a place for personal finance in everybody's life, especially young musicians (and models) on the rise.

4. I HAVE ENOUGH ANXIETY AS IT IS

While anxiety related to financial issues like school debt, paying monthly bills, and saving for the future is 100 percent legitimate, it shouldn't serve as a major barrier to capitalizing on your personal financial education.

You see, emotions and human behavior are a subset of what personal finance is all about. It's called behavioral finance.

Behavioral finance is the study of how human emotions affect your financial decisions (or indecisions). It deals with why people act on emotions rather than facts, how people tend to act against their best interests, and so much more.

So, while personal finance may initially cause you some anxiety on the surface, know that learning about these anxieties can help you to overcome your fears and make you financially smarter. To be sure, avoiding personal finance is only going to make your anxiety much worse.

5. IT ALL SOUNDS TOO COMPLICATED TO DEAL WITH

While we agree that the media can spit out complicated things like, "the "S&P 500 is up 7 percent," and, "the Dow slid 200 points," this shouldn't be a barrier to your personal finance education. There are a lot of credible resources that break down the basics so that it sticks. Take what you're reading right now, for example—it's not too scary, is it?

To overcome your fear, we suggest that you also consider reading a number of classic books on personal finance that are both quick and light reads. Try *The Wealthy Barber* and *The Richest Man in Babylon* for starters. What's unique about these books is that they are delivered in a storytelling platform that we think you'll find less intimidating and leave you wanting more.

6. I DON'T HAVE ANY TIME FOR PERSONAL FINANCE

Another common excuse for why musicians lack in personal finance skills is because they believe it will take up a lot of time that they really don't have. After all, it is hard enough to write and record new songs, schedule all of your social media posts, and try to get played on Spotify playlists.

Well, it's true that personal finance will take up some of your time, but it is definitely something that is doable and that you can schedule into your life's routine.

For instance, just taking an hour to create a budget and then saving your daily expense receipts is a huge step in the right direction. Then, at the end of the month, you can take another hour to add up your actual expenses against your budgeted expenses to see where you stand. If you are a little bit off your target budget, you can make adjustments and try again the next month. Each month you'll get better and better at running that little ol' business of "you."

So, as you can see, personal finance doesn't have to be about sitting at a desk counting pennies all day like the miserable Scrooge character in Charles Dickens's classic tale. It could take no more than adding a few hours—once per month—to your life's schedule and changing a few of your daily habits. So why not start scheduling personal finance into your life today?

7. IT DOESN'T RUN IN MY FAMILY'S BLOOD

Some musicians blame their lack of personal finance education (and financial interest) on their families, stating that it is something that just doesn't run in their blood.

While we agree that children can inherit certain talents and skills from their parents (like having an analytic mind, possessing certain creative skills, and having an entrepreneurial spirit), learning how to handle your personal finances more responsibly does not have to be something that your family practiced successfully before you.

Contrarily, it could be your parents' lack of interest in personal finance that serves as your true inspiration. Do you know how many millionaires (and even billionaires) there are in the United States who came from complete poverty? Here's a short list: Dolly Parton, Jay-Z, Oprah Winfrey, Ralph Lauren, Drake, and many more.

So, make no mistake folks, the apple *can* fall far from the tree if you shake the branch hard enough. Saying that personal finance does not run in your family is a BS excuse, and your parents will likely be the first people to agree—whether they are financially successful or not!

8. THERE'S PLENTY OF TIME TO GET MY SHIT TOGETHER

Using time as a barrier to getting your financial shit together is also completely misguided and foolish. We get that you feel things like retirement, cutting coupons, and saving money is only for old folks in rocking chairs. But take note—you could not be more wrong. The best time to start worrying about personal finance is right now.

By getting started in personal finance today, you have the golden opportunity to build your credit scores, save your money for your future, and watch your invested money grow in value over the next fifty years (due to the power of compounding interest: interest on interest).

Furthermore, you have the opportunity to aggressively ride the inevitable ups and downs of the stock market for several decades and—as a result—to statistically end up with some really big returns. In fact, if you make all the right moves now, you could set yourself up nicely as a musician who doesn't have to worry about changing musical trends or the success of your next record.

But if you continue to hold the same attitude and wait "to get your shit together" (like most musicians—and Americans), you'll only be playing catch-up in your later years. And while it is never too late to start thinking about personal finance, you will only look back on your youth and realize the wonderful opportunity of time you ultimately let slip right through your fingers.

So yes, you do have all the time to get your shit together, but only if you start today!

9. I'M GONNA HIT THE JACKPOT ONE DAY!

Another common barrier to personal finance literacy for musicians is their egos and their true belief that they are going to hit the jackpot one day and everything will be fine.

Just look at artists like Lil Nas X. He was literally broke, making beats out of his sister's apartment one day, and breaking streaming charts and signing big record deals the next. Hey, if it could happen to him, it could happen to you to, right?

Well, while "insta-famous" artists do seem to be popping up all over the place, the truth is that they still represent a small percentage of all the artists out there like you, who are trying to make it big. This is not meant to crush your dreams of instant success but, rather, to inject you with a little sense of reality and the fact that there is a place for personal finance education in everyone's life—even your own.

Make no mistake, it's okay to dream big, but it's so much better to dream wisely.

10. MONEY IS GONNA KEEP ON COMING IN FOREVER

Yet another major barrier to personal finance for musicians is the belief that once they hit it big, the money will keep coming in for the rest of their lives. In other words, they'll be on a "non-stop money train." But this is typically the furthest thing from the truth.

Take Xzibit for example. Xzibit was a successful rapper with a platinum record, two gold albums, and a gig as the host of a popular MTV show called *Pimp My Ride*. This meant, of course, that he also lived the life of a rap star with the awesome mansions, cars, and jewelry.

But after *Pimp My Ride* was canceled and his music career fizzled out, Xzibit's income (or lack thereof) could no longer support his lifestyle, and he found himself in deep trouble. To make matters worse, he also owed back taxes to the IRS, which he couldn't afford to pay. Sucks!

Rapper Lil' Kim is another example. Lil' Kim was one of the first super successful female rappers—long before Cardi B and Nicki Minaj. With her success, of course, also came the expensive lifestyle—it was "all about the Benjamins" for Lil' Kim and she even rapped about this. But when Lil' Kim's career fizzled out, she found herself behind on mansion payments and owing millions in back taxes to the IRS. Yikes!

So, as you can see, the money does not keep on coming in for many successful artists. But with wise financial planning and good money habits, you could certainly live out the rest of your years comfortably.

11. I PLAN TO HIRE SOMEONE TO DO IT WHEN I GET SUCCESSFUL

Finally, many musicians lack personal finance skills because finance (and other important business issues) is just something that they plan to outsource to a professional team when they make it big. While it's true that a smart strategy for success is to surround yourself with strong people who can make up for weaknesses, this doesn't always turn out the way you want it to.

Rapper NAS found himself in a debt of $6.5 million in taxes to the IRS. He indeed had a professional team to look after his finances, but the business manager thought the accountant was handling the taxes, and the accountant thought the business manager was handling the taxes.

Had NAS acquired even just a little knowledge about personal finance, and he checked in once in a while just to make sure that everyone was doing what they were supposed to, then he would have been far better off than he is today. Remember, it's up to you to watch your own ass.

So as you can see, folks, there's really no excuse not to learn the basics of personal finance, no matter your personal situation, age, or philosophy on life. By reading a few books, taking a few classes, and just forming smart habits about how you handle your money, you can significantly improve your chances for securing a bright and long-term financial future.

So, stop making excuses, and get busy developing your finance skills today. Peace!

2

INCOME

The value of your human capital over the next forty years will likely dwarf any other asset you own.

—Jonathan Clements, author of
How to Think About Money

3

Fifteen Types of Money that Independent Artists Can Make

Money makes the world go round. It pays bills so you can function sanely as a musician, covers vital insurance to protect your personal assets, and builds savings and investment accounts to secure your financial future. It also helps you to have some fun and enjoy your life, too.

While there are many factors that ultimately determine the kinds of money that musicians will make in their careers, below are fifteen types of income that are related, specially, to what an independent artist (who owns his or her songs, masters, merchandising, etc.) can earn in his or her career.

Just be clear that these monies trickle into an artist's life rather slowly early on, but they can also snowball into tremendous streams of income as an artist builds his or her profile. Enjoy!

1. MECHANICAL ROYALTIES

Mechanical royalties are licensing fees that you earn when your songs are copied or reproduced. For instance, when your songs are streamed from interactive digital service providers like Spotify, a copy of your song is made on the computer cache of the consumer interacting with Spotify, and a mechanical royalty is generated.

Or, in another instance, when your songs are licensed by an outside record company for release on an album in music stores across the country, a copy of your songs is made on vinyl and CD and a mechanical may be paid.

FIFTEEN TYPES OF MONEY THAT INDEPENDENT ARTISTS CAN MAKE

The amount in mechanical royalties generated from interactive digital service providers is difficult to nail down, but it is based on a percentage of the digital service provider's revenue, which ultimately amounts to a fraction of a penny per stream.

The amount in mechanicals from record company licenses for CD and vinyl is more easily defined at 9.1 cents per song (per record made and distributed), but more typically at 6.8 cents per song sold after the record company reduces the rate (usually by 25 percent) it must pay.

Just don't expect much from mechanical royalties in the beginning of your career. But if you score a big hit song and your career gains traction, mechanicals can add up quickly. Rates subject to change.

2. PERFORMANCE ROYALTIES

Performance royalties are licensing fees that you earn when your songs are performed publicly by a variety of different music users.

Performance royalties may be earned when your songs are performed by digital service providers like Spotify, Apple Music, and Tidal, or when they are performed by internet radio stations like SiriusXM or Pandora.

Performance royalties may also be earned when your songs are performed by music users like terrestrial radio stations, television networks, and shopping centers and malls.

The amount in performance royalties generated by music users is also complicated to nail down, but it is generally based on a percentage of the service's revenue and the amount of times your songs are "counted" as being performed or streamed.

In the beginning of your career, the amount you earn in performance royalties may be minimal. However, if your song is a hit and streamed on stations or playlists around the country or regularly broadcasted on a popular television show, you can indeed expect performance royalties to rain down on you from the heavens above.

3. SYNCHRONIZATION FEES

Synchronization fees are monies that you earn when your songs are merged with visual images.

For example, when your songs are used in a film, television show, or a video game, a synchronization fee (or synch fee) must be paid.

A synch fee must also be paid when someone wants to use your song in a music video, such as when someone wants to cover your song or use your music in "user-generated content" they create and post on YouTube.

The amount you can earn in synch fees from a film, television show, or game can range dramatically, from $0 in the beginning of your career to hundreds of thousands of dollars when you're more established.

The amount you can earn from user-generated content in videos is usually based on a percentage of advertising revenue (from 15 to 50 percent), which could add up based on your popularity and the number of people viewing the content.

The cool thing about synchronization in general is that once your music is synched in a TV show, for instance, there is inevitably a "performance," which means that you also get a back-end performance royalty too. It's like double the pleasure and double the fun. All hail to synch.

4. PRINT ROYALTIES

Print royalties are monies that you earn when your songs are used in printed form.

For example, when your songs are used by printers in sheet music and music books like the ones you see at Sam Ash music stores, a print royalty can be earned.

Or, for example, when your songs are used by lyric websites like Genius, a print royalty might also be generated.

The amount in print royalties you earn from sheet music and music books as the author/owner of your songs is typically around $1 and $2.50, respectively.

The amount in print royalties you earn from music websites is typically a percentage (around 50 percent) of the advertising revenue earned from the lyric website.

Since the demand for your music in printed form in the early stages of your career will be low, you should not expect to see much in print monies early on. In fact, even when you hit it big and become a star, print monies will still dwarf the other types of income (discussed above) that you'll make from writing/owning your songs. But hey, every little bit of income is income.

5. MASTER MONEY

Moving away from the money you can make from your songs, master money is the income that you'll make when the actual sound recording you own and/or performed on is sold or streamed.

So, to illustrate, when your vinyl recording is sold in an independent shop like Amoeba Records, you may earn master money.

Or when your master recording is streamed on digital service providers like Spotify or Apple Music, you may also earn master money.

As with the other royalty streams, the exact amount you get in master monies is difficult to nail down because of the many variables that are at play, such as the record's selling price, distributer charges, and so much more. But, for example, if you are a DIY artist who is self-releasing his or her vinyl record for $10 and selling it on consignment from a local record shop, the shop will typically take $5 (50 percent) and give you the rest.

As for the master monies from digital service providers, the amount you'll make is also very difficult to nail down. But generally, it is a percentage of the digital service provider's revenue, which amounts to fractions of a penny per stream.

No matter what you'll make in master monies, you'll typically have to sell a lot of units—and stream even more—for the dollars to add up to being substantial sums for you. But hey, the harder you work and the luckier you get, you just might start making a lot of dough here.

6. MASTER-USE FEES FOR SYNCH

Master-use fees are the money you'll make when the actual sound recording you own and/or performed on is licensed and synched with a variety of visual media.

For example, when your master is licensed in a film, television show, or video game, a master-use fee (or master fee) must be paid.

Or, when someone wants to use your master in a video, such as when a YouTube creator produces user-generated content to post on his or her channel, a master-use fee must also be paid. The amount you can earn in master fees from a film, television show, or game can range dramatically from $0 in the beginning of your career, to even hundreds of thousands of dollars when you're more established. But note that it is typically equal to the synch fee that you would get for being the songwriter. So, if the songwriter gets $10,000, the master owner gets $10,000.

The amount you can earn from user-generated content on a site like YouTube is usually based on a percentage (about 35 percent) of YouTube's advertising revenue, which could certainly add up over time based on the number of views and total watch hours a piece of content receives.

Just in case you're not putting all of the different income streams together, a synch in something like a TV show can generate three different incomes payments: a synch fee for the song, a master fee for the master, and a performance royalty when it is broadcasted. Not bad!

7. NON-INTERACTIVE MASTER PERFORMANCES

Master performances are the monies you'll make when the actual sound recording you own and/or performed on is streamed on non-interactive platforms (a.k.a. internet radio).

For example, when your master streams from platforms like SiriusXM or Pandora, master performances must be paid.

As with many of the other types of digital income discussed above, the exact amount you'll get in master performances is difficult to nail down. However, given that master performances are a relatively new type of income born out of the the Digital Performance Right in Sound Recordings Act of 1995, most master owners are grateful for whatever amount they receive. Note, there is currently no other income that is generated from the performances of masters (including performances on radio), which is something master owners have been fighting for decades. So be sure to stay tuned for updates in this highly contentious area.

8. LIVE PERFORMANCE MONIES

Moving on from master monies discussed above, live performance monies are the income you make when you perform live on stage.

Live performance fees may be earned when you play live in a club, in a theater, or in a large concert venue.

Live performance fees may also be earned when you perform live on stage in alternate venues like colleges and military bases and when you perform live on television shows like *Jimmy Kimmel Live*.

Other incomes associated with live performances, such as VIP package monies (monies generated from fans who will pay extra to meet you backstage or hang out at a backstage BBQ), may also be generated here.

Depending on your level of success, live performance fees can range anywhere from zero to several hundreds of thousands of dollars per night.

Early in your career, the amounts offered might be strictly arbitrary based on your worth in the eyes of a club owner. But as you advance in your career, a guaranteed fee is typically negotiated on the gross potential (i.e., the average ticket price multiplied by the capacity of the venue), *or* on a percentage (80 to 90 percent) of the gross receipts less approved expenses, whichever is greater.

While it's true that it is costly to tour, some of the biggest artists can make millions.

9. MERCHANDISING MONIES

Merchandising monies, which also go hand in hand with live performing and touring, are the income you receive for the sale of merchandise that bears your artist name, logo, and personal image (or any graphic design you create).

Merchandising monies may be earned, for instance, when a T-shirt bearing your band name and logo is sold at a concert venue.

Merchandising monies may also be earned, for instance, when your personal image is sold on the back of a jacket in a retail store.

Finally, merchandising monies may also be earned, for instance, when your logo is sold on a lunch box from an online website.

Depending on your status as an artist, T-shirts typically range in price from $10 to $40, jackets can range from $70 to $125, and lunch boxes can range from $20 to $50. While there are fees for manufacturing, credit card processing, and venue commissions before you get your cut, merchandising monies can certainly add up to very substantial amounts. Big league artists like Madonna have been known to gross $100,000 and more in merchandising sales per night. Cool!

10. SPONSORSHIP MONIES

Sponsorship monies, also related to live performing and touring, are the income you receive when entering into promotional relationships with other company brands.

For example, when you agree to promote an energy drink brand like Monster during one of your concert tours, sponsorship monies may be paid to you.

Or, when you agree to promote an equipment manufacturer like Dean Markley Guitar Strings and perform clinic performances, sponsorship monies may also be paid to you.

Sponsorship monies depend on so many factors, such as your level of success, the terms of the deal, the rights you give the sponsor for advertising purposes, and much more. At first, you might just get free products to use yourself or give out to your fans. But, as your career evolves to superstar status and your face ends up on the side of a Pepsi can for a concert tour, you can probably expect the sponsorships monies to be hundreds of thousands, if not millions.

11. CELEBRITY APPEARANCE FEES

Celebrity appearance fees are the monies you make when promoters and other event organizers hire and book you to make a public appearance.

To illustrate, when a club promoter is promoting a special night in a hot club in Hollywood, California, and he or she asks you to show up to the event and simply make yourself "seen," or to hang out in the DJ booth for a while, a celebrity appearance fee might be paid.

Or, when a restaurant entrepreneur is opening up a new location and wants to attract a hip and cool clientele, and you are asked to show up to the opening night and dine in the restaurant, a celebrity appearance fee might also be paid.

Finally, when a music business convention is organized and you are asked to perform or just come in and be a keynote speaker, celebrity appearance fees might also be paid.

At the beginning of your career, when you are not a bona fide celebrity, don't expect much in celebrity appearance fees (unless, of course, you are indeed a local hero).

But make no mistake, when you eventually make it big in music (and you are going to make it big, right?), celebrity appearance fees can add up to the tens of thousands of dollars, if not into the millions of dollars. Would you believe that actress/model/musician Paris Hilton reportedly takes in from $100k to $500k just to travel to your event and party with you. Wow!

12. RECORDING SESSION FEES

Now moving away from the monies you can make via live events, recording session fees are the monies that you make when you are contracted to go into the recording studio and perform on record.

So, for example, when you are asked by another artist to "guest" perform on his or her record in a recording studio, recording session fees will likely be paid for your services.

Or, when you are asked by a branded company, such as an energy drink or favorite cola brand, to go into the studio and cut an advertisement, then recording session fees will likely be paid for your services.

Depending on the success level of the person or company asking you to record, as well as your professional status, recording session fees are usually based on a minimum payment scale mandated by two unions—the American Federation of Musicians (AFM) and the Screen Actors Guild/American Federation of Television and Radio Artists (SAG/AFTRA).

For example, to record guitar as a side musician on a single song demo intended to be pitched (but not for release), the amount might be $156 for a three-hour session.

To record guitar as a side musician on an album, the scale rate might be $450 for a three-hour session.

Make no mistake, if you're doing a lot of sessions, this money adds up quickly and is a great source of income. Just be sure to check the websites of the AFM and SAG/AFTRA unions for current rates and detailed information for joining.

13. UNION SPECIAL PAYMENT FUND MONIES

While on the topic of unions, union special payment fund (SPF) monies are the extra payments you will receive for performing on records that are monitored by the musicians' unions mentioned above.

To illustrate, if you are asked to guest perform on a major label artist's record and you are indeed signed up to participate in the unions' Sound Recording Special Payments Fund, then you can earn extra income (above the session fee) in special fund monies.

The amount you receive in SPF monies is collected by the unions from the record companies and issued to you based on a percentage (ranging from 20 to 80 percent) of the scale dollars you earned on union-covered recording sessions performed in the prior year. This payment will continue for the next five years.

If you are only playing smaller level recording sessions (outside the major label or major-indie level), and you're not yet signed up for the Sound Recording Special Payments Fund, then don't expect to earn anything in this type of income.

However, as you advance to doing a lot of union-covered recording sessions, know that you can earn several thousands of extra dollars per year just for the recording work you do. This is a union benefit to which many musicians are completely blind. So, know your shit folks and never leave any money on the table. Remember, the more income, the better your outcome.

14. UNION REUSE FEES

Keeping with unions, reuse fees are the extra monies you receive as a union member when your union-covered sound recordings are used in a way other than originally intended.

For instance, if you record on a union-covered record intended for the purpose of sales and streams, and then that recording is used in a film or TV show, the union collects residuals called "new use" fees and pays you because the master was used in a new way.

Again, the amount you get is difficult to nail down, but just be clear that reuse fees are typically received only if you are indeed affiliated with a professional musicians' union. That being said, when you get to a point in your career when you are performing on a lot of union-covered recording sessions, be sure to check out the websites of both the AFM and SAG/AFTRA to learn more. Again, as a musician, you can never afford to leave any money sitting on the table.

15. NFT MONIES

Finally, NFT (non-fungible token) monies are the monies that you might receive from the initial sale of an NFT to a collector, as well as the subsequent royalties you might receive per an agreement for resells of that NFT.

To be sure, an NFT is essentially a unique cryptographic token on a secure electronic database of information, known as the blockchain, that generates trust. NFTs can be tied to both digital or physical products and experiences consisting of artworks, songs, exclusive pictures, and even lifelong memberships to clubs. They can be one-of-a-kind

FIFTEEN TYPES OF MONEY THAT INDEPENDENT ARTISTS CAN MAKE

(only one is minted for sale) or a short-run-of-a-kind (several are minted for sale).

The amount you can get for an NFT is all over the place, because it is based on the perception of value today and what fans believe it may be worth if they resell it in the future. While artists like Grimes, Blau, and Kings of Leon have all had great success selling their NFTs, remember that these artists also have built-in demand. Meaning, until you have a fanbase of people who give a shit about you, don't expect your NFT to generate thousands "just because."

So, there you have it gang—as you can see from above, there are a variety of revenue streams that exist in the music business, especially when you own the rights to your songs, masters, merchandising, and more. It might take some time before these monies start pouring in, but when they do, the key is to hang on to as much as you can and make them grow.

To learn more about the above-mentioned revenue streams, particularly about how to collect these incomes using a variety of professional organizations, be sure to check out the books *Business Basics for Musicians*, by Bobby Borg, and *Introduction to Music Publishing*, by Bobby Borg and Michael Eames. Peace!

4

Twenty Money-Making Ideas and Side Hustles for Musicians

While there are several income streams available to independent music artists today, ranging from streaming royalties to live performance fees, the truth is that it can take a long time before most artists will see sizable amounts of any of these monies (if ever at all).

This is why it's crucial for musicians to consider all of the flexible money-making ideas and side hustles that exist today. After all, you can only couch surf at your buddies' apartments for so long before you're forced to find a more sustainable approach to your music career.

While many of the suggestions below won't be right for everyone's personal situation, and there are no guarantees that these ideas will always generate enough income for you to survive, what follows is meant to inspire you to get creative, get busy, and start making some steady money while still pursuing your ultimate dream of becoming a music artist. Let's do this!

1. TEACH MUSIC LESSONS

Teaching music lessons is an extremely popular and often lucrative gig for musicians.

With the average rate of $55 per hour, just ten students per week can add up to a sizable amount of money per month. And besides, music lessons can be taught in the comfort of your own home, the client's house, a music store, or even online.

When I (this is Bobby) graduated from Berklee College of Music way back when, I had thirty students at $30 an hour (that's $900 a week and $3,600 a month). I had enough money to cover my bills, and still had plenty of extra time to devote to my own original band and career.

2. PLAY IN COVER BANDS

Playing in cover bands for bar performances, weddings, and corporate parties can be a great way to make steady money and keep your chops up too.

To supplement teaching music lessons, I (this is Bobby again) joined an R&B/soul cover band that held a residency in a small Cambridge club for three nights a week for six years—now that was some steady cash!

Additionally, the group played weddings and corporate parties around the state of Massachusetts on the off nights.

The good news about cover bands, for me as a drummer, was that it kept my hands moving while also keeping my bills paid. As long as I was playing and not digging ditches, I was happy.

3. GET A CHURCH GIG

Getting a church gig and playing faith-based hymns and originals is not a bad way to bring in the bucks. The musicians are typically great and the music ranges from gospel to rock or R&B.

And one of the best parts about church gigs is that many are residencies where you're playing three or more times per week for several months or years—and the money is not bad, too.

We know one indie artist who makes thousands playing synagogues around California. Amen!

4. WORK ON A CRUISE SHIP

Working on a cruise ship is yet another option for musicians looking for a money-making idea.

Would you believe that famed vocalist Jennifer Hudson worked on a Disney Cruise Line as an entertainer before auditioning for *American Idol* and becoming a star? Pretty cool, right?

While taking on a cruise gig will require you to be out at sea for long periods of time, the good news is that you have a lot of personal time during which you can continue to work on your own songs and record right on your laptop computer—all while making good money, too. Not bad!

5. BECOME A THEME PARK PERFORMER

If the thought of working on a cruise ship makes you seasick, becoming a theme park performer just might be the thing for you.

Drummer Josh Freese, of the highly respected band A Perfect Circle, actually got his start playing in top forty bands at Disneyland.

What's that you say? You don't live near Disneyland? That's okay, there are all types of theme parks around the country that are looking for entertainers just like you. So why not give theme parks a try?

6. HIT THE STREETS AND BUSK

Hitting the streets and busking can be another cool gig to help bring in the bucks. As long as you've got an outgoing personality and can deal with uninterested passersby, you're good!

You wouldn't believe the number of successful artists who have literally "hit the road"—from Rod Stewart (who played the street corners of London) to Ed Sheeran (who played the subways of London), to BB King (who played the famous streets of Memphis—in fact, BB's original name was Beale Street Blues Boy). If these famous artists can busk, then so can you!

7. WORK AS A MOBILE DJ

Working as a mobile DJ spinning other people's records at parties, weddings, bar mitzvahs, and more can bring in a lot of money and be a fun gig too.

While nearly everybody and their mom is a DJ these days, and there appears to be a lot of competition for gigs, someone's always throwing a party and needs cool music to set the mood.

So, if you can mix music from different genres and have enough of a personality to occasionally talk between songs on a microphone as the MC, then why not give this gig a spin?

8. HIRE OUT YOUR SERVICES FOR STUDIO WORK

Hiring out your services in the studio to other artists is a highly coveted gig for most musicians.

But let's not get carried away—we're not just referring to the bigger studio gigs with major artists (which are hard to come by) but, rather, the more realistic money-making side hustles.

You can hire out your services on online platforms like SoundBetter and AirGigs and pick up a variety of freelance work (laying vocals, doing guitar solos, and more) for people making records in their own bedrooms all around the country and world.

If you've got some recording chops and are also a versatile musician, getting started is as easy as logging on to the various platforms out there and listing yourself as a provider. Go for it!

9. MAKE AND SELL BEATS

Making and selling beats might be another way to bring in quick cash and pay some bills too.

Utilizing platforms like Airbit, BeatStars, SoundClick, and more, musicians can make their beats available and close some deals with independent music makers around the world.

As long as you've got some production skills, know some theory, and have extra time to build up a library of different beats, we think this could be your next gig.

10. HELP OTHER ARTISTS PRODUCE/ENGINEER THEIR PROJECTS

While on the topic of production and engineering, helping other artists record their own projects may be another money-making idea for you while waiting for your big break.

Hey, why not?—if you've got some dope home recording gear, a place where you can record vocals, and you're good at making music, lend a hand to your fellow musicians and make some decent money in return. You could earn several hundred dollars per song, to several thousand for a full EP or LP. And you'll still have time to focus on your own music! Why not?

11. DO LIVE SOUND

Many musicians who are good with production also do live sound. If this is you, know that many venues typically hire sound engineers on an ongoing basis (meaning, it's a steady gig).

Look, if you don't mind tying up some of your evenings, the money can be pretty good and the work environment is a lot of fun. Who knows, you might even make some great contacts too.

12. SELL MERCH FOR A BAND

Another good gig that deals with live performances is selling merch for a live band in clubs.

If you are outgoing, good at handling money, and responsible when around liquor, then selling band merch is a good way to make a few extra bucks. And if the band decides to hit the road, it could also be a good way to get some road experience and make contacts too.

13. WORK AS AN EQUIPMENT TECH

While on the topic of being out on the road and earning a few extra bucks, working as an equipment tech could also be a sufficient gig for you.

If you're not too proud to schlep someone else's gear, you'll get a lot of road experience and make some really important contacts too.

Would you believe that Tupac was the roadie for Digital Underground before becoming a big star? It's true! If he can do it, so can you.

14. WORK AT A REHEARSAL/RENTAL COMPLEX

Speaking of tech jobs, working at a rehearsal/rental complex like SIR could also be an excellent place to make money and contacts too.

A friend of ours who worked at SIR studios actually got a gig touring with the artist Cher after meeting her at one of her SIR studio rehearsals. The two hit it off and she asked him to audition. Hey, what better place to work than where professional tours actually start!

15. DO STAGE PRODUCTION WORK

Staying with tech jobs, doing stage production work for concerts and events could also be an awesome and flexible way to bring in some quick cash.

If you're fairly strong, have a good back, and don't mind climbing, this could be an easy way to make some dough and be around some really cool concerts and events, too.

Check out Superior Staging, Stage Ops, and Bigger Hammer to see if they are hiring.

16. BECOME A PIANO TUNER

Moving on to yet another tech side hustle, if you play piano, have a good ear, and are good with people, becoming a piano tuner could help you make thousands of dollars monthly.

With just a few tools, you can start your own business tuning pianos in homes and schools, or work for a piano gallery who will send you out to various places fully equipped. Try it!

17. TRANSCRIBE MUSIC

Transcribing music is also a great side hustle you might pick up as long as you're good with theory, notation, and have experience with transcription software tools like Sibelius.

You know those music books you see on the back shelves of stores like Sam Ash and Guitar Center? Well, someone has to transcribe all those notes, so it might as well be you!

Contact a publisher like Mel Bay to see if they need help, or become a freelancer (using platforms like Fiverr) and work for people like music teachers who are creating their own books.

18. FREELANCE AS A GRAPHIC DESIGNER/PRO TOOLS EXPERT OR OTHER

Since we just mentioned freelancing on platforms like Fiverr, hiring out as a graphic designer, Pro Tools expert, or drum programmer could also help to bring the bucks in.

Check out freelance platforms like Fiverr, Upwork, and Outsourcely, and start getting paid for your special music skills today.

19. WORK AS A SALESPERSON AT A MUSIC STORE

Working as a salesperson at a music store like Guitar Center, Sam Ash, or some other great music store in a city near you, could also turn out to be an excellent gig.

Not only do these gigs pay decently, Guitar Center is known for being flexible with staff who need to go on the road for a few weeks. So, you can work, leave, and come back! Pretty dope!

20. WORK AT A TICKET AGENCY

Finally, if selling instruments is not the job for you but you're good at sales and love concerts, perhaps working at a ticket agency (or ticket re-seller) can help you to pay the bills while working toward being a music artist.

As long as you're good on the phone and skilled at customer service, this gig just might be what you're looking for. And hey, the pay rate and commissions can be good too. Good luck!

BONUS: TEN (NON-MUSIC RELATED) SIDE HUSTLES FOR MUSICIANS

Now that we covered twenty music-related side hustles, let's take a look at a few non-music related side hustles out there that can help you pay the bills. Again, these might not be for everybody, but they are all flexible and won't steal you away from your music career. Enjoy.

1. **Drive for Ride Share Companies (Uber or Lyft):** Flick on the Uber app whenever you want, drive customers from point A to B, and make a few bucks to pay your rent too. Simple gig!
2. **Deliver Food (DoorDash or Uber Eats):** Turn on the app at your convenience, pick up people's food and bring it to them, and get paid. That's it!
3. **Deliver Groceries (Instacart):** Turn on the app in between writing songs (or whatever), make runs to the grocery store for people, and deliver their groceries—all for cash!

4. **Become a Mobile Notary:** Drive around to various businesses, screen the signers of important documents for their true identity, and make up to $4k a month! Seriously!
5. **Work as a Telemarketer:** Work part-time hours making calls to people, practice your communication and sales skills, and pay your rent! Perfect!
6. **Become a Personal Trainer:** Kill two birds with one stone—make good money and keep your body fit for the musical stage too. Excellent!
7. **Participate in Surveys:** Join up with survey companies (like Cash Crate, Survey Monkey, and Swagbucks), assist other companies with their research, and get paid.
8. **Become a Secret Shopper:** Sign up with secret shopper companies (like BestMark, IntelliShop, and Market Force), report on customer service issues at select stores, and bring in some cash! Perfect for you shopaholics out there.
9. **Work at Starbucks:** Serve people their coffee, work on your customer service skills, and make money. Simple! And besides, there's a Starbucks on every freakin' corner too.
10. **Become a Dog Walker:** Finally, take care of other people's pets, hang out with super friendly animals, and make up to $40 per walk, per hour! As one of our music students says, "A dog a day keeps the bill collectors away."

Okay peeps, so that's our list of twenty money-making side hustles for musicians (and a few bonus tips too). Just remember that till the money starts rolling in from your ultimate gig of being a successful music artist, there's no shame in making some "cash in a dash." You'll be able to cover your bills, save some money, and even start investing a little cash, too. So, get working and have fun doing it!

Extra Tips at a Glance: Getting and Staying Hired

Knowing the various types of side hustles out there for you to make money is one thing, but now you need to know how to get—and keep—the job. Here are a few quick tips to ensure that you put your best foot forward every time. Use these tips well.

- **Make a Good First Impression:** Remember, first impressions might be your only chance to make an impression.
- **Make People Like You:** Understand that people usually hire those they really like.
- **Add Value:** Remember, it's not what people can do for you, it's what you can do for them.
- **Respect Your Job:** Treat the company as your own, and one day you'll have your own.
- **Be Passionate:** Put your heart into your job, because your job is feeding your dream.
- **Have a Positive Attitude:** Maintain a positive outlook for life no matter what job you've got.
- **Be Cool with Everyone:** Remember that today's secretary can be tomorrow's CEO.
- **Smile a Lot:** Don't forget that a genuine smile radiates and attracts good energy.
- **Be Grateful:** Remember that no one owes you anything in this world.
- **Don't Be Late:** Remember, "If you're not ten minutes early, you're late."
- **Make Your Boss Look Good:** Make your boss a star and you will go extra far.
- **Stay Up to Date:** Keep up with the world around you and you'll always be employable.
- **Know That Everything You Do Matters:** Understand that even taking a shitty telemarketing job as a side hustle is an opportunity to work on your pitching and communication skills.
- **Don't Complain:** Know that no one likes a toxic whiner, so don't whine.
- **Work Hard:** Know that nobody likes a deadbeat corpse, so come to work ready to kill it.
- **Listen Well:** Remember that taking direction and paying attention to detail are paramount.
- **Move to the Big City:** Appreciate that big cities typically have greater opportunities.
- **Be Patient:** Finally, know that it is a long road to the top if you want to Rock 'n' Roll. Remember that your day will come if you can just hang in there and go the long haul.

3

SAVINGS

"Saving doesn't mean being miserable today so you can live a good life tomorrow. It's about setting aside enough money each month to reach your wildest dreams."

—Bill Schultheis, author of the *Coffee House Investor*

5

Ten Tips for Spending Less and Saving More

We once heard a great quote about money that went something like this: "Having more money isn't just about making more money [from writing a hit song, winning the lottery, or getting a raise at your job]; it's also about spending less money and cutting back wherever you can."

While the above quote makes so much sense, so many people (especially young musicians) are guilty of spending more than they can really afford. Part of this comes from lacking practical money skills, being subjected to peer pressure, and needing the emotional high that comes from spending money and acquiring new things.

Whatever your personal "spending excuse" (hey, we're not judging), know that by adapting a more frugal lifestyle, you'll have more money to pay off debt, cover emergencies, and tuck away money in investments to achieve your dreams. All good stuff!

What follows are ten tips—from cutting back on gear to setting a budget. We're not suggesting you have to make all of these changes, but even if you can make just a few, you'll be far better off financially. Okay? So, grab your yellow highlighter and let's do this.

1. CUT BACK ON THE MUSIC GEAR YOU REALLY DON'T NEED

The first and most useful tip for any musician on spending less and saving more is to cut back on the music gear you really don't need.

While buying a new vintage guitar for the stage or new EQ for your home studio might be totally dope, remember, "it's not always what you got, but how well you use what you got."

Even the basic gear you need to succeed in the music industry like Pro Tools won't make you a pro, Logic won't make you logical, and Ableton won't make you able.

All jokes aside, don't get caught up in the trap of paying more money than you can afford on the premise that "better gear makes you a better musician."

Bottom line, learn to use what you already own more efficiently instead of purchasing more. You can do this by subscribing to numerous YouTube channels, joining Facebook groups, and merely practicing. You'll spend less, save more, and get a far greater return on your investment.

2. DON'T SPEND A FORTUNE ON YOUR MUSIC CAREER EARLY ON

Don't spend a fortune on your music career early on when you're just starting out and honing your craft.

It always surprises us when a young musician writes their very first song and then spends several thousand dollars hiring a producer and recording it in an expensive studio.

Then, if that were not enough, they hire the big video crew with all the bells and whistles to record a top-notch music video that looks like a brand commercial.

Okay, some of you are wondering, "What's wrong with that, aren't you supposed to put your best foot forward?"

Our answer is simple: all the money and production in the world won't make a bad song good. A clear, simple, and less expensive recording and video is all you need when first starting out to get feedback and help you to improve.

As you get better and better, you can start investing more into your career for your first big release. And who knows, in time, investors may even swoop you up and pay for all the rest.

So, take our advice on this, folks, and you'll end up spending less and saving much more.

3. DON'T PAY FOR MUSIC PROMOTION THAT REALLY DOESN'T WORK

Don't pay for music promotion that really doesn't work in an attempt to make a larger-than-life first impression.

Many musicians fall into the social media trap of wanting to appear more popular than they really are by purchasing Instagram followers, Spotify streams, and TikTok followers.

But while it might make for a good look, know that "buying success" could eventually lead to your accounts getting banned and even taken down.

Not only that, many music professionals know that your success is fake when they see 100,000 followers and no engagement at all.

So, look gang, rather than wasting your precious hard-earned money, you'd be better off posting regularly and engaging fans like the rest of us. To be sure, avoid "get rich quick" promotion tactics. You'll spend less, save more, and have more cash for far better purposes.

4. FORM A BAND AND SPLIT THE COSTS

Form a band and split the costs between all four members as a way to spend less and save more. Take note: $100 divided by one is $100, but $100 divided by four band members is $25.

If being in a band united in a common vision is right for you creatively and business-wise, then splitting costs is a solid cost benefit for all musicians involved.

However, if being in a band is just your master plan as a solo artist to manipulate others into thinking the band is a band, then partnering up to split costs is not advisable. Enough said!

5. DRESS THE PART, WITHOUT PARTING WITH ALL YOUR CASH

Dress the part of the pop star you truly are, but without spending all of your hard-earned cash.

We totally get how creating the image of success in the minds of fans is important in pictures, videos, and on album covers, but "where there's a will to save money, there's a way."

Fashion experts claim that avoiding the latest trends and sticking with classic pieces that transcend the trends—like a fitted pair of jeans, a black jacket, or pencil skirt—is the way to go.

Other experts claim that indulging in a few expensive pieces you can use every day (like a great bag, expensive glasses or cool boots you can mix with your "not-so-expensive" stuff) is another way to "look the part" of a rock star, when you don't have much money at all.

Finally, shopping at second-hand shops, going to estate sales in rich neighborhoods, or just buying knock-off brands are additional methods to help you to spend less and save more.

So, why not give a few of these tips a try? Your wallet will be really glad that you did!

6. GET SPONSORS TO MAKE UP FOR SOME OR ALL OF YOUR COSTS

Get sponsors to make up for some—or all—of your costs if you're really looking for a resourceful tip to spend less and save more.

Sponsorships are a symbiotic relationship between company brands (fashion, cosmetics, accessories, etc.) and music artists (like you) where the sponsoring company gives away or loans products in return for exposure.

If a sponsor feels that you have the attention of a large audience, your audience is made of their target customer, and you fit with their values, you might be able to get everything from instruments to designer clothes and loaner cars for absolutely free.

Getting in touch with potential sponsors is not difficult to do. All it takes is finding the brand manager at a company and giving them a benefit-packed pitch. So, why spend hundreds of dollars when you may be able to do a deal with a brand sponsor today? It's worth the try!

7. KEEP PERSONAL HOUSING COSTS AS LOW AS POSSIBLE

Now as a more general method of spending less and saving more, try to keep your personal housing costs as low as possible. Remember folks, housing is one of your biggest expenses and there are definitely ways that you can cut your housing costs if you want.

Sure, it's cool when you can rent the "rad pad" perfect for hooking up with your new date, hosting after-parties, and making YouTube videos of y'all acting like fools in the pool.

But, living in a cheaper part of town, getting a roommate to help split all of the rental costs, and keeping utilities like air and heat to a minimum will really make a difference in your financial health. And besides, if you're frugal now, you'll be far better equipped to manage the millions and mansions you'll get when you're a big rock star.

Oh, one more thing: if you really want to save on housing, there's nothing wrong with living at home with your folks till you get your financial shit more together. As long as you and your parents are cool and you live in a "good music city," there's no shame in it for a short while.

8. ROLL UP TO THE PARTY IN A CAR YOU CAN AFFORD

As another general method of spending less and saving more, try to keep your transportation costs as low as possible by getting a practical car you can truly afford. This is really where the economic principle of "wants versus needs" comes into the conversation.

Most musicians "want" that new Escalade, Range Rover Sport, or Mercedes Benz to make a cool appearance in front of clubs and parties on the weekends. But what most musicians really "need" is a cheaper, used car brand that is easy to maintain and reliable. Just remember: you are not what you drive, and neither is anyone else.

Okay, we know what you're probably thinking right now: we sound like your boring parents. So, if you really don't want to be practical (or consider alternatives like ride share services, or rentals like Zipcar), you might buy a cooler used car through a reliable company like CarMax and rent it out to people using an app like Toro to help make back some of your money. Additionally, you can double down on another tip herein to help you spend less and save more.

9. STAY ENTERTAINED WITHOUT GETTING OVERLY DRAINED

For our next-to-last tip on spending less and saving more, try to find new and creative ways to stay entertained without burning a hole in your wallet. Since small expenses have a way of adding up super quickly, you really need to cut entertainment costs everywhere you can.

Here a just a few of things that you can do:

- **Slash Your Bar Tab:** For the cost of just one beer in a club, buy a whole six pack from the grocery store and hang out with friends at home. You can play guitars and pump out a new tune too. Say goodbye to all those huge bar tabs for good!
- **Avoid Eating Out:** Instead of splitting the bill at a fancy restaurant and getting charged $40 for a taco, cook up a big meal at

home with a couple friends for a more chill evening. You can literally save thousands per year.
- **Cut Back on Music Festivals:** Instead of going to every music festival known to man, pick your favorite—preferably the one closest to your hometown—and save hundreds and potentially thousands in airfare, hotels, and more.
- **Kick the Starbucks Habit:** Finally, for the cost of just one $6 Starbucks Caramel Frappuccino with whipped cream and extra chocolate chips, mix up several coffees in a blender at home. Would you believe one musician we know saved $1,200 a year doing this! Wow!

Look gang, we don't want to cramp your fun lifestyle but, rather, we want you to understand that every dollar you save on entertainment matters. By monitoring your spending closely and making more practical decisions, you will end up spending less and saving more.

10. CREATE A BUDGET, AND LIVE AND DIE BY IT

Finally, remember the key to everything we've discussed about spending less and saving more is to create a well-written budget and to live and die by it.

A budget involves accounting for all your incomes and outflows, projecting an amount of money you can afford to spend, and then monitoring for any variances between your budgeted and actual expenses.

This is really not as difficult as you think and can be done using an Excel spreadsheet, a filing cabinet to keep receipts, and an hour of your time at the end of the week or month.

The website NerdWallet offers simple budgeting tips any musician can follow. So, why not create a budget today? You'll be glad you did.

So that's our ten tips on spending less and saving more. Remember that by adapting a more frugal lifestyle, you'll have more money to pay off debt, cover emergencies, and tuck away money in investments to achieve your dreams. The rewards are super worth it. So do it!

And just remember, when you start making more money as a successful musician, that's no excuse to start spending more too. You can lighten up in certain areas for sure, but maintain good spending habits throughout your lifetime. Okay peeps! Cool! Good luck!

More Cost-Cutting Tips at a Glance

Methods to cut costs are so numerous, we could probably fill an entire book of them. Now that we've got more of the general methods out of the way above, what follows are another fifty tips presented in a short, rapid-fire, bullet-point style. Some of these tips are over-the-top (intended to be funny) and some are things you should really consider. Have fun with this. But just remember one thing: most people who become rich, live like they're broke. Give it a try!

- **Weed:** Smoke your friend's stash, or kick the lifestyle.
- **Cigarettes:** Roll your own, or quit smoking.
- **Groceries:** Shop at less expensive places, eat less, and never shop when you are high.
- **Bulk Food/Stuff:** Get a membership card to Sam's Club, and buy in bulk.
- **Meat:** Eat less of it, or go vegan.
- **Water:** Get a Brita filter, and stop polluting our oceans with plastic bottles.
- **Leftovers:** Don't throw away what you can't eat—freeze it for another day.
- **Lunch Breaks:** Bring a can of tuna to work with a carrot and a handful of almonds.
- **Grocery Receipts:** Check your receipts for mis-charges.
- **Electricity:** Shut off the lights when you're not using them.
- **Air Conditioner/Heater:** Wear a sweater or buy a plug-in fan.
- **Home Internet:** Use the public library's internet instead.
- **Cable:** Read a good book instead—you'll learn more!
- **Mobile Phones:** Hang on to your old phone a little longer (you don't need the latest model).
- **Subscription Services:** Get rid of subscriptions you don't use (the Rocket Money formerly known as Truebill, app can help).
- **Cell Phone Bills:** Move down to a cheaper data plan.
- **Plastic Garbage Bags:** Use small bags you get from the grocery store.
- **Paper Towels:** Use a sponge instead (they last longer).
- **Tin Foil:** Wash and re-use that perfect sheet of tin foil you just used for baking your lasagna.
- **Sandwich Baggies:** Rince, dry, and use them again.

TEN TIPS FOR SPENDING LESS AND SAVING MORE

- **Car Insurance:** Lower your monthly premium by raising your deductible and always shop for the best deals.
- **Gasoline:** Use your bicycle more often and get some exercise while you're at it.
- **Car Wash:** Go to DIY car washes or do it at home with a bucket and soap.
- **Movie Theaters:** Get a subscription to Netflix instead.
- **Movie Theater Refreshments:** Smuggle in your own popcorn (but not if you're trying to impress a date).
- **Massages/Spa:** Get a girlfriend or boyfriend with strong hands.
- **Airline Tickets:** Buy tickets six months in advance and use a discount travel company like Expedia (oh, and don't fly first class, one-way, or on the weekends).
- **Vacations:** Do a staycation in a nice local hotel instead of the long-distance trip.
- **The Gym:** Buy an exercise bike together with a set of dumbbells and stay at home.
- **Clothes:** Try bargain basements, thrift shops, and trendy off-the-rack shops rather than going to department stores at the mall.
- **Sneakers:** Clean your kicks, and change up the color of the shoestrings once in a while.
- **Store Sales:** Remember the best deal is when you don't buy anything.
- **One-Click Online Buying:** Deactivate this feature—it promotes compulsive buying.
- **Retail Therapy:** Meditate instead, if you're feeling stressed or depressed.
- **Vinyl Records:** Cut your vinyl obsession down to one record a month and then play the shit out of that record till your neighbors hate you.
- **Music Supplies:** Change guitar strings and drum heads only for gigs or sessions.
- **Late Fees:** Pay your bills on time.
- **Stamps:** Pay your bills online.
- **Bank Fees:** Balance your freaking checking account and stop using out-of-network ATMs.
- **Credit Card Statements:** Check your statements regularly for mis-charges.
- **Credit Card Usage:** Use cash instead of credit cards. You'll spend far less money.

- **Birthday Cards:** Take a picture of yourself and write a short letter telling the person how much they mean to you (no more $5 pieces of cardboard from Hallmark).
- **Xmas Presents:** Buy gifts for your immediate family, not every friend you have.
- **Loans to Friends and Family:** Just don't do it.
- **Husbands/Wives:** Marry someone with similar spending habits and never get divorced.
- **Children:** Get a pet instead. They are cheaper and don't talk back when they turn seventeen.
- **Pets:** Hold off on getting Fido, and get a goldfish instead.
- **Taxes:** Save your receipts and speak to your accountant about what you can write off.
- **Houses:** Shop for a house only when you are really ready to buy and maintain one. And don't get "more house" than you can afford. Would you believe that Warren Buffett (one of the richest investors in the world) still lives in the first house he bought for $32,000? Crazy, but true!

4

ACCOUNTING

With my mind on my money, and my money on my mind.
—Snoop Dogg

Get Your Financial and Business Records in Order: Twenty-Four Tips

An important step in managing your finances and handling business matters efficiently is to organize all of your important business documents in one place. This includes your monthly bills, annual tax returns, investment statements, and so much more.

Doing this will facilitate paying your bills on time, filing taxes correctly, and monitoring your investments. You'll also be able to respond quickly to any number of requests from creditors, the Internal Revenue Service, investment brokers, your bank, and even employers, too.

Using a filing cabinet, personal computer, and/or home safe, you'll be able to securely store each of the twenty-four documents that we discuss below. We present enough items to make your eyes glaze over, but note that not all of these items will apply to you. Thus, feel free to skim our list and pick those that are most relevant. Okay? Cool! Now, let's get to organizing!

1. CASH RECEIPTS, CHECK COPIES, AND PAY STUBS

File copies of all of the employee and/or independent contractor payments you receive during the year. This includes cash receipts, copies of physical checks, and even regular pay stubs.

This will help you to keep track of all the money you earn, provide a total of your annual income for tax purposes, and match important information with tax forms you receive from employers at the end of the year.

2. INVOICES

Additionally, keep invoices for all employers who have not yet paid you.

After every job you do (particularly independent contractor work where the employers may claim, "I'll pay you later"), submit an invoice, and keep a copy of that invoice in a file named "accounts receivable."

After proper payment is collected, mark the invoice "received" and move it to the appropriate income file we mentioned in tip one.

Doing this will help you track any unpaid income, which you might otherwise lose sight of should you get extremely busy.

3. BILLS

Be sure to also create folders for all of your monthly bills and title them (phone bill, credit card, auto lease, mortgage, etc.). Then fill these folders with corresponding monthly statements after paying them, dating them, and marking them paid in full (PIF).

Doing this will help you to keep track of all your payments, maintain records of certain expenses you claim on your annual tax returns, and respond appropriately should there be any misunderstandings about your bill terms or payment options.

4. SPREADSHEETS OF MONTHLY BILLS AND BUSINESS EXPENSES

Also be sure to create Excel spreadsheets to track monthly bills and business expenses and keep a physical and electronic version in your files. Consider the following:

- **For Monthly Bills:** Indicate the date, transaction number, purpose, amount and mode of payment (e.g., September 1, check #305, rent, $1,300 by mail).
- **For Business Expenses:** Indicate the date, the cost, and the business purpose of the expense (e.g., July 4, $12, drumsticks for USC parade gig).

Spreadsheets will come in handy should you ever have to reflect back on a particular transaction, or need the data for preparing your annual tax return. It might take some time to maintain these spreadsheets but, in the end, it will be absolutely worth it.

5. BANK ACCOUNT STATEMENTS

Make sure to also file monthly bank account statements after confirming that all of your withdrawals, deposits, and checks were correctly accounted for.

Any online statements should also be carefully checked by logging on to your bank's website and reviewing all of your transactions.

Remember that banks are known to make occasional mistakes, so tracking all of your transactions is a very sound idea.

6. PHYSICAL RECEIPTS

Be sure to also create a file for the physical expense receipts you receive! This includes expense receipts related to the work you might do as a hired employee or independent contractor.

In either case, be sure to create a neat system (both physically and digitally) for organizing and storing your receipts. Your receipts will come in handy when calculating yearly taxes that you may owe and/or for correcting discrepancies in your tax return should you be audited by the IRS.

We'll share more specific ideas about storing receipts in another piece. Promise!

7. TAX RETURNS

Make sure to also categorize annual tax returns together with W4 and 1099 forms you receive from your employers.

Note that older tax returns can serve as useful references should you ever need to prove your income when applying for loans, or should you ever get audited by the IRS.

So, for the sake of absolutely clarity, keeping your tax returns filed safely is crucial!

8. CREDIT REPORTS

Additionally, file your credit reports from the three major credit bureaus in the United States: Equifax, Experian, and TransUnion.

Credit reports include information about your personal bill paying history and are useful to lenders when determining your credit worthiness.

They can also be useful in spotting fraudulent activity (such as identity theft) and any misinformation that a creditor may have reported.

To get your free annual credit report, visit annualcreditreport.com.

9. INVESTMENT INFORMATION

Also, file statements, letters, and other information associated with the investments you hold.

These include statements from employer retirement funds, money market accounts, savings bonds, certificates of deposit, and more. Don't worry if you don't know what these investments are. In yet another piece, we'll cover this to ensure you are totally up to speed.

10. DMV-RELATED INFORMATION

Make sure to also create a file titled "DMV" (Department of Motor Vehicles) for all correspondence you receive regarding your driver's license, vehicle registration, and any violations. On the latter note, this information can help you to keep track of paid and unpaid tickets. After all, you don't want to get your car towed due to delinquent tickets, do you? Nope!

Also be sure to file your motor vehicle title for the automobile you currently own. Never keep your vehicle title in your car. Should someone break into your automobile and grab your title, it's gonna cost you a lot of headaches dealing with the DMV to set things right. Yuck!

11. PASSPORT

Also be sure to file your current passport and all related correspondence received (i.e., the place where you applied for the passport, the photographer who snapped the photo, proof of your payment, etc.).

Remember, you will need your passport "on the fly" when traveling in and out of the country for music tours. And the last thing you need is to misplace it. Hey, it's been known to happen.

Also, remember that should you ever find that your passport has expired, having all of the information on file about your photographer, renewal location, and more will come in handy.

12. NATURALIZATION PAPERS, CITIZENSHIP CERTIFICATES, AND VISAS

Also file important correspondence and payment records related to any naturalization, citizenship, or visa documentation you may have. Don't know what these are? Here's a breakdown:

- **Naturalization Papers:** Show that you are a legal US immigrant and are entitled to all of the liberties of being a US citizen.
- **Citizenship Certificates:** Show that you are a US citizen who was born to US parents, or who was otherwise born to a foreign parent who became naturalized before you turned age eighteen.
- **Visas:** Show that you have the right to travel in and out of the country during a certain period of time for things like going to school.

If any of these documents apply to you, know that you might be asked to furnish originals when applying for a job or leaving and entering the country. So, be sure to keep them safe.

13. SOCIAL SECURITY CARD

Be sure to also file your Social Security identification card in a safe place and never carry it with you.

Social security cards are identification cards issued to US citizens at the time of birth. They are used to help the government track an individual's records and financial information.

You'll need your Social Security card when applying for a job, applying for certain credit, and for receiving Social Security benefits later in life. If you are a legally admitted non-citizen authorized to work in the Unites States, you will also need to get and file a Social Security card.

A lost card in the hands of a criminal could lead to identity theft and so much more. So, keeping your card in a secure place is a wise safeguard. For more info, contact www.ssa.gov.

14. BIRTH CERTIFICATE

Filing your birth certificate in a safe place is also a very wise idea.

You may need to refer to your birth certificate to verify both your identity and age when registering for school, when getting a driver's license, or when renewing a passport.

Should you ever be asked for your birth certificate and don't have it, you could easily lose valuable time waiting for a copy in the mail or paying extra money for expedited delivery.

Would you believe that I (this is Bobby) almost missed the application process for grad school while waiting several weeks for a copy of my birth certificate? Yup, it's true. What a pain!

15. PROOF OF MILITARY SERVICE

Be sure to also file any military discharge papers (including those belonging to a deceased parent who served). This will help you to access a number of government benefits for which you may be eligible.

Some of these benefits may save you thousands of dollars in education, health care, dental, guaranteed home loans, and so much more. So, you don't want to miss out.

While I (this is Bobby again) was not entitled to receive any military benefits (because I didn't serve), would you believe I actually had to show proof of "non-military service" when I applied to grad school? Yup, I thought this was pretty weird, too. Oh well, as long as I got in!

16. INSURANCE RECORDS

Make sure to also categorize files that include medical, auto, renter or home insurance policies, including corresponding photographs (or videos) of the insured items. On the latter note, yes, this means actually taking and filing pictures of your automobile, your apartment, and other valuables.

Know that these physical and digital files will particularly come in handy should you ever have to file a personal claim resulting from injury, theft, or damage. Insurance companies will want to see proof of ownership and the original condition of the items for which you are filing a claim.

17. PASSWORDS AND ACCOUNT NUMBERS

Also log all of your important passwords in one electronic file on your personal computer and keep a physical printout of this file in your office filing cabinet. Include passwords to bank accounts, investment websites, social media sites, and more.

Note: with your passwords in one safe and accessible place, you'll be able to create more complex passwords, thus decreasing the likelihood your accounts will get hacked.

If you'd prefer, you might also try a phone app like Dashlane to store your passwords.

18. IMPORTANT CONTACTS (DOCTOR, LAWYER, ETC.)

Be sure to also keep a physical and digital printout of your important contacts, including your doctor, dentist, lawyer, parole officer, social worker, and emergency contact person (parent, brother/sister, best friend, etc.).

While digital storage "in the cloud" and on your phone may seem satisfactory in that it is more permanent, it pays to have contacts at your fingertips in a file—particularly if something ever happens to you and someone else needs to access this information on your behalf.

19. INCORPORATION PAPERS AND RELATED DOCUMENTS

Make sure to also file paperwork related to your corporation or limited liability company (LLC).

This documentation might include notes on meetings, corresponding bank account numbers, business licenses, operating agreements, and tax identification numbers.

All of these documents could come in handy when filing (or refiling) your business entity and when filing taxes at the end of the year.

Note that the IRS.gov has handy info on business entities if you want to learn more.

20. FREQUENT FLYER STATEMENTS AND CARDS

Also be sure to file statements, account numbers, and mileage cards from the various frequent flyer programs in which you are enrolled.

Even when you track your mileage online, it helps to keep a convenient desk file containing a running tally of your miles, expiration dates, and account numbers and passwords.

Remember that free miles come in handy, especially for musicians and other business persons who may need to book regular flights across the country for work and auditions. I (this is Britt) can't tell you the number of free business flights I've received. So, file those miles!

21. PRODUCT WARRANTIES, GUIDES, AND SERIAL NUMBERS

Also make sure to file product warranties, user guides, and serial numbers associated with the important equipment that you purchase (e.g., keyboards, computers, microphones, etc.).

This is important given that all equipment replacements and/or repairs require a warranty registration number as well as the product serial numbers.

Furthermore, keep in mind that when selling a product, you can often charge more when you provide the original user guide and other important information initially received.

Would you believe I (this is Bobby) still had my owner's manual for a classic 1977 dirt bike I recently sold? Yup, and the collector who bought it expressed his happiness in cash! Oh yeah!

22. PHOTOCOPIES OF ITEMS IN YOUR WALLET

Also create a file marked "My Wallet" and keep an updated photocopy of everything in your wallet.

This might include a copy of your driver's license, automobile registration, auto insurance card, credit card, frequent flyer card, medical insurance card, dental cards, union cards, customer loyalty cards, gym membership cards, and more.

If anything at all, this serves as a reminder of everything you store in your wallet and facilitates the process of getting all of these items replaced should you ever lose your wallet. Trust us people, we are talking from hard experience on this one. Copies totally come in handy!

23. EDUCATIONAL RECORDS

Make sure to also file official school transcripts, copies of diplomas, and exam results of any placement tests taken (SAT, GMAT, GRE, etc.).

All of these documents could come in handy should you decide to further your education and apply for undergraduate, master's, or doctorate programs to study music or something else.

Keep in mind that there are way more opportunities in music for musicians than just trying to be a huge rock star, and a degree could "potentially" improve your annual income. Remember, the more income you make, the more you can invest and grow your personal wealth.

24. WILL AND OTHER ESTATE PLANNING ITEMS

Finally, also be sure to file important estate documents. These may include the following:

1. **A Will:** That essentially documents how you want your possessions to be distributed should you die
2. **A Health Care Directive:** Which outlines your wishes should you no longer be able to make decisions for yourself because of illness or incapacity
3. **A Financial Power of Attorney:** Which gives a person the authority to handle your financial needs should you no longer be able to make financial decisions because of illness or incapacity

Other "estate planning" items (like a trust, or life insurance policy) may also be useful to store in this file. We'll talk more about this stuff in another writing, we promise.

Wow! Congratulations! You've made it through our long and exhaustive list. But just remember that organizing your business and financial life is a crucial step in responsible personal finance.

Again, not all of the things we discussed will apply to you. But if you can get just a few items we mentioned secured in a safe place, you'll be a finance superstar. As someone once said, "For every minute spent organizing, an hour is earned." Sounds like good financial advice to us.

Now get organizing!

Three Accounting Documents to Examine Your Financial Health

While there are many financial and business documents that all play an important role in personal finance, perhaps the three most important are: (1) net worth statements, (2) cash flow analyses, and (3) personal budgets.

These documents all serve slightly different functions, but they overall help you to assess your financial well-being and make important financial decisions.

Utilizing Google Sheets, Microsoft Excel, or just a pen and paper, what follows is an expanded explanation of these three accounting documents and how to create them.

So, with no further ado, open your laptop or grab your pen and paper, and let's get this party rockin'.

I. NET WORTH STATEMENTS

The first step in taking account of your financial health is to create a net worth statement.

Usually created annually, at the beginning of the month, a net worth statement presents a current snapshot of everything you own (assets) versus everything you owe (liabilities).

The benefits of creating a net worth statement include:

- **Financial Inventory:** By taking note of all your assets (guitars, computers, savings accounts) and liabilities (school loans, credit card bills, personal loans), you'll have a complete, evaluated inventory in one place. Believe it or not, many musicians are

unaware of the value of everything they own and owe, until they take inventory and add it all up in a net worth statement.
- **Wealth Assessment:** By taking the sum of everything you own, and then subtracting the sum of everything you owe, you will have a clear understanding of your financial situation or net worth—you'll either have a positive or negative wealth rating. This information will serve as the foundation for your entire financial plan and even serve as an immediate wake-up call for your need to reduce debt.
- **Loan Worthiness:** Finally, by dividing your total liabilities by your total assets, you'll have an understanding of your debt-to-asset ratio. This helps to determine the likelihood that you'll be approved for important loans (to buy a car, house, etc.).

Now to create your own net worth statement, reference the net worth graphic (see Figure 7.1) while following these four steps:

1. **Assets:** Make a list of all of your personal holdings and their value in dollars. This includes: money in savings or checking accounts (income from your side hustle or freelance gigs), investments (inheritance from grandma and grandpa), and personal possessions (resale value of your automobile, musical instruments, studio gear, computers, and more). Now find the sum of all of your assets (e.g., $100,000).
2. **Liabilities:** Make a list of all of your personal liabilities and their value in dollars. This includes all of your debt (student loans, credit card balances, car loans, and personal loans like the one from your buddy for those Coachella tickets). Now find the sum of your liabilities (e.g., $40,000).
3. **Net Worth:** Subtract your total liabilities from your total assets to arrive at your net worth. For example, $100,000 in assets, minus $40,000 in liabilities, equals a net worth of $60,000. Just don't be shocked if your own personal net worth is negative. Should this be the case, you'll need to start lowering your liabilities immediately.
4. **Debt to Assets Ratio:** Finally, check your debt to assets ratio by dividing your total liabilities by total assets. Personal financial advisors say that your debt should be no more than 40 percent of your assets. Or said another way, your assets should be financed by no more than 40 percent of your debt. Keeping with the above example, $40,000 liabilities divided by $100,000

assets equals a debt to assets ratio of 40 percent. This is right on target.

That's about it for net profit statements. As we told you, it's a simple but very powerful tool to measure financial health. Now be sure to check out the sample net profit statement below.

NET WORTH STATEMENT		
Assets		**Own**
3 Gibson Guitars	$	15,000.00
Laptop Computer	$	3,000.00
Recording Studio Gear	$	12,000.00
Chase Checking Account	$	9,000.00
Emergency Fund	$	7,000.00
Individual Retirement Account	$	54,000.00
Total	$	100,000.00
Liabilities		**Owe**
Credit Card Outstanding Debt	$	4,000.00
School Loan Oitstanding Debt	$	30,000.00
Car Loan Outstanding	$	6,000.00
Total	$	40,000.00
Net Worth Analysis		**Wealth**
Total Wealth	$	60,000.00
Debt to Assets Ratio		**DAR**
Total		40%

2. CASH FLOW ANALYSES

Now that you understand the importance of a net worth statement and how to create one, it's time to look at another critical accounting document called a personal cash flow analysis.

Usually reviewed annually, at the first of the month, a cash flow analysis tells you how much cash you have (or don't have) available to use at your discretion.

To be sure, unlike a net worth statement that examines the value of what you own (cars, guitars, and other stuff that cannot be easily converted to cash), a cash flow statement only examines cash on hand that you have to pay your bills, make investments, and more.

The primary benefits of a cash flow analysis include:

- **Cash Generation:** You'll have a clear picture of where your money is coming from, how much money is flowing into your accounts, and whether the amounts are adequate to meet your goals.
- **Expense Reduction:** You'll have a detailed picture of every single expense category, how much of your cash is outflowing, and where you can cut down on your spending.
- **Improved Confidence:** Finally, you'll have a clear understanding of your monthly cash position, how much surplus money you can put toward your investment accounts, and whether you need financing to get by.

Now to create your own cash flow analysis, reference the cash flow graphic below (see figure 7.2) while following these five steps:

1. **Inflows:** List each and every income source, including the dollar amount, that you typically have throughout the year. This can include money that you get from your job (less taxes and other deductions), payments you receive from the military, or even money that is being sent by your family members. Now find the sum of these inflows.
2. **Outflows:** List each and every expense category that you typically have over the year. This can include "fixed" expenses that don't change like rent, auto loans, and insurance, and also estimates of "variable" expenses that can fluctuate month-to-month like your monthly gas usage, food costs, entertainment, coffee, cigarettes, weed, and miscellaneous expenses. Now find the sum of all of these outflows.
3. **Surplus or Deficit:** Now subtract your outflows from your inflows to arrive at your surplus or deficit. The goal is to have a positive (or surplus) cash flow and not a negative (or deficit) cash flow. We'll cover what happens when you have a deficit in number five below.
4. **Savings Ratio:** Now determine the percentage of your surplus (assuming you have one). Surplus money can be used for preparing for emergencies, making investments, and securing your future. According to good ol' Ben Franklin, your goal is to have a surplus of at least 10 percent of your total inflows. You can calculate your savings ratio by dividing your surplus by your total inflows and converting that number to a percent.

5. **What-if Analysis:** Finally, if you have a low or negative cash flow, you definitely must experiment with ways of how to eliminate your deficit and create a surplus. Do this by plugging in different estimates for your expenses, asking the question, for instance, "What if I only spend $100 on gas? What if I only spend $1,000 on food?" The idea is to help you see where you can reduce or even eliminate certain outflows. Bottom line, anywhere that you can spend less and save more is golden.

That's about it for cash flow analysis. As we told you, this is also a powerful tool to help measure your financial health. Now be sure to check out the sample cash flow analysis below.

PERSONAL ANNUAL CASH FLOW STATEMENT	
Inflows (After Mandatory Medicare, SS, Health/Dental)	**Annual**
Guitar Center Sales Gig	$ 36,520.00
Independent Guitar Teaching (Average Yearly Net)	$ 10,000.00
Guitar Sessions (Average Yearly Net)	$ 6,000.00
Total Inflows	$ 52,520.00
Outflows (Fixed/Variable Expenses)	**Annual**
Rent	$ 12,715.68
School Loan	$ 3,000.00
Car	$ 4,080.00
Phone	$ 600.00
Internet	$ 600.00
Electric	$ 365.00
Car Insurance	$ 1,140.00
DMV License Fees	$ 480.00
Accountant	$ 400.00
Web Hosting	$ 250.00
Gym	$ 240.00
Food	$ 18,000.00
Gas	$ 600.00
Car Wash	$ 120.00
Books	$ 500.00
Health Care Co Pays	$ 500.00
Travel (flights, trains, Uber, food)	$ 2,000.00
Business Mailing	$ 200.00
Holiday Presents	$ 200.00
Parking	$ 144.00
Total Outflows	$ 46,134.68
Surplus or Deficit	$ 6,385.32
Savings Ratio	12%

3. PERSONAL BUDGETS

Last, but not least, it's time to create a personal budget—perhaps the most frequently used among the three accounting documents: net worth, cash flow, and budget.

Typically updated monthly (or even weekly and/or daily if you so choose), a personal budget presents a complete spending plan for all of your money.

Benefits include:

- **Goal-setting:** By focusing on short-, mid-, and/or long-term objectives, you'll be able to estimate how much of your hard-earned money you intend to spend and/or save each month to meet those goals.
- **Money-management:** By regularly tracking your inflowing and outflowing dollars, you'll be able to (1) see whether you are satisfying your monthly targets and then (2) make adjustments accordingly.
- **Peace of mind**: By knowing exactly where you stand with every dollar and cent, you can eliminate the stress of not knowing whether you'll be able to meet all of your financial obligations at the end of every month. What's more, your control and new-found respect for money will allow you to make sane, rational decisions that will lead to building your wealth.

Now, to create your own personal budget, reference the monthly budget graphic (figure 7.3) below while following these six steps:

1. **Goals:** Forecast what you are trying to accomplish (e.g., "To meet all monthly expenses while investing 10 percent of monthly inflows into retirement accounts"). Whatever your personal goals might be, give them some serious thought right now.
2. **Inflows:** List estimates of all of your monthly income less taxes and deductions (e.g., payments from side hustle jobs, money from freelance sessions, and more). Now find the sum of these incomes.
3. **Disbursements:** List estimates of the money you'll have available for monthly disbursements into investment accounts. (This is a system called "paying yourself first" or "forcing yourself to save.") Note that, typically, the amount of your disbursements

carries over from any surplus monies you calculated in your cash flow statement. Now find the sum of these monies.
4. **Outflows:** List estimates of each and every expense you have (e.g., rent, school loans, food, and gas). Now find the sum of these outflows (including your disbursements) and make sure they equal—or are balanced with—your inflows. This is what is called a "balanced budget." To plug in some real numbers, if your monthly inflows equal $4,376.66, then your monthly outflows and disbursements must also equal $4,376.66. Every dollar is budgeted. Okay? Good. Let's move on.
5. **Monthly Actuals:** Create an "actual" column (next to your "estimated" column) to plug in the "real" dollars you make, invest, and spend (remember, budgets only present "estimates" of where you'd like to be each month, but these numbers are not where you will always fall). Plug in actual numbers by counting pay stubs, adding up investments, and counting receipts you saved that month. Now find the sum of all these numbers.
6. **Variances:** Finally, create a "variance" column (next to your "actual" column) to help you determine any monthly budget fluctuations. Where there are variances in your budget, make necessary adjustments where needed and then try again for the next month (and so on). It's hard to always be right on budget due to changes in your lifestyle. But as long as you are closely in tune, you should be pretty cool.

So that's it for a personal budget. Be sure to review the sample monthly budget below. By the way, while were aware of budgeting apps like Mint and Wiley, we feel that when starting out, creating your own budget with Google Sheets, Microsoft Excel, or a pen and paper is simpler, more customized, and even safer (with respect to the potential security breaches of online apps). So, again, review the monthly budget below and then try plugging in your own numbers.

CHAPTER 7

PERSONAL MONTHLY BUDGET			
Inflows (After Mandatory Taxes)	Monthly Est	Monthly Actual	Variance
Guitar Center Sales Gig	$ 3,043.33	$ 2,916.67	$ (126.66)
Independent Guitar Teaching (Average Net)	$ 833.33	$ 933.33	$ 100.00
Guitar Sessions (Average Net)	$ 500.00	$ 400.00	$ (100.00)
Total Inflows	$ 4,376.66	$ 4,250.00	$ (126.66)
Disbursements (Emergincies & Investments)	Monthly Est	Monthly Actual	Variance
Individual Retirement Account	$ 437.67	$ 437.50	$ (0.17)
Emergency Fund	$ 94.44	$ 94.44	$ -
Total Disbursements	$ 532.11	$ 531.94	$ (0.17)
Outflows (Fixed/Variable Expenses)	Monthly Est	Monthly Actual	Variance
Rent	$ 1,059.64	$ 1,059.64	$ -
School Loan	$ 250.00	$ 250.00	$ -
Car	$ 340.00	$ 340.00	$ -
Phone	$ 50.00	$ 50.00	$ -
Internet	$ 50.00	$ 50.00	$ -
Electric	$ 30.42	$ 30.40	$ 0.02
Car Insurance	$ 95.00	$ 95.00	$ -
DMV License Fees	$ 40.00	$ 40.00	$ -
Accountant ($400 1x Annually spread out)	$ 33.33	$ -	$ 33.33
Web Hosting	$ 20.83	$ 20.00	$ 0.83
Gym	$ 20.00	$ 20.00	$ -
Food	$ 1,500.00	$ 1,600.00	$ (100.00)
Gas	$ 50.00	$ 75.00	$ (25.00)
Car Wash	$ 10.00	$ -	$ 10.00
Books	$ 41.67	$ 62.00	$ (20.33)
Health Care Co Pays	$ 41.67	$ 30.00	$ 11.67
Travel (flights, trains, Uber, food)	$ 166.67	$ -	$ 166.67
Business Mailing	$ 16.67	$ 35.00	$ (18.33)
Holiday Presents	$ 16.67	$ -	$ 16.67
Parking	$ 12.00	$ 36.00	$ (24.00)
Total Outflows	$ 3,844.57	$ 3,793.04	$ 51.53
Total Disbursements and Outflows	$ 4,376.68	$ 4,324.98	$ (0.17)

So, to wrap up this entire piece on important accountant documents, we hope that creating a net profit statement, cash flow analysis, and personal budget helped you to understand your financial position and direct you toward financial health. We realize that setting up these documents at first might take a little time, but we promise that once you get the hang of them, they will be totally worth your effort. Good luck with this, gang! Now get to work!

5

BANKING

Banks are not an accident. They have developed over thousands of years to meet commercial needs and will go on developing to survive.

—Sir Andrew Likierman,
professor at London Business School

8

Twenty-Four Reasons to Use a Bank

Banks come in many shapes and sizes. There are traditional commercial banks (like Bank of America), credit unions (like Connexus), and online banks (like Discover).

While banks are regularly stigmatized as being evil (especially in movies like *Hell or High Water*, where they foreclose on poor mama's farm), the truth is that banks provide a number of wonderful benefits—from protecting your money to investing it. This is good news, right? After all, you can't hide money under your mattress forever.

What follows are twenty-four reasons to use a bank. While our focus is primarily on traditional brick-and-mortar establishments, know that many of the same services (give or take) apply to credit unions and online banks too. So, grab that yellow highlighter, and get ready to learn.

1. A SENSE OF COMMUNITY

Community and personalization are major benefits as to why you should use a bank. When you work with a bank, you're essentially part of a family.

The same friendly tellers, loan officers, and managers working at your corner bank will likely be serving you three to five years from now.

Let's face it, when dealing with your hard-earned money, it's comforting to be greeted by a familiar face.

2. MONEY IS SAFE FROM FIRE AND THEFT

Theft and fire protection are also major benefits that banks provide.

Banks have sophisticated security systems and technologies to protect your money and guard it against potential disasters.

Think about it, how protected is your money from fire in your little studio apartment, constructed from stucco and fiber board? Thought so!

And how protected is your cash from theft when stuffed in a cardboard cookie box in your kitchen cupboard? Double thought so!

Therefore, consider using a bank to hold your cash (especially in the short term), unless you like the chance of becoming cashless.

3. MONEY IS COVERED BY THE FEDERAL DEPOSIT INSURANCE CORPORATION (FDIC)

FDIC protection is yet another reason using a bank is a smart choice for you.

Dating back to after the Great Depression when thousands of people lost their money to bank closures, FDIC protection has kept depositors safe under a variety of economic conditions.

You see, with FDIC insurance, your deposits are backed by the full faith and credit of the US government. You receive coverage up to $250,000 in combined total balances. And best yet, FDIC coverage is free when you use a bank.

So, this is a no-brainer. Use a bank and get the protection your hard-earned cash deserves.

4. OPPORTUNITY TO EARN INTEREST IN A SAVINGS ACCOUNT

Interest on the money you tuck away in a savings account is also a useful convenience banks provide to its customers.

Savings accounts allow you to store the extra cash you get (from birthday gifts and side hustle jobs you hold) for some future goal—all while earning interest for letting the bank hold and use your money over time.

While the interest rate banks pay you is total crap, know that a savings account is usually the gateway to more profitable investments you'll make down the road.

So, open a savings account with a bank today, and start building good savings habits.

5. OPPORTUNITY TO EARN INTEREST IN A CHECKING ACCOUNT

Interest on the money you put in a checking account is another reason you might use a bank. Checking accounts allow you to use your money for everyday purposes (paying bills and making purchases), while also earning a little interest too.

Okay, we'll admit . . . the interest rate on a checking account is even shittier than on a savings account. But where else in the world are you going to earn interest on money that easily flows in and out of your account for the purpose of paying bills?

There are no mathematicians needed here, gang. The answer is crystal clear on this one!

6. ABILITY TO TRACK YOUR MONEY

Access to monthly account statements that allow customers to view every transaction easily is yet another valuable service offered by banks.

Knowing where every penny is going is just good financial management. It helps with budgeting, gathering financial information for tax preparation, and identifying fraudulent activity too.

So, no matter how you slice it, your ability to easily track money is a great reason to use a bank.

7. ABILITY TO CASH CHECKS

Check cashing services can also be an important bank benefit for customers still conducting business the old school way.

Should your current employer pay by check, you'll need a bank to cash that check.

Sure, you can go to one of those check cashing places next to the liquor store and cannabis shop. But keep in mind those places charge up to 4 percent plus a flat fee for their services. Do you really want to throw away $30 to $40 on a $500 check? Your answer is, NO!

Banks are an easy fix.

8. ABILITY TO ENABLE DIRECT DEPOSIT

Direct deposit—a modern form of transferring money between an employer and employee—is also a reason you might use a bank.

Compared to waiting for old-fashioned checks to arrive in the mail, direct deposits are fast, easy, and super simple to set up.

Since most employers use direct deposit, a bank account will be necessary to get paid.

So, speak with a bank representative and your employer today to set up direct deposit.

9. ACCESS TO CASH EVERYWHERE VIA ATMS

Cash accessibility via ATMs, a huge convenience for customers, is another advantage that banks provide.

With access to thousands of ATMs nationwide, you'll never have to worry about those "cash only" places like restaurants, street vendors, or laundromats when you're out on the road.

So, rejoice, with the help of your trusted bank, you will never be cash deprived again.

10. ACCESS TO A CHECKING DEBIT CARD

Debit cards, widely used by most customers, are another reason you might use a bank.

Linked to your everyday regular checking account, they require no more than a quick swipe at a store register to process your day-to-day payments. Welcome to the 2020s. LOL.

One cool feature of debit cards is that they can be linked to your savings account, providing you with "overdraft protection." This allows the bank to draw money from your savings should your checking ever hit zero. So, rejoice! With a checking debit card, you'll never get rejected at the grocery store again.

11. ACCESS TO CREDIT CARDS

Credit cards, also widely used by customers, are an extremely valuable service banks provide.

Here are a few of the benefits:

- **They Provide a Line of Credit:** Unlike debit cards, credit cards are not linked to your checking or savings account but, rather, to a line of credit approved by the bank. This means you can make purchases with money you don't really have, and pay for those purchases at a later date.
- **They Provide Reward Features:** Whenever you use your card, banks give you cash back on purchases, air miles, and even purchase discounts. Not bad! And finally . . .
- **They Help to Build Credit:** Building your credit history is perhaps the biggest benefit of bank credit cards. As long as you use your credit card responsibly, you'll become more credible to your bank, and improve your chances for future loan approval.

So, why not skip over to your local bank and get your credit card today?

12. WIRE MONEY SERVICES

A money wire, another benefit provided to bank customers, is a formal method of sending money to someone in a hurry.

Let's dream that the house you want to buy with your rock star money closes escrow (meaning you have about forty-eight hours to finalize the purchase) but you're on a European tour.

Guess what?! The only acceptable form of payment would be through a wire transfer.

So, thanks to your smarts for opening a bank account, you now have a place to call home.

13. ABILITY TO PAY BILLS ONLINE

Online bill payment, a convenient and modern method for paying bills today, is yet another reason you might use a bank.

All it takes to get started is:

1. Open your bank account,
2. Link your bill collectors' info to your checking, and . . .
3. Begin paying your bills online . . . from home, work, or on tour.

And to make it even easier, you can set up "automatic" bill payment so your bills are paid every month on the specified day and time. Boom! More time spent writing new songs!

With online bill payment and its automatic services, you'll never write an archaic check again or get charged fees for paying your bills late.

14. MOBILE BANKING

Mobile banking via your smartphone is another modern convenience provided by commercial banks. You can check your balances, pay bills, and deposit checks "on the go," 24/7.

To get started, you can just:

1. Download your bank's app to your phone,
2. Answer a few security questions, and . . .
3. Create a log-in name and password.

That's it!

So, should you ever get caught up in the studio and can't afford the time to visit your local bank, just open the app and take care of your banking needs on the go! Pretty convenient.

15. ABILITY TO WRITE CASHIER AND CERTIFIED CHECKS

Cashier and certified checks are also useful bank products, particularly when the person you're paying requires a more secure form of payment than a personal check.

While there are many similarities between a cashier and certified check, here is a basic breakdown:

- **Cashier Checks:** A cashier check is drawn against the bank's account (you give them the money and they write the check).
- **Certified Checks:** A certified check is drawn against your account (the bank designates the funds to be taken out of your account via a certified check that proves you have enough money).

In either case, should you ever need to transfer large sums of money to persons with whom you are unfamiliar, they just might request a cashier or certified check. Thanks to your local bank, you'll be able to fulfill that request.

16. ABILITY TO WRITE MONEY ORDERS

Money orders, another service offered by banks, can also be quite useful to some customers.

Similar to cashier checks, money orders are drawn against the bank's account (you give them the money and they issue the money order).

The major difference, however, is that money orders are usually used when dealing with less formal transactions and smaller dollar amounts. The fee for money orders is also far less.

Yes, in lieu of a bank, you could always get a money order from a 7-Eleven or another convenience store. But would you feel safer walking into a bank with $500 cash, or a 7-Eleven store? You get the point!

17. QUICK PAYMENT FEATURES LIKE ZELLE

Zelle, a useful tool for sending and receiving money, is another reason you might use a commercial bank.

Let's have a little fun and imagine that you just finished the last song of a big concert, when you get a text from your medical marijuana dispensary saying, "can't deliver to your hotel in Los Angeles tonight, till you pay the fee in advance."

At first, you're like, "bugger!" but then remember you have Zelle and can send that payment immediately through your online banking app.

Problem solved! Thanks to your bank, everyone is super high (we mean happy).

18. OPPORTUNITIES TO GET LOANS (AUTO, MORTGAGE, AND MORE)

Getting loans is yet another bank benefit—and this one ranks high on reasons to use a bank.

Cash is king, but unfortunately, we never have enough of it to buy a car, go to school, or purchase a home.

You won't get approved for every loan you apply for, but the longer you're with a bank, the greater a candidate for loans you become.

Look, no matter how you look at it, with banks and bank loans, the possibility of achieving your wildest dreams becomes a far greater reality.

19. ACCESS TO FINANCIAL ADVICE

Free financial advice is also a huge advantage of using a commercial bank.

Bank employees will show you how to grow your money through bank products like certificates of deposit (CDs), money market accounts (MMAs), and even stocks and bonds.

So why not take advantage of the free financial services your bank offers? Make an appointment with an investment officer and pick their brain today.

Remember, as Ben Franklin said, "An investment in knowledge pays the best interest."

20. OPPORTUNITY TO INVEST IN MONEY MARKET ACCOUNTS

Money market accounts (MMAs), which are popular money-making investments, are also a valuable service provided by commercial banks.

While an MMA is similar to a regular savings account in that it is a safe—FDIC insured—low-risk way to save money, MMAs provide more flexibility via check writing and debit card privileges and usually pay a higher interest rate too.

The downside is the high balance requirement to open an MMA (about 1k), limited account transactions, and fluctuating interest rates (with the possibility of falling below your savings account interest rate).

Just be sure to speak with the bank's financial advisors for advice. Okay? Cool!

21. OPPORTUNITY TO INVEST IN CDS

Certificates of deposit (CDs) are also popular money-making investments that banks offer.

While a CD is similar to both a regular savings account and an MMA in that it is a safe—FDIC insured—low-risk way to save money, CDs pay a potentially higher interest rate than both a savings account and an MMA.

The downside is that CDs are bound by fixed-term maturity dates ranging from three months to five years and impose penalties, should you withdraw money before the maturity date. So, if you're uneasy about tying up your money, CDs are probably not for you.

So again, please take advantage of your bank's financial advisors for advice.

22. BROKERAGE FIRM ACCESS

Brokerage firm access, yet another popular money-making benefit, is also offered by some banks.

While savings accounts, MMAs, and CDs are certainly safe low-risk forms of investment, brokerage firms can help you earn significantly higher interest rates via investments like:

- stocks (fractional ownership of companies),
- bonds (loans to companies), and . . .
- mutual funds (pooled money from a variety of investors in stocks, bonds, and other investments).

The downside to these investments, however, is that they are "higher risk" and the balances in your accounts can drastically fluctuate given a number of economic factors.

So, if risk is something you can't handle, then these investments are not for you.

Examples of banks with brokerage firm access are Bank of America (with Merrill Edge) and Chase Bank (with J. P. Morgan Wealth Management). Be sure to check them out today!

23. CUSTOMER SERVICE ACCESS 24/7

Yet another valuable service offered by most banks, 24/7 customer service access can be quite beneficial to anyone in an emergency.

Let's say you're getting ready to pay for dinner while touring out of country and your card is rejected. Immediately, you call your bank and the problem is resolved.

Thanks to good customer service, you're not washing dishes while adoring fans watch and wonder, WTF!

With 24/7 access, you can avoid very embarrassing moments.

24. ACCOUNT ALERTS

Finally, the account alert function is another reason you might use a bank.

Text and email alerts keep you fully informed of all suspected fraudulent activities, and may even trigger an automatic account freeze until you're able to get in touch with the bank.

After all, when you're out on the road or deep in the studio, the last thing you need is money worries. But with account alerts, you can feel confident your bank has got your back.

So that's it on the various benefits of why you might consider using a commercial bank. While our focus was primarily on traditional brick-and-mortar establishments, remember that many of the same services (give or take) apply to credit unions and online banks too.

Should you ever be eager to compare and contrast all three banks, be sure to check out helpful websites like creditkarma.com and investopedia.com. Also, be sure to check out our piece on the pros and cons of online banks. Who knows, that piece just might be coming up next.

9

Major Pros and Cons of Using an Online Bank

Taking rise in the digital revolution—and expanding significantly during the COVID-19 pandemic—there is a new type of cool, hip, and convenient bank known as the online bank.

While online banks perform many of the same functions as traditional banks, they are unique in that they function entirely online and thus have lower overhead. This allows them to pass on their savings to their customers in the form of attractive benefits.

But, don't get too excited yet—where there are advantages there are also some disadvantages.

What follows are the pros and cons of online banks. We hope these points will inspire you to consider your banking needs and, ultimately, to find the best banking option for you.

PRO #1: BETTER INTEREST RATES ON YOUR MONEY

Probably one of the greatest benefits of using an online bank is that you'll earn a greater percentage rate on your money in savings and select checking accounts.

For instance, the average interest rate of a savings account for a traditional brick-and-mortar commercial bank is just 0.01 percent.

On the other hand, the average rate of an online bank is 0.50 percent (and as high as 1 percent). While these rates are subject to frequent changes depending on the bank (and the economy), these rates are still higher than any other commercial bank today.

Whether your money is in a savings account for some future event, or it's in a checking account for everyday use, who wouldn't want to earn a higher percentage rate on their money? After all, banks use your money as loans to other people at rates ranging from 3 to 20 percent, so why shouldn't you get a little more too?

PRO #2: LOWER (OR NO) FEES

Another advantage of using an online bank is that you'll find lower or no banking fees.

While traditional brick-and-mortar commercial banks are known to charge you for a host of different fees, many online banks tend to take a different approach, as follows:

1. When you open a checking or savings account, the bank may not charge you a "maintenance fee" for keeping your account open.
2. When you make a payment or purchase that exceeds your balance, and the bank allows the transaction, the bank may not charge you an "overdraft fee."
3. When you make a payment or purchase that exceeds your balance, and the bank declines the transactions, the bank may not charge you an "insufficient fund fee." And finally . . .
4. When you use an ATM that is out of your bank's network, the bank may not charge you an "out-of-network" fee.

While many of the above fees can be avoided at a commercial bank just by being more financially responsible, it's nice to know that you're not going to get railroaded with an online bank should you happen to make a few mistakes once in a while. After all, musicians are humans too.

What's that, you say, "How bad can an occasional fee here and there be?" Well, according to a recent GoBankingRates Survey, the average American spends $7 in banking fees per month. Yikes! That's $94 extra per year you can be earning in a higher interest account at an online bank. Um, those online banks are starting to sound pretty good! Don't you think?

PRO #3: AN EQUAL NUMBER OF ATMS (IF NOT MORE)

Another pro of online banks is that they have an equal number of ATMs (if not more) available for their customers to use around the country.

Yup, it's true—while many of us may initially feel that online banks are not as ubiquitous as commercial banks (because there are no big signs on every street corner), online banks do indeed have partnerships with networks of ATMs numbering into the several thousands.

Here are some actual numbers from the best-rated online banks:

- Axos Bank provides access to more than 91,000 ATMs
- Quontic Bank provides access to more than 90,000 ATMs
- Discover Bank provides access to more than 60,000 ATMs
- Ally Bank provides access to 43,000 ATMs
- NBKC provides access to 37,000 ATMs

Now here are some numbers from the best-rated commercial banks:

- Citibank provides access to 72,000 ATMs
- PNC provides access to 19,000 ATMs
- Chase Bank provides access to 16,000 ATMs
- Bank of America provides access to 16,000 ATMs
- Wells Fargo provides access to 13,000 ATMs

As you can see, online bank ATMs are quite competitive to commercial bank ATMs. They can be found in large retail stores, small businesses, and even other banks (the latter being the most secure). There are even apps that help you find an ATM near you. Pretty cool, right?

So, if you're a musician who loves ATMs and is out on the road a great deal, or just jetting around locally from one gig to the next, you will always have access to your cash. Sweet!

But don't get too excited just yet. First, we have to review the cons of online banks.

CON #1: WEAKER BRAND RECOGNITION

Brand recognition refers to how recognizable a company is (i.e., how well we know its name, its logo, and personality). Brand recognition is important because familiarity builds trust.

Take a look at the top-ten rated online banks by *Forbes*. Do you recognize any of them?

1. Quontic Bank
2. Discover
3. Axos Bank
4. Ally Bank
5. NBKC bank
6. iGObanking
7. Salem Five Direct
8. TIAA Bank
9. Vio Bank
10. Capital One 360

If you're like most people, you probably recognized about two of the above online banks (Discover and Capital One 360). Just two! What the F?

While all of these banks are indeed highly rated, you might initially feel uncomfortable trusting your money with most of these online companies. Because, let's face it, you simply don't hear much about—or even see—the majority of these names in everyday life.

Come on peeps—you can't deny the power of branding. Branding makes the consumer world function more efficiently. It's all about heuristics—you're driving down the street, you see that big Chase Bank sign, and you feel a certain level of comfort. I mean, after all, John Pierpont Morgan Sr. is the freakin' guy that helped fund the development of electricity, had a major hand in steel (which helped build our nation), and reorganized several major railroads (which helped connect our nation). Chase is a promise.

Branding is probably something you can get over quickly, but this is an initial hurdle.

CON #2: CASH CHALLENGES—GETTING AND DEPOSITING IT

Okay, so if you can get past the branding hurdle, then the next greatest con of online banking is withdrawing and depositing your cash.

Imagine being out on the road and suddenly needing a large sum of cash. Maybe your van breaks downs and the mechanic will only accept cash. Really? Does this happen? Yup, it happened to me (this is Bobby) in the middle of the Nevada desert. So, what the heck happens next?

Well, with online banking, there are no branches you can walk into and take out $3,000 for the new radiator, water pump, and thermostat. Sure, you can find one of many ATMs in the online bank's network, but most online banks have limits on the amount of cash you can withdraw in a day—on average it is between $400 and $1,000. Yikes!

Okay, so changing gears, now imagine being out on tour and getting paid cash that you would rather not hold for the full trip. Say you're getting paid cash from the promoter or pulling in cash at the merch table from T-shirt sales. What the heck do you do with all the dough?

Well, with online banking, there are no branches you can walk into to deposit the money. And most (if not all) of the ATMs for online banks will not allow you to deposit cash. This means that you either have to hang on to your cash and risk something happening to it, or devise some kind a slick work-around? Sucks! Right?

All this will probably change in the near future (as online banks know this is a problem they need to fix ASAP), but for now you're screwed when it comes to cash peeps. Hey, we're just trying to be critical and present both sides of the story to you. As we said, where there are advantages, there are also disadvantages. And this one can be a major hassle. Don't ya think?

CON #3: LESS PERSONALIZED SERVICES (CHATS, ROBOTS, OH NO)

Less personalized face-to-face customer service is yet another disadvantage of using online banks.

Imagine this real-life replay:

1. I (this is Britt) get on my mobile phone to call an online bank. Crap, no cell service, so I move to a spot where there is better reception.
2. After dialing the 800 number, I am greeted by a recording that gives me a long list of number options to choose from. Wait, I don't hear the choice that I want, so I say, "operator."
3. Now the operator doesn't understand, so it (the robot) repeats the long list once again all while I am now yelling "operator" several times in a high voice. LOL. Yes, I am getting annoyed.
4. Finally, I decide to hang up and jump online to use the chat service that is available. I type in the reason I am reaching out

(e.g., "Want to talk about cash deposit work-arounds"), but the chat robot also doesn't understand what I want. I am now extremely frustrated and log off without finding a solution to my problem.

Could this type of scenario exist when calling the customer service department of a commercial bank too? Yes! But the good news with commercial banks is that you can visit your local branch to talk to real-life people, which, let's face it, is sometimes nice.

We don't know about you guys, but as much as we love technology with all of its great conveniences, it has not entirely replaced human beings. With human beings, you can talk face to face, communicate a problem, and feel as though your emotions and body language are being understood. In that moment, you get a sense that you are being heard and that the person is going to work hard at getting the job done before you split.

So, like yeah, less personalization can be a major disadvantage of using an online bank.

CON #4: SECURITY CONCERNS

Another potential disadvantage of online banks are security issues.

Though most online banks boast about how safe and secure they are, accidents really can happen. One recent *Wired* article wrote, "A Massive Fraud Operation Stole Millions from Online Bank Accounts." Yikes!

According to *Wired*, "Crooks used 20 emulators to mimic more than 16,000 phones belonging to customers whose mobile bank accounts had been compromised."

While it's true that people with commercial bank accounts also use their mobile phones "some of the time," people with online banks use their mobile phones "100 percent of the time." So, the risk is greater. Remember, online banks are "online" only.

CON #5: SERVICE INTERRUPTIONS

Finally, service interruptions can be another potential disadvantage of online banks.

Service interruptions could occur when an online banking's system gets overwhelmed by too many users trying to log on at once. Or, they can also occur when the bank is conducting an update or regular maintenance.

In any case, when you need to take care of important business, no one wants to deal with temporary closures. After all, you've got hit songs to write and gigs to play! Right? Right!

So, in closing, online banks and traditional banks provide similar services to their customers. However, the advantages and disadvantages might sway you one way or the other.

You can also do a trial with both banks, and see what works best for you. Perhaps you can use the online bank exclusively for your savings (to get the higher interest rates), and a commercial bank for everyday services.

Just be sure to do your homework and consider your banking needs before making a decision. Good luck, gang!

6

CREDIT AND DEBT

If you can't buy it twice, you can't afford it.

—Jay-Z

Ten Steps to Building "Rock" Solid Credit

Credit is short for credibility. It tells creditors, like credit card companies and others, that you are capable of paying them back tomorrow for the things you need today.

Whether a loan for music school, or a credit card to buy that new guitar, without credit you would have to save your money for several years before moving your career forward. And that would totally suck, right?

So, below are ten steps to building rock-solid credit that you can start using today.

Warning: While credit can be an absolute godsend to many people, it can also be the devil in disguise to those who are financially irresponsible. So, always use restraint and only rely on credit when absolutely necessary. The end goal is to use cash whenever possible, and minimize the use of credit. Understand? Good. Now, let's get started.

1. ESTABLISH A STEADY FLOW OF INCOME WITH A "SURVIVAL" JOB

The first step in building rock-solid credit is to establish a steady flow of income via a survival job. Remember, creditors will want to know you have the ability to pay them back, and holding a steady job that pays the bills (until your music can) is a great way to reassure them.

There are numerous survival jobs today that are quite flexible. Consider the following:

- You could give music lessons online from the comfort of your own home.
- You could sell gear at a music store, like Guitar Center. Or . . .
- You could drive for Uber, Postmates, or DoorDash. These gigs are so flexible you can work whenever you want to.

Look gang, remember that creditors are not going to extend credit to those with inconsistent income. So, get a survival job, prove to the creditors you are capable of paying your bills, and start establishing the rock-solid credibility you need to succeed.

2. DON'T MOVE AROUND A LOT—MAINTAIN A STEADY RESIDENCE

Now that you understand the concept and importance of a survival job, it's time to recognize the significance of maintaining a steady residence.

When you move around a lot, it creates "red flags" and indicates to creditors that you can't pay your rent.

Our best advice: rent a small, affordable apartment, commit to it for several months or years, and eventually get an account summary from the landlord for all of the months you've paid rent. This will come in handy when dealing with future creditors.

Look, if you still don't understand the creditor's viewpoint on "consistency," think of it this way. Let's say you and your fellow band members are looking for a drummer to join your band. Would you want a drummer who's been with twenty bands in the last year? No, because that drummer's inconsistencies and lack of commitment and responsibility would be a huge turnoff. Make sense?

So, find a crib you dig and stay in it for a while. You'll be really glad that you did.

3. OPEN A CHECKING ACCOUNT

So, you've got the job and a place to live. Now, let's talk about opening up—and maintaining—a checking account to pay your bills.

Your ability to successfully maintain this account without incurring any penalties for overdrafts, insufficient funds, or negative balances will be a major step in building credit.

Now, here's how to do it:

1. Contact a reputable bank (like Chase or Wells Fargo) and choose an account that does not require a minimum balance or charge you monthly or annual fees.
2. Sign up for direct deposit so you always have a steady flow of money coming in from your job.
3. Pay your bills on time and absolutely never spend more money than you have in your account.

If you can do all of the above successfully over several months, the bank and other creditors will start to see you as a credible customer. The more credible you are, the more credit products (credit cards, lines of credit, personal loans, etc.) you will eventually be offered. But it's gonna take some time. So, just open a checking account first! Okay? Cool! Now, let's move on.

4. BECOME AN AUTHORIZED USER ON YOUR PARENTS' CARD

Since it might take some time to build credibility with your bank and be offered your very own credit card, you might consider asking your parents to make you an authorized user on their credit card. This is especially smart if your parents maintain low balances on their credit cards and have a good credit history.

You see, even if you never use your parents' card, you can still reap the benefit of their good credit standing by just having your name on their account. Yup, you heard right! Their good credit history will eventually rub off onto you and make you a more viable candidate to creditors.

So, while your parents might initially freak out at your request to become an authorized user on their card, let them know they'll actually be helping you build your own financial independence.

5. GET A SECURED CREDIT CARD

If becoming an authorized user on your parents' credit card may not be an option, another strategy might be getting a secured card.

A secured card acts like a regular credit card, in that the bank issues you a line of credit, you make purchases, and then you pay for these purchases at a later time.

However, the primary difference is that a cash deposit is required when opening a secured card. And your credit limit will be the amount of your initial deposit. The deposit is not used for paying your monthly bill, but in the event you completely default on paying off your card, the deposit ultimately protects the lender from your irresponsibility (hence the name "secured card").

The point of a secured card is to get you comfortable using a card without the possibility of accruing massive debt. After you prove you're credit worthy, you can apply for a regular credit card and get your deposit back.

A few examples of secured cards are Platinum Select Mastercard, the Secured Visa OpenSky card, and the Credit One Platinum Secured credit card. There are many more possibilities, so do your research.

6. PAY YOUR BALANCE IN FULL EVERY MONTH

So, you've done your research, spoken with a few banks, and now have that shiny new secured credit card. Congratulations! But don't screw this up! Now you have to pay the balance in full every month for all the purchases you make.

You may be thinking: "Why do I have to pay the balance every month if the bank has my security deposit?" Good question! But remember, the bank does not use your deposit to cover your monthly bill (they only use it if you completely default). Instead, they'll charge you interest every month on any remaining balance from all your purchases.

To put this into perspective, if you purchase a guitar for $500 and only make the average minimum required payment of 3 percent ($15) on a card with a 15.99 percent annual interest rate, you will end up paying a total of $643 for your guitar by the time it's paid off. That's $143 more. Yuck!

So, why pay interest if you don't have to? Just pay all your balances in full every month.

7. PAY YOUR BILLS ON TIME

Paying your bills on time is yet another important strategy in elevating your credit history to the top of the charts. Be clear that just one late payment can drop your credit score to the floor. Even worse, that one late payment will stay on your credit history for seven years. Holy crap!

But what happens if you fall on hard times? Don't freak and let your ego get the best of you. Call your credit card company and explain the situation. Oftentimes, they will give you a one-time extension. Or they will work out a payment plan without the adverse effects of damaging your credit history.

So, pay your bills on time. And if you can't, call your creditor. You'll be glad you did!

8. APPLY FOR A "REGULAR" CREDIT CARD (I.E., VISA OR MASTERCARD)

The time has come. It's been almost twelve months since you opened your secure credit card. You've consistently used your card, paid off your balance on time each month, and maintained a good relationship with your bank. Now it's time to apply for the real thing . . . a regular credit card.

Apply for either a Visa or Mastercard first, since these cards are accepted worldwide at most merchants. All you need is one card for now, so pick a card that offers you the best deal.

Consider the card's interest rate, annual fees, and special perks it might offer. Don't worry about the credit limit—we wouldn't want you going retail crazy and maxing out your card. On the latter note, this brings us to the next topic of our discussion on overcharging. Read on . . .

9. DON'T OVERCHARGE YOUR CREDIT CARD

Okay, you've played by the rules and followed our advice, and now you've got yourself a "regular" credit card with a higher credit limit than your secured card had. On average, your new limit will be about $3,000 to $5,000. That's enough to make you want to go on a rock star spending spree.

But look, maxing out your credit card is irresponsible. The goal should be to keep your credit card "utilization" to under 30 percent of your total limit. This means if your credit limit is $5,000, you should *never* owe more than $1,500 (30% x $5,000 = $1,500). Seriously gang!

Remember, credit card companies are testing you to see how well you manage credit. If they sense your spending is getting out of hand, they may lower your credit limit, suspend your card temporarily, or even cancel your card. Now, you're back in the dumps where you started.

So, remember, always practice good spending habits. Think of it this way: you're out on stage in front of the credit world and you don't want to get booed off. Show those banks how good you are and continue building credit. You'll be glad you did!

10. DON'T APPLY FOR TOO MANY ACCOUNTS AT ONCE

You've come a long way toward building your credit. Once again, congratulations! But we're not done yet. There's one more important tip to share: don't apply for too many accounts at once!

You see, once people are on the road to building their credit history, they tend to begin applying for multiple credit card accounts. While having multiple accounts (in good standing) is indeed beneficial to solidifying your credit score, you have to approach this with patience.

You see, each time you apply for a credit card, the bank checks your credit history, which places an "inquiry" on your credit report. The multiple inquiries generated on your credit report all at once can actually kill your good standing. This may prevent you from getting that future loan for equipment, a car, or even your first house. Wow, major buzz kill!

So, do this instead: Continue to use your regular credit card responsibly for about twelve months. After this, close your secured card, get your deposit back, and replace it with another "regular credit card," which you should also use responsibly for say another six months. After this, you can apply for another card (or some other line of credit), and so on and so forth. All you'll only need is about three or four lines of credit to solidify your credit history.

Okay gang, so remember, slow down on the applications. Start with one regular card for a year add then add one new card every six months or so. Patience is your virtue. Good luck!

So, that's about all we have to say on building credit for now. But remember, while having access to credit is great, there is also that saying, "Credit Kills." This means if you overindulge in credit, it could become your worst nightmare.

Eventually, when you have enough money to pay cash, you should minimize the use of your credit altogether. This is the name of the game, people. Play wisely, build credit, and thrive.

Monitor Your Credit via Reports and Scores: Nine Steps

Your personal credit (or credibility) helps creditors decide whether you are capable of paying them back tomorrow for the things that you need today.

With a good credit report and score, you can usually do everything from leasing a car, to renting an apartment, to buying that new guitar for upcoming gigs. This is why it is so crucial to initially build good credit and then monitor and maintain it (the latter of which is the focus of this piece). Failure to monitor and maintain your credit could lead to denied credit applications, embarrassment, and zero money when you need it.

From understanding credit reports (or history) to knowing the best FICO score apps, be sure to take the following nine steps extremely seriously. Okay? Let's do it!

1. UNDERSTAND CREDIT BUREAUS AND REPORTS

The first step in monitoring your credit is understanding the basics of credit bureaus and reports.

A quick breakdown as follows is really all you need:

- **Credit Bureaus:** Credit bureaus (like Equifax, Experian, and TransUnion) are data collection agencies that compile data about your credit history in credit reports.
- **Credit Reports:** Credit reports typically include information like your name, address, date of birth, Social Security number, and—most importantly—your payment history. Credit reports

help to tell any creditor inquiring about your credit whether you are "credit worthy."

2. OBTAIN YOUR PERSONAL CREDIT REPORTS

Now that you know the basics of credit bureaus and reports, the second step in monitoring your credit is to obtain copies of your personal credit history.

Follow these three simple steps:

1. Log on to AnnualCreditReport.com and enter basic personal information.
2. Choose the bureau report you desire (we suggest a report from all three bureaus). And finally . . .
3. Download the reports online or request physical copies to be sent by mail.

3. SCAN FOR POTENTIAL ERRORS ON YOUR CREDIT REPORT

After obtaining copies of your personal credit reports, now you'll want to scan them for "fixable" errors. Know that credit errors—even the smallest inaccuracies—can lead to denied credit.

Here's what to look for:

1. **Duplication Errors:** When creditors mistakenly report one of your accounts multiple times, making it appear you have more accounts than you actually do.
2. **Insufficient or Blank History:** When creditors fail to report your information to the credit bureaus and your report is missing accounts you know you have.
3. **Clerical Errors:** When creditors incorrectly enter your name or address from an application you filled out.
4. **Multiple Variations of Your Name:** When you fill out credit reports unintentionally using different variations of your name (like Rich, Richie, and Dick).
5. **Omission of Information:** When you fill out credit reports, accidentally omitting key information (like your address, phone number, and employers' info). And finally . . .
6. **Accounts that Aren't Yours:** When scammers fraudulently open new credit accounts in your name and default on making

payments. (Yikes! Hold this thought, this is identity theft and we'll address it later.)

4. CORRECT SIMPLE MISTAKES ON YOUR CREDIT REPORT

Should a thorough scan of your credit reports reveal any simple errors, you'll want to correct these blunders immediately. Remember, even the smallest mistakes can lead to denied credit.

Follow these three steps:

1. **Contact the Appropriate Credit Bureau:** Contact the appropriate credit bureau where the mistake exists, identify each disputed item with supporting documents to prove you are in the right, and then request a deletion or correction be made to your report.
2. **Write to the Appropriate Creditor:** Write to the appropriate creditor who initially reported (or omitted) the erroneous information and explain that you've filed a dispute to have the information reviewed. Be sure to include any documentation that you may have to support your claim. And finally . . .
3. **Be Patient:** Know that the entire process may take thirty to ninety days. Sucks, we know. But as the old adage proclaims, "patience is a virtue."

5. RESOLVE SERIOUS IDENTITY THEFT ISSUES ON YOUR CREDIT REPORTS

Also be sure to immediately resolve far more serious errors—like identity theft—you might find after conducting a thorough scan of your reports. Identity theft can really screw up your life, since it essentially involves someone taking over your life.

Be sure to follow these six steps:

1. **File a Police Report:** Visit your local police department and tell them that you want to file an identity theft report. Be sure to get a copy of the report as you will likely have to show it to creditors in the coming weeks.
2. **Contact the Federal Trade Commission (FTC):** Get in touch with the FTC at identitytheft.gov and file an identity theft report. This will not only provide proof to creditors that your

issues are legit, but will give you certain consumer protection rights under law.

3. **Contact All of Your Creditors:** Contact the fraud departments of all the companies where you spotted fraudulent purchases and activity. They will also need to see a host of information including police reports, the FTC identity theft report, and proof of your identity to investigate the matter. You should also ask them to immediately close all the accounts that were fraudulently opened in your name.
4. **Request a Fraud Alert or Freeze:** Contact the three credit bureaus and place a fraud alert or freeze on your account. A fraud alert makes it much more difficult for any person applying for credit in your name to be issued credit. A freeze makes it impossible for anyone to open up credit under your name (including you).
5. **File a Claim with the Credit Bureaus:** Contact the three credit bureaus and file a claim requesting that all of the questionable accounts on your file be removed. Typically, they will need to see the FTC identity theft report, proof of your identity, and a letter identifying the fraudulent accounts on your report. Follow through with this until your report is eventually clean and back to normal. And finally . . .
6. **Obtain Credit Reports Regularly:** Obtain a free credit report from annualcreditreport.com once per year and purchase additional statements from the three major credit bureaus throughout the year. Remember, credit monitoring is the whole point of this piece, so you need to remain diligent in keeping reports clean—especially after being a victim of identity theft. So, stay on top of this!

So, that's pretty much it for dealing with the shit show of identity theft. By now, you should also be clearer, in general, about monitoring credit and keeping error-free reports.

But what the heck is that thing called a FICO score you've been hearing about in the news? Aren't they also important to a discussion on monitoring credit? Good question! Read on!

6. KNOW WHAT A FICO SCORE IS

A FICO score is a credit ranking assigned to your credit report by the Fair Isaac Corporation.

Ranging from 300 to 850 points, a FICO score helps lenders quickly determine whether or not they'll extend you a line of credit. Bottom line, lenders simply do not always have the time to look at line-by-line items in your credit report every time you apply for a loan, they just need a quick numeric calculation. This is where your FICO score comes into play. Pretty cool, right?

7. UNDERSTAND FICO SCORE CALCULATIONS

FICO scores are calculated from data in your credit report grouped into five categories:

1. **Payment History:** 35 percent
2. **Debts Owed:** 30 percent
3. **Credit History Length:** 15 percent
4. **New Credit Accounts:** 10 percent
5. **Credit Mix:** 10 percent

Notice how "payment history" and "debts owed" rank as the two highest categories that creditors look at. This is why it is so important to pay your bills on time and keep the amount of credit you charge to no more than 30 percent of your credit limit. Don't mess this up!

8. UNDERSTAND FICO SCORE RANGES

Now if you're scratching your head trying to figure out what the above FICO percentages mean and what a good FICO score actually is, it's rather complex. Lenders all have different criteria and expectations, but here is a good rule of thumb when it comes to a general FICO score range:

- **580 and Below:** Poor
- **580 to 669:** Fair
- **670 to 739:** Good
- **740 to 799:** Very Good
- **800 to 850:** Exceptional

For those who skipped math class to party and play music, clearly the only math you need to know here is that the higher the score, the better the rating. But you're probably wondering: How can I check my own FICO score? Is there a website or app that I can use? Yup! Read on . . .

9. CHECK YOUR FICO SCORE VIA APPS

When it comes to checking your FICO score, the easiest method is to use a reputable, free app.

There are many apps that allow you to pull your FICO score as often as you like. Some are offered through your bank or financial institution, some via the credit bureaus and some from random third-parties. In either case, here are our favorite top six FICO Score apps:

- Credit Karma
- Credit Sesame
- myFICO
- WalletHub
- TransUnion Credit Score, and . . .
- Experian FICO Score

Just visit the Apple Store or Google Play Store to download the FICO app of your desire and begin checking your score today!

Oh, and, if apps aren't your thing, you can always access the web-based versions of these apps from your home computer. Personally, we prefer this option, since we'd rather not use our phones for any important business, especially since phones can get lost or stolen.

In any case, whether you use an app or computer, be sure to get your FICO score today!

Well folks, that's pretty much it for monitoring your credit via reports and scores. Just remember that it is not enough to build good credit. You have to continually monitor your credit to maintain a strong rating.

Also remember that good credit can help you achieve your wildest dreams, but bad credit can also put you into your darkest nightmares. So, be diligent monitoring your credit and thrive!

Good luck with this, gang! Peace!

12

Twenty Ways to Protect Yourself from Identity Theft and Fraud

Identity theft and fraud exist when a less-than-desirable person gets ahold of your personal information, uses it to open new lines of credit, and racks up debt in your name. It also exists when someone uses your info to withdraw money from your existing financial accounts.

While we could go on and on with examples of identity theft and fraud, the bottom line is that it can temporarily ruin your life and good credit standing. This is why learning a variety of safety precautions to protect yourself from thieves is an important part of personal finance.

What follows are twenty tips—from storing your personal information safely to utilizing identity theft prevention services. There's a lot of stuff here that can seem a bit overwhelming, so feel free to skim the list to get a general idea of the important steps you can start taking today.

1. STORE YOUR PERSONAL INFORMATION IN A SAFE PLACE

The first step in protecting your identity is to make sure no one has access to your personal information.

This means securing things like your Social Security number, credit card number, and bank and retirement account numbers. You can use a secure computer hard drive, file cabinet with locking drawers, or home safe.

Also, be sure to limit to whom you give important information like your date of birth, address, and mother's maiden name. You can simply keep that information tucked away in your pretty little head. In other words, zip your lips!

Remember, there's only one of you on this earth. Don't let someone else try to be you. Protect your personal information like you would the "rights" to your award-winning songs.

2. SIGN YOUR NEW CREDIT CARD IMMEDIATELY

Signing the box on the back of your credit card immediately upon receipt is great practice in minimizing your chances of identity theft.

To ensure your signature sticks, use a permanent Sharpie pen just like the ones you use to sign autographs for your beloved fans.

Or, if you don't want to sign your name, simply write, "Check ID" in the signature box on the back of the card. This way, the clerk will ask for your ID each time you make a purchase.

Whichever approach you use, it's far better than just leaving your credit card blank.

3. NEVER LET YOUR CREDIT CARD GET OUT OF YOUR SIGHT

Keeping your eyes on your credit card each time you use it is another preventative measure.

Yes, we know this isn't always possible like when that server walks away to run your card. But as a general rule, never lose possession or sight of your credit card for more than a couple of minutes.

This means don't loan out your credit card, don't leave it at the club because you were too drunk to remember to pay your tab, and don't leave it with the front desk at the rehearsal studio where you rent space. There are many other examples, but you get the gist! Watch it, or else!

4. REVIEW CREDIT CARD BILLS TO ENSURE TRANSACTIONS ARE YOURS

Though it can be time consuming, looking at your monthly credit card statements is plain smart.

People usually don't find out about illegal charges until they've reviewed their statements. And for those that never look at their statements, they end up paying for purchases that are not even theirs. Do you really want to pay for three rounds of drinks you never drank? Nope!

Look, when credit card companies are alerted of dispute charges early enough, they may remove it from your account and not hold you liable. So, always inspect to protect!

5. ASK FOR ALL YOUR RECEIPTS

Ask, ask, ask! Having receipts as documentation for your purchases is a great way to protect yourself from theft.

Since most of us can't remember all our purchases or recognize transaction names on our statements, you'll now have receipts as a reference. If there's a charge on your credit card that you can't match to a receipt, you may be the victim of fraud. OUCH! Should this happen to you, notify your credit card company immediately and dispute the charge.

6. BE CAREFUL USING ATMS

Cash is king. And sometimes you need a little of it in your pockets. But just remember that ATMs are hotspots for identity thieves.

So, the next time you visit an ATM, keep the following tips in mind:

- Look for suspicious skimming devices on the front of the ATM.
- Do not use ATMs that look jank or have shifty keypads or card slots.
- Never leave your ATM receipts behind. And finally . . .
- Watch for people looking over your shoulder.

Bottom line, use common sense when using ATMs, and you just might thwart the thieves!

7. UPDATE ALL YOUR ONLINE PASSWORDS

Okay, we know . . . it's a pain in the ass keeping track of all your passwords. But making sure your passwords are fresh and newly updated is one of the best fraud prevention techniques out there.

To minimize fraudulent access to your online accounts, create strong passwords with random letters, numbers, and symbols. Just never use words, names, or phrases that can be easily connected to you. For instance, don't use your personal name or band name for one of your passwords. While this might sound like common sense, remember that sense is not always common. Okay! Now. Let's move on!

8. INSTALL SOFTWARE THAT DETECTS SPYWARE AND OTHER VIRUSES

One of the sneakiest ways thieves can obtain your personal information is through the internet.

Therefore, always install antivirus and anti-spyware software on your computer. For a small subscription charge, you can get top-rated products by Norton, Bitdefender, and McAfee.

Warning: Criminals posing as legit websites commonly offer free giveaways of "antivirus" protection software in hopes that your greed will get the best of you. Should you fall for this and download their free product, spyware may be installed on your computer. So, be mindful of everything that you download from the internet, or you could end up regretting it.

9. ACTIVATE TWO-STEP AUTHENTICATION ON YOUR ACCOUNTS

Since criminals can easily crack one online password, it makes sense to activate two-factor authentication (2FA).

2FA is an extra step added to the log-in process, such as a code sent to your phone, that helps verify your identity. It offers an extra level of security that cyber thieves can't easily access.

Typically, sites that offer 2FA will ask you to activate it every time you log on. Other sites, like the college where I work (this is Bobby) will insist you sign up for it, or you won't be able to log on. Ha ha. I guess this is my college's way of using tough love to cause change.

10. BE CAREFUL WHEN USING PUBLIC COMPUTERS

Be careful when using public computers in libraries, schools, and hotel business centers, especially when logging on to your business and financial accounts.

Personally, we'd recommend not using public computers at all for business use. But when you're out on the road with your band and you have no other options, at least do the following:

1. Log off of every account you visit.
2. Don't allow the computer to save your log-in information.
3. Delete your history.
4. Watch out for over-the-shoulder snoops.
5. Never leave the computer unattended while logged on to an account. And finally . . .
6. Never enter any sensitive information.

By practicing these few tips, you'll keep your info safe and keep the thieves away.

11. DON'T FALL FOR PHISHING AND OTHER SCAMS

Don't fall for phishing and other scams that are devised by criminals to catch you off guard.

With a phishing scam, you'll typically receive an email with an internet hyperlink that directs you to a criminal website that contains fields for you to enter your personal information.

To protect yourself against phishing scams, follow these six tips:

1. Ignore outrageous or overly urgent emails.
2. Be extra cautious of people asking for personal information.
3. Do not open attachments you are not expecting no matter who it is from.
4. Avoid clicking on embedded email links.
5. Watch for suspicious emails even when they appear to be from a friend. And finally . . .
6. Be wary of emails with improper grammar/spelling and shoddy graphics.

Remember, folks, if you happen to fall for a phishing scam, the hacker will be "gone fishing" with your personal information. So don't let this happen to you. Enough said!

12. PURCHASE ONLY FROM SECURE SITES (HTTPS://)

Purchasing from sites that begin with https:// is another smart way to beat the fraudsters.

Sites using this protocol are secure and on a legit server.

So before whipping out your credit card on your next online purchase, heed our advice.

13. WIPE (OR DESTROY) ALL ELECTRONICS BEFORE PARTING WITH THEM

Taking extra precautions before selling, trading in, or disposing of electronics is also a good bet in helping you secure sensitive data.

When selling or trading in electronics, always wipe your computer hard drive and phone's SIM card. If you don't know how to do this, have an expert assist you.

When disposing of electronics, drill holes through your computer hard drive and smash your phone's SIM card as well. Hell, blow them up for all we care!

This one is a no-brainer, guys. So, just do it!

14. CHECK YOUR CREDIT HISTORY FOR SIGNS OF FRAUD

Checking your credit history for signs of fraud is something you should do on an ongoing basis. This is often overlooked, and thieves know this.

You can obtain a free credit report from www.annualcreditreport.com once per year and purchase additional statements throughout the year from the three major credit bureaus: Equifax (www.equifax.com), Experian (www.experian.com), and TransUnion (www.transunion.com).

A good rule of thumb is to get your free report in January, and then pay for the others in April, July, and October. While some people may think this is overkill, we say it's just smart!

15. FREEZE YOUR CREDIT SO FRAUDSTERS CANNOT OPEN ACCOUNTS

If you are not planning on opening new accounts or applying for new loans in the immediate future, then you may want to freeze your credit by calling the three credit bureaus.

A credit freeze prevents unauthorized persons from opening credit in your name, and also blocks creditors from checking your credit profile. You really can't get any safer than this.

Just don't forget you'll have to unfreeze your credit (or thaw it) should you ever decide to apply for new lines of credit. All this requires is a simple call to the credit bureaus. That's it!

16. OPT OUT OF ZERO CREDIT CARD SOLICITATIONS AND JUNK MAIL

Opting out of credit card solicitations and junk mail is also a good idea in protecting you from potential fraudsters. Someone could steal one of your credit card offers and attempt to open a card. Or you might fall for some silly junk mail offer and end up getting scammed.

So, to cover your ass, follow these three steps below:

1. Call the Consumer Credit Reporting Agency to opt out of new credit card offers. Their number is 1-888-5optout (1-888-567-8688)
2. Send a letter to: "Direct Marketing Association" to opt out of junk mail offers. Their address is: Attention Mail Preference Service. PO Box 9008. Farmingdale, NY, 11735-9008. And finally ...
3. Contact DMAchoice in an additional effort to set preferences for what you want to receive in the mail. Their website is https://www.dmachoice.org/static/learn_more.php.

Just don't be surprised if you still receive solicitations after going through these processes. But remember, anything you do to get rid of these annoying solicitors (even if just a few), is better than doing nothing at all.

17. PROTECT YOUR INCOMING MAIL

Probably one of the easiest ways to protect yourself against identity theft and fraud is to protect your incoming mail from lurking thieves. That's right!

Mail theft has been on the rise, especially after the 2020 COVID-19 pandemic that changed the world. People got used to having everything delivered to them via Amazon and the US Postal Service, and thieves have been jumping all over this opportunity to rip you off.

So, be sure to follow a few or all of these simple tips:

1. Retrieve your mail ASAP after delivery.
2. If leaving town (i.e., touring) inform your post office to hold your mail.
3. Report suspicious activity around your mailbox to the police.
4. Get a Ring Doorbell Cam for renters or home owners. And finally . . .
5. Get a post office box at a post office or UPS store.

Look, the last thing you want to do is have thieves get ahold of any important packages or letters that contains sensitive personal information inside. It's yet another way they can steal your identity and fuck up your credit. Not to mention humiliate you. So, take this tip seriously.

18. MAIL BILLS AT THE POST OFFICE ONLY

We know it's a pain in the ass, but consider using the post office exclusively for outgoing mail, especially those pieces that contain sensitive information.

I (this is Bobby) actually got a few checks stolen from the mail when thieves ripped the entire USPS metal mailbox right out of the cement. Can you believe that? Fortunately, I noticed the missing mailbox just after the incident took place, and made the decision to cancel my checks before they could be cashed. Of course, now, I mail everything from my neighborhood post office.

So, make no mistake, simply leaving sensitive outgoing mail in your mailbox is a recipe for both mail and identity theft. Take care. Don't let this happen to you!

19. BUY A PAPER SHREDDER AND SHRED IMPORTANT "TRASH"

Stop throwing away important information in your trash. This includes credit card offers, deposit slips, bank checks and statements, canceled checks, and medication or prescription receipts.

Instead, get yourself a paper shredder from Staples or Office Depot that crosscuts your information (not strip cuts). This is the best way to protect yourself against dumpster-diving thieves. You know that so-called transient who is searching for bottles to recycle? Think again!

Yup, trashing important info is like feeding hungry sharks.

20. USE A SECURITY MONITORING SERVICE (LIKE LIFELOCK)

Finally, a secure way to help prevent identity theft is to use a security monitoring service.

While we do like LifeLock, some other security monitoring services are Aura, Identity Guard, and Identity Defense, to name just a few.

These services range from credit monitoring to data recovery and offer multi-layer protection for your personal information. They even have insurance of up to $1 million.

So do yourself a favor and let others watch your back, 24/7. This could pay off, big time.

Okay, so that concludes our twenty tips to protecting yourself against identity theft and fraud. Since identity theft and fraud can temporarily ruin your life and good credit standing, we highly recommend that you practice as many tips as possible. Even if you can practice just a few, you'll be far ahead of most musicians. So, what do you say? Get to work at protecting yourself today!

13

Ten Tips to Getting (and Staying) Out of Debt

Debt can be a four-letter word when it comes to personal finance.

Debt refers to the outstanding money that you owe to lenders like credit card companies, automobile financiers, school loan organizations, and more.

When mismanaged, debt can destroy your financial credibility, lead to repossessions and evictions, and even cause bankruptcy. Even worse, it can lead to stress, anxiety, and depression.

This is why it's so important to learn a few basic tips on getting (and staying) out of debt.

Below are ten pointers (and then some) to help you get started. And don't be afraid to seek additional credit counseling advice if you're really up shit creek. Okay? Now, let's do this!

1. USE THE "GRANDMA'S SAVINGS" APPROACH

Use the "Grandma's savings" approach as your first financial strategy for getting out of debt.

That's right! It's time to bust out Grandma's birthday card money from your savings account and put it to good use. Straight up, this may be one of the smartest investments you ever make.

If you're only earning 0.01 percent interest on a regular savings account, but paying 20 percent interest on a credit card loan, you're winning by paying off the loan.

Yes, yes, we know it's nice having that little nest egg in the bank. But the truth is that you fucked up your situation by getting into debt, so now you simply need to un-fuck your situation.

2. UTILIZE A "DEBT CONSOLIDATION" STRATEGY

Utilize a "debt consolidation" strategy as another method to start digging your way out of debt.

Debt consolidation is the process of moving your debt to another creditor who can offer you better terms.

Here's how it works: Suppose creditor A is currently charging you 20 percent interest on your debt. Along comes creditor B that offers to take over your debt from creditor A, at a 0 percent interest rate for an introductory term of twelve months. Fabulous, right? As long as you make on-time payments, and knock out your debt in a year, this can be an effective strategy.

However, this can also turn out to be a disaster if you're financially irresponsible. You see, if you make new charges, miss payments, and fail to pay off your balance before the twelve-month statute, your new creditor could shoot your interest rates to 24 percent. Now, you're worse off than when you started.

So, peeps, consolidate all of your debt only if you are ready to rock, otherwise run!

3. USE THE "DEBT AVALANCHE" STRATEGY

Use the "debt avalanche" strategy as yet another smart tactic to pay down all of your debt.

This is a strategy where you essentially tackle your highest interest loans first in effort to save thousands on interest payments.

It works like this: double-down consistently on your highest interest rate loan so that you can be done with that loan more quickly, all while covering at least the minimums on your other debts. Once paid off, take the amount of money you allocated for the highest interest rate loan and add it to the minimum payments on the next highest interest rate loan, and so on, until you no longer have debt.

This is an easy concept and only requires that you rank your debts from the highest to lowest interest rate. Pay in that order and you'll be debt free and save thousands in interest too.

4. USE THE "DEBT SNOWBALL" STRATEGY

Use the "debt snowball" as an alternative to the avalanche to help pay down all of your accounts.

This is a strategy where you essentially tackle the loans with the smallest balance first (instead of the highest interest rate first). This strategy is designed to boost your motivation.

It works like this: double-down consistently on your smallest balance loan so that you can be done with that loan more quickly, all while covering at least the minimums on your other debts. Once paid off, take the amount of money you allocated for the smallest balance loan and add it to the minimum payments on the next smallest balance loan, and so on, until you no longer have debt. Scratching off the debts more quickly serves as a motivator.

So, while paying off lower balances first may cost you a little more (in interest fees) over time, you will reap the benefit of having fewer debt accounts overall, which is a really good start.

5. UTILIZE THE "LUMP SUM" STRATEGY

Utilize the "lump sum strategy" as another useful tactic for knocking out your debt in a flash.

This is where you use windfalls of cash from gambling winnings, tax refunds, royalty checks, and other blessings bestowed upon you to double down on all of your debt payments. Doing this will obviously help you to knock out debt quickly and eventually become debt free.

We realize it's hard to part with easy cash and you'd rather do something fun with it. But the longer you wait to pay creditors, the more money they'll make off of you. So, just pay up!

6. UTILIZE THE "PAY DOWN THE PRINCIPAL" APPROACH

Utilize the "pay down the principal" strategy as another clever tactic to dig your way out of debt.

This is where you ask your creditors if extra payments you make can be applied to paying down the loan's principal only (no interest). Not all creditors will allow this, but you should ask anyway.

Creditors are sneaky. If you don't say anything, instead of applying those extra payments to the immediate principal, creditors will apply those extra payments to future monthly payments with interest, and then tell you that you do not owe them for the next few billing cycles.

That way, they still make interest and you really get no benefit from the extra payments.

Trickery at its finest! So again, be sure to speak with your creditor.

7. USE A "DEFERMENT" STRATEGY (AND MORE) FOR STUDENT LOANS

Use a "deferment" strategy as one of many methods to help graduate your student debt for good.

Don't waste a lot of energy worrying about all of the payments you'll have to make after graduation (or you're currently paying back as a graduate). Know that there are several useful financial strategies available to get the job done.

Depending on your personal situation, you might be able to:

- delay payments for up to thirty-six months through deferment or forbearance programs,
- adjust payments based on your current income through income-driven repaying,
- get the remaining balance of your loans forgiven through loan forgiveness programs, and/or
- refinance or consolidate your loans at lower interest rates.

Since student loans can be a complex matter due to government and private institutions having different rules and regulations, check out organizations like the National Foundation for Credit Counseling (www.nfcc.com), the Consumer Financial Protection Bureau (www.consumerfinance.gov), and Federal Student Aid (https://studentaid.gov/) to see which of the above options are best suited for you.

But make no mistake, while student loans could very well make up the bulk of your debt problems, you don't have to freak out just yet. There are several options you can explore.

8. GO WITH THE "CREDIT COUNSELOR" APPROACH

Go with the "credit counselor" approach as another helpful method for smashing all of your debt.

Credit counselors can sit down with you and map out an appropriate plan to help you climb out of your deep, dark hole. And the best part of it all is that many credit counselors are nonprofit, meaning they won't charge you a single cent.

To find a nonprofit counselor, check out organizations like the National Foundation of Credit Counseling (www.nfcc.org) or review the list of approved counselors offered by the US Department of Justice (www.justice.gov/ust).

9. USE THE "DEBT SETTLEMENT" METHOD

Use the "debt settlement" method as another tactic to negotiate your way out of your living hell.

Know that you can negotiate with creditors to forgive a portion of your debt (sometimes as much as 50 percent or lower) as long as you agree to stringent payback terms. We suppose creditors would rather get some of their money back than none of it at all. This doesn't leave the best mark on your credit history, so you want to leave this strategy as one of your last resorts.

Typically, you should be able to call up your creditors yourself and negotiate with them.

However, if unsuccessful, you should know that there are debt settlement companies that will be willing to do the job for you, at a cost. Just watch out for companies that ask for upfront payments, provide only one option for you, and are not part of the American Fair Credit Council (AFCC). There are so many scammers out there, so you really need to be extra careful with this.

10. TAKE THE "BANKRUPTCY" APPROACH

Finally, take the "bankruptcy" approach as the Hail Mary last-ditch attempt to get out of debt.

Believe it or not, thousands of people and businesses file for bankruptcy, so you would not be alone. Just be sure to hire a seasoned bankruptcy attorney if you decide to go this route.

Your bankruptcy attorney will suggest one of two options depending on your situation:

- **Chapter 7:** Debts are discharged and your assets may be sold to repay creditors.
- **Chapter 13:** Debts are not discharged but are put on a modified repayment plan of up to five years.

Listen folks, bankruptcy is no doubt awful. It can taint your credit history for up to ten years. But remember that bankruptcy can also get you out of debt, provide a sense of relief from nasty creditors, and give you the chance that you need to start over and rebuild your credit.

It's a last resort, but definitely a solution! Think it through before you act. Good luck!

11. BONUS: PRACTICAL ADVICE FOR STAYING OUT OF DEBT FOR GOOD

Now that you've worked your ass off to get out of debt, the last thing you want is to fall back into it. This is why we thought you need a few parting thoughts on staying out of debt for good.

Consider the following:

- **Don't Be Afraid to Get Another Job:** Remember that one of the best ways to stay out of debt is to make more money so you can cover your ass. An extra job does not have to be stringent and permanent. Instead, it can be flexible and temporary so that it doesn't take you away from your music. Consider jobs where you can set your own hours like driving for Uber, Postmates, and Grubhub, or teaching guitar lessons to kids.
- **Keep Unnecessary Expenses Out of Your Budget:** Remember that an even better way to stay out of debt is to spend less money and never get into debt. Don't eat out in expensive restaurants, keep housing costs to a minimum, and remember that you are not what you drive. Know that "frugal" is your best friend when trying to stay out of debt. If you can learn to sacrifice a little today, you'll be better off now and tomorrow.
- **Avoid Payday Loans:** Never take out a loan from one of those cheesy payday stores at the corner strip mall. Payday loans are high-interest, short-term loans that give you an advance on your paycheck before you have even received it. One payday loan creates the need for a second and third loan because borrowers usually pay off one payday loan with another. Clearly, these loans are just stupid and can only lead you back into debt all over again. Stay away from payday loans and stay on top of debt.
- **Avoid Pawnshop Loans:** Keep away from pawnshops and pawnshop loans. Pawnshop loans are high-interest, short-term loans that require collateral (like your prized guitar). When you pay back the loan (with super-high interest), you get your guitar back. But if you fail to repay, then you lose your guitar, and the opportunity to play that gig that could have made you some dough. Again, this is just a stupid money move that can lead to problems. If you want to stay out of debt, stay away from pawnshop loans.
- **Avoid Cash Advances on Credit Cards:** Don't ever be tempted to take a cash advance on your credit card to pay for something you need. While a cash advance might feel like a simple solution,

cash advances are just high-interest loans that can dig you into a deep dark hole. Stay away from cash advances and stay ahead of debt.
- **Avoid the Urge to Dodge Creditors:** Never play a game of hide and seek with creditors. Changing your phone number or pretending you're not home is just a bad idea when it comes to staying on top of your debts. Your accounts are not going to magically disappear and will only get worse with accruing interest and penalties. This is the stupidest money mistake there is. Deal with your shit, and stay legit.
- **Admit When You Have a Money Problem:** Remember that denial is the biggest enemy to remaining debt free. Recognize when you are slipping back into your financially irresponsibility, so that you can nip your money issues in the bud. Never "fake it till you make it." This is a bullshit phrase that will only dig your hole again.
- **Never Feel Like There is No Way Out:** Finally, never panic when you feel debt creeping back into your life. Remember there are numerous strategies you can employ. By taking action and not allowing yourself to slip, you'll remain debt free for life.

Well, there you have it, gang—ten tips for getting (and staying) out of debt—plus a few bonus tips for good measure as well. Debt is a four-letter word when it comes to personal finance, but with these tips, you can be on the road to rebuilding credibility as soon as you want.

Paying down your debt can seem like it will take a lifetime, but good things come to those who stick to their plan. There are countless stories of people who have dug themselves out of their holes, and you can certainly do it too. Patience will be a major factor in your success.

So put on your fighter face, roll up your sleeves, and get to work. You'll be glad you did!

7

RETIREMENT PLANNING

We need to retire the phrase retirement. Retirement is about freedom.

— Ben Stein and Phil DeMuth,
authors of *Bulletproof Investing*

14

Twenty-Six Questions About Retirement Planning for Musicians

The last thing on the minds of most young musicians is retirement. After all, retirement is for old fogies who are fed up with their corporate jobs and just want to play golf all day in Florida. LOL.

If this is how you look at retirement, you could not be more wrong. In fact, retirement (or, more specifically, retirement planning) is one of the most relevant parts of your personal finance education—and it's something that you should already be thinking about in your early twenties. Yup, It's true. The good news is, it's never too late to strategize a plan. Now is better than never.

What follows are frequently asked retirement questions by our students and clients. Given the complexity of this subject, we provide merely the basics and strongly urge you to speak with a certified financial planner (CFP) who can map out a customized plan for you. Sound good?

Now, with no further ado, sit back, get comfortable, and let's get ready to rock this.

1. WHAT, REALLY, IS RETIREMENT?

This is the perfect first question! Retirement is about freedom of choice. It's a time in your life where you've amassed enough money to live out your days stress and worry free. The money you save is like your "fuck you" fund of the future that allows you to call all of your own shots!

Consider the following scenarios:

- Tired of hitting the road as a musician and want to do something different like spend more time with your family? No problem!
- Feel like getting away from your party lifestyle and former bandmates to write scores you hope to place in film and TV? No problem!
- Feel like giving back to the world and spending more time volunteering to an important cause that betters the planet? No problem!

Look, retirement can mean a lot of different things to a lot of different people. But one thing is for absolute sure: retirement is about doing mostly everything on your very own terms.

2. WHY DO I NEED TO "PLAN" FOR RETIREMENT?

The reason you need to plan for retirement is that life doesn't come with a crystal ball. That being said, to ensure you have enough resources, you really do need to plan for life's "what-ifs."

Consider the following:

- **Inflation:** What if "inflation" rapidly increases prices and you need three times as much money forty years from now to cover basic costs?
- **Disability:** What if you have an injury at age forty and can no longer walk or work?
- **Health:** What if you experience a prolonged health issue that requires a lot of money in housing, equipment, or the level of care not covered by your health insurance?
- **Poverty:** What if your popularity as a musician fizzles, and you completely run out of money because you spent it like a "big pimp" in your prime on mansions and Ferraris?
- **Total Failure:** What if you never make it as a professional musician? Yikes!

Look, retirement is not about being paranoid; it's about being smart. Remember, your Mom and Dad (and Uncle Joey) are not always going to be around to save you. You need to make sure that you have enough tucked away to be able to save yourself.

3. BUT WON'T SOCIAL SECURITY BENEFITS BE ENOUGH?

Social Security is a benefit established by the US government to help ensure (in theory) that working citizens do not end up living in tents in their golden years.

By paying required Social Security income taxes throughout your life, the Social Security Administration will give it back to you in small monthly payments after age sixty-two. These payments will be based on your lifetime earnings and the age you start collecting. Although you can start collecting at age sixty-two, if you wait until age seventy, you will get much more.

On average, payments are approximately $1,555 per month in today's dollars, which is not quite enough to survive. What's worse, many experts fear that the Social Security system may run out of funds unless major improvements are made. Yikes! So, no—Social Security benefits are not enough to survive and may not even be around.

4. SO, WHEN SHOULD I START SAVING FOR RETIREMENT?

The time to start saving for retirement is right now. Even if it is just a matter of saving a dollar here and there, the longer you wait, the harder it will be to ensure a secure, safe retirement.

The problem is that most of what we've already said about retirement falls on deaf ears to most young musicians. Young musicians aren't worried about what's going to happen in forty years; they're worried about getting more TikTok followers and getting on Spotify playlists.

But pay attention; through the power of compounding interest (interest on interest), simple math shows that you are so much better off in your retirement years if you start saving in your twenties (rather than waiting till your thirties, forties, or fifties). Bottom line, the more time your money has to compound, the more you'll save. So, heed this advice, and get started today.

5. SHOULD I START SAVING FOR RETIREMENT EVEN IF I AM IN DEBT?

The short answer is, *yes*! If you have a steady flow of decent money coming in from your gigs and side hustles, you should put some of it into your retirement, and the rest toward your debt.

But what if you're totally strapped for cash and can barely afford to make the minimum payments on your debt obligations? Then in these extreme cases, it makes more sense to focus on paying off your debt and not risk screwing up your credit history.

6. HOW MUCH DO I NEED FOR RETIREMENT?

The amount you need for retirement depends on many factors. This includes the average monthly amount of money you think it will take to live comfortably (adjusted for inflation), the amount that you estimate you will receive in Social Security payments, and the number of years you'll spend in retirement before you die. The last part is difficult to predict, but experts say plan for age one hundred.

Retirement calculators are available online to help you determine approximately how much dough you'll need in your golden years, but spoiler alert—it's going to be around one million dollars. But don't let this number scare you into inaction. With discipline, hard work, and this book, you can certainly do it. So, get saving for your retirement today. You'll be glad you did!

7. WHAT ARE THE VARIOUS TYPES OF RETIREMENT ACCOUNTS?

Great question! There are a multitude of retirement accounts with fancy buzz names to help you save up for a groovy retirement. Some of the more common examples include:

1. Traditional IRA (individual retirement account)
2. Roth IRA
3. 401(k)
4. Roth 401(k)
5. 403(b)
6. 457(b)
7. SEP IRA

Since a description of these accounts is literally a book chapter, just know they are all government established with each having special tax perks. In short, if you don't take advantage of these perks, you're a fool! By the way, we'll cover more on this in another piece. Promise!

8. GENERAL ADVANTAGES OF RETIREMENT ACCOUNTS?

Listing every advantage of each retirement account is beyond the scope of this question piece.

But generally speaking, all the plans provide huge tax advantages that can save you thousands of dollars in dues to Uncle Sam over the course of your working life. In fact, this is why retirement accounts are often called "tax-advantaged accounts."

Look, no matter which account you use, and no matter which one is right for you, you'll be far better off saving for retirement using any one of them, than none at all. So, start today!

9. GENERAL DISADVANTAGES OF RETIREMENT ACCOUNTS?

The biggest disadvantage of most retirement accounts—from the perspective of a young musician—is that they are designed to keep your money tied down for potentially decades.

While there are ways you can break out your money (or part of it) depending on the type of retirement account and your personal situation, the government generally imposes penalties if you withdraw your money before fifty-nine and a half. This may be difficult for young folks (like you) who are more interested in immediate gratification than delayed fulfillment.

But trust us, unless you plan on being part of the unlucky "27 club" and dying a beautiful corpse, then sacrificing a little bit of your money today will pay off *big time* tomorrow.

10. CAN I HAVE MORE THAN ONE RETIREMENT ACCOUNT?

Having more than one retirement account is very possible. However, know that there are often limits to how much you can contribute to the total of all of your retirement accounts.

For instance, you can open up a traditional IRA (or Roth IRA) and contribute up to $6,000 yearly (and $7,000 if you're fifty or above). But, if you have both accounts, the IRA and the Roth IRA, then the total contributions of both accounts must not exceed the above figures.

In another example, you could have a 401(k) maxed at $20,500 yearly (and $27,000 if you're fifty or above) and a Roth IRA maxed at $6,000 yearly (or $7,000 if you're fifty and above).

So, yes, you can have more than one plan, but you must understand the maximum limits.

11. SHOULD I TAKE ADVANTAGE OF MY EMPLOYER'S PLAN?

Yes! It's typically a great idea to take advantage of any benefit that an employer offers you, especially when it is an employer-based retirement plan like a 401(k) (one of the most common plans).

A 401(k) plan is essentially where your employer (at a normal job like Guitar Center) will put a percentage of your money directly into an account on a tax deferred basis (meaning you won't get taxed until you start taking qualified withdrawals).

Not only is a 401(k) a good forced savings plan at a tax savings, but it could also mean "free money" if your boss is cool enough to "match" a percentage of the portion of the money that you contribute. Not all bosses are cool and participate in matching, but no matter how you look at it, 401(k) plans are typically a smart move. So, yes, enroll in your 401(k) today!

12. SHOULD I OPEN UP AN INDIVIDUAL RETIREMENT ACCOUNT?

You should definitely open up an individual retirement account, especially when you're a self-employed worker who doesn't have access to an employer-based 401(k) plan.

A traditional IRA, for instance, will also allow you to contribute money into an account on a deferred tax basis (meaning you won't get taxed until you start taking qualified withdrawals). As long as you are disciplined enough to make the contributions yearly, this is a no-brainer move. So just do it!

13. WHAT INVESTMENTS SHOULD I PUT INTO RETIREMENT ACCOUNTS?

Great question! When your employer offers you a retirement plan like a 401(k), they'll typically have a limited number of investment fund choices offered by an administrator. Some administrators will have more (and better) choices than others, but all will typically be presented to you in pie chart drawings. These pie charts are composed of investments like index funds, bond funds, foreign funds, and large and small cap funds. It's enough to make your eyes glaze over and want to crack open a beer. (Forget about small cap, give me a night cap! LOL.)

So, perhaps one simple solution is to go for a "target-dated fund" with the target year that you think you'll retire. The Vanguard Target Retirement 2060 Fund, for instance, allows you to "set it and forget it." This means you can invest your money with little to no management and not worry about all of those investment choices. The account even adjusts the allocation of stocks to bounds over time to be less risky as you get older. Not bad! Remember that sometimes the simplest approach to investing is the best.

14. IS THERE A GENERAL PHILOSOPHY OF RETIREMENT INVESTING?

The time horizon for most young musicians to save up and invest for retirement is forty to fifty years. This presents the opportunity to invest more aggressively in higher-risk stocks to achieve the needed gains while still being able recover from the inevitable downturns of the market.

So, the rule is: the more time you have, the more investment risk you can generally take.

15. SHOULD ANYTHING CHANGE WITH MY INVESTMENTS OVER TIME?

As you age, one of the most important investment changes you should make is the allocation of stocks to bonds in all of your accounts marked for retirement.

Stocks typically have the greatest potential for growth, but are also more volatile. Therefore, the allocation of stocks in your account should decrease as you age and are close to retirement.

Experts say that the percentage of stocks should be one hundred less your age. Thus, at age twenty, you might have 80 percent of your money for retirement in stocks, at age forty, 60 percent in stocks, and at age seventy, 30 percent in stocks. Changing the allocation of your retirement investments in your account is designed to preserve your money, not lose it.

16. SHOULD I MAKE BIGGER CONTRIBUTIONS (PER LAW) OVER TIME?

The IRS increases annual retirement contribution limits as you get older.

For instance, in a 401(k) plan, older employees (fifty and up) can contribute as much as $27,000 yearly, while young employees can contribute only $20,500 yearly. Given that this money is tax deferred (meaning you're taxed much later in life), most experts will say to take advantage of the bigger contribution limits.

17. WHAT IF I MAX OUT MY YEARLY CONTRIBUTIONS?

If you max out the yearly contributions in your "tax-advantaged" retirement accounts, and you still have money to invest for retirement, then you can open up additional "taxable accounts."

While taxable accounts don't have the same tax benefits as your tax-advantaged retirement accounts, they offer far more flexibility (i.e., you can withdrawal "all" of your money "penalty-free" whenever you want).

Taxable accounts are fine for long-term retirement planning, but they are also useful (and recommended) for mid- and shorter-term goals, too (like buying a house and newer car).

18. WHAT IF I LEAVE THE COMPANY THAT I AM WITH?

When you leave the company where you have an employer-based retirement plan, you will typically have a variety of different options to choose from including the following:

1. **Do Nothing**: Let your money sit in your previous employer's plan.
2. **Roll It Over:** Transfer it from your old employer's plan into your new employer's plan.
3. **IRA It:** Open up a new account like a traditional IRA and move the funds over, or . . .
4. **Withdrawal It:** Take the funds out with no penalty (but only if you're fifty-nine and a half or older).

The strategy you take will depend largely on your individual situation and any fees and penalties associated with your retirement plan. So, be sure to do your homework before making a move.

19. WHEN DO MOST PEOPLE START TAKING WITHDRAWALS?

Different people have different goals when it comes to retirement.

For example, some folks with a 401(k) or a traditional IRA will start withdrawing penalty-free at age fifty-nine and a half, while others will hold out till they are legally required to start withdrawing at age seventy-two.

And other folks, perhaps with a Roth IRA (which is a more flexible plan), will keep their money in for as long as they wish.

Always check the rules for your specific plan.

20. WHEN DO MOST PEOPLE START COLLECTING SOCIAL SECURITY?

The debate about which age to begin collecting Social Security is all over the place. Some say to wait until age seventy, and thus get a larger chunk (hell, why not take the larger sum?).

Others say to take it early at sixty-two and invest it (hell, who knows if Social Security—or even you—will be around till age seventy?).

So, there is no single answer.

21. WILL I NEED TO RETHINK MY LIFESTYLE WHEN I RETIRE?

Most smart people rethink their retirement lifestyle through the creation of a specific budget.

While budgets can contain everything from downsizing your home to moving to another state where it's less expensive, the most important thing your retirement budget will monitor is the rate at which your money is withdrawn from your accounts designated for retirement.

The recommended withdrawal rate is 4 to 5 percent of the value of your retirement funds per year, but you need to keep this in close check in case you need to take much less.

After all, the last thing that you want is to see your accounts dry up.

22. WHY DO SO MANY PEOPLE RETIRE IN STATES LIKE FLORIDA?

Besides being warm and free of burdensome snow, many people retire to states like Florida and Nevada because there is no state income tax.

Remember, Social Security and your retirement distributions are considered income.

So, if you can avoid paying state taxes on this money, who wouldn't want to move to a state like Florida or Nevada?

23. DO I REALLY NEED TO PLAN TO LIVE TILL I AM ONE HUNDRED?

Most financial planners suggest you estimate your life expectancy to age one hundred, so yes, we believe it is a good idea that you take their advice very seriously. Why? Because here is the gamble:

1. Don't save enough and struggle in your senior years till you die (sucks being you).
2. Save enough but die early (sucks, but at least the kids and dog will benefit).
3. Save enough and die comfortably old (perfect, you're a senior big pimp).

Yup, we'll take choice three any day! By the way, if you want to know your life expectancy, click on the handy Social Security calculator right here: https://www.ssa.gov/cgi-bin/longevity.cgi.

24. WHAT HAPPENS IF I OUTLIVE MY MONEY?

If you outlive your money, you better hope that you have family members that you can rely on.

As for health care expenses, Medicare (a federal health insurance program for low- to no-income earners) might become available to cover health needs. But know that the services Medicare covers are limited.

25. IS HEALTH AND NUTRITION A FORM OF RETIREMENT PLANNING?

People like Keith Richards of the Rolling Stones lived a life of drinking and drugs and he still seems to be going strong (at the time of this writing).

But given that he is more of a rare breed, you shouldn't consider his lifestyle as the standard. So yes, generally, take care of your health today, and you'll be better off tomorrow.

26. IS INSURANCE PART OF RETIREMENT PLANNING?

Yes! Some people purchase annuities (which pay you a guaranteed income). Other people buy long-term care insurance (which covers housing with on-site nurses to boot).

If you live a very long life, then these plans can really pay off in your retirement big time. On the other hand, if you die early, then they can be a bit of a waste of money. That's the gamble of life!

So that's our twenty-six FAQs on retirement planning. Hope all this stuff about your future and aging didn't depress you but, instead, inspired you to get your shit together starting today. There's a lot of stuff to consider, so be sure to read more about retirement plans and meet with a CFP to guide you based on your own personal needs. Remember, your parents are not always going to be around to save you. You have to save yourself. Start planning today.

15

The Seven Most Common Retirement Accounts (and Then Some)

Retirement means different things to different people. To some, it might mean kicking back on a beautiful boat on turquoise waters while fishing for sea bass. To others it may mean opening up a new recording studio in your back yard and making music and touring only when you want to.

But no matter what retirement means to you, two things are for certain—you'll need decades of smart retirement planning and a boatload of money to comfortably retire. The good news is that there are several tax-advantaged retirement accounts to help you reach your goals.

What follows are the top seven most common retirement accounts. Since there is no one-size-fits-all retirement plan, we present only an overview of the available accounts. As usual, we suggest you sit down with a certified financial planner to map out a strategy that fits your needs.

Note: Because these plans are similar in many ways, we've boldfaced key words in the introductions to highlight the differences and summarized the plans in Fig 15.1. Nonetheless, reading about these plans can be a little tedious given their details, so feel free to skim the list to get a general gist of their primary functions. Enjoy.

1. TRADITIONAL IRA

A traditional IRA (individual retirement account) is a **personal plan** designed to help **individuals** invest **"pre-tax"** dollars to grow and be **taxed upon withdrawal** in retirement. **Self-contributions**, as long as they are diligently made, make saving for retirement super easy.

Here is a basic breakdown of the plan:

Contribution Details

- personal contributions made by individuals (you)
- individuals determine the contribution amount and frequency
- $6,000 yearly contribution max
- $7,000 yearly contribution max (age fifty and up)

Benefits

- tax is deferred, which may lower your current tax bracket
- money grows tax-free until withdrawal
- you have an unlimited number of investment choices

Withdrawal (Distribution) Rules

- penalty-free withdrawals starting at age fifty-nine and a half
- special circumstances where money can be withdrawn early penalty-free
- must start taking withdrawals by age seventy-two

2. ROTH IRA

A Roth IRA (individual retirement account) is a **personal plan** designed to help **individuals** (who makes less than **$144,000**) invest **"after-tax"** dollars to grow and be **withdrawn tax-free** at retirement. **Self-contributions**, as long as they are diligently made, make the Roth IRA a very convenient way to save for retirement.

Here is a basic breakdown of the plan:

Contribution Details

- personal contributions made by individuals (you)
- individuals determine the contribution amount and frequency
- $6,000 yearly contribution max
- $7,000 yearly contribution max (age fifty and up)

Benefits

- money grows tax-free with no taxes at withdrawal

- can continue to contribute for as long as you live
- you have an unlimited number of investment choices

Withdrawal (Distribution) Rules

- penalty-free withdrawals starting at age fifty-nine and a half (as long as you've had your account for five years)
- special circumstances where money can be withdrawn early penalty-free
- "contributions" can always be withdrawn early penalty-free
- can keep money in your Roth for as long as you live

3. 401(K)

A 401(k) retirement plan is an **employer-based plan** designed to help **employees** invest **"pre-tax"** dollars to grow and be **taxed upon withdrawal** in retirement. **Employee contributions**, deducted directly from the employee's salary each pay period, make retirement saving easy. **Employer matching** contributions, when offered, can really sweeten the deal.

Here is a basic breakdown of the plan:

Contribution Details

- direct from each paycheck
- employee determines contribution percentage
- $20,500 yearly contribution max
- $27,000 yearly contribution max (age fifty and up)

Benefits

- tax is deferred, which may lower your current tax bracket
- money grows tax-free until withdrawal
- some employers match (up to a certain percentage)

Withdrawal (Distribution) Rules

- penalty-free withdrawals starting at age fifty-nine and a half
- special circumstances where money can be withdrawn early without penalty

- must start taking withdrawals by age seventy-two
- loans against your 401(k) may be possible

4. ROTH 401(K)

A Roth 401(k) is an **employer-based plan** designed to help **employees** invest **"after-tax"** dollars to grow and be **withdrawn tax-free** at retirement. **Employee contributions**, deducted directly from the employee's salary each pay period, make retirement saving easy. **Employer matching** contributions, when offered, are a big plus.

Here is a basic breakdown of the plan:

Contribution Details

- direct from each paycheck
- employee determines contribution percentage
- $20,500 yearly contribution max
- $27,000 yearly contribution max (age fifty and up)

Benefits

- money grows tax-free with no taxes at withdrawal
- some employers match (up to a certain percentage)

Withdrawal (Distribution) Rules

- penalty-free withdrawals starting at age fifty-nine and a half (as long as you've had your account for five years)
- special circumstances where money can be withdrawn early penalty-free
- pro-rated "contributions" can always be withdrawn early penalty-free
- must start taking withdrawals by age seventy-two
- loans under specific contract terms may be possible

5. 403(B)

A 403(b) is an **employer-based plan** designed specifically to help **employees** of **nonprofit organizations** (donor-based schools, charities, and religious organizations) invest **"pre-tax"** dollars to grow and be **taxed upon withdrawal** in retirement. **Employee contributions**, deducted directly from the employee's salary each pay period, make retirement saving easy. **Employer matching** contributions, when offered, make participation in this plan irresistible.

Here is a basic breakdown of the plan:

Contribution Details

- direct from each paycheck
- employee determines contribution percentage
- $20,500 yearly contribution max
- $27,000 yearly contribution max (age fifty and up)

Benefits

- tax is deferred, which may lower your current tax bracket
- money grows tax-free until withdrawal
- some employers match (up to a certain percentage)
- Roth designations of the plan may be available

Withdrawal (Distribution) Rules

- penalty-free withdrawals starting at age fifty-nine and a half
- special circumstances where money can be withdrawn early without penalty
- must start taking withdrawals by age seventy-two
- loans against your 403(b) may be possible

6. 457(B)

A 457(b) is an **employer-based plan** designed specifically to help **employees** of **state and local government** (public schools, post offices, and lifeguard stations) invest **"pre-tax"** dollars to grow and be **taxed upon withdrawal** in retirement. **Employee contributions**, deducted directly from the employee's salary each pay period, make retirement saving easy. Employer **matching contributions are rare**, which kind of sucks.

Here is a basic breakdown of the plan:

Contribution Details

- direct from each paycheck

- employee determines contribution percentage
- $20,500 yearly contribution max
- $27,000 yearly contribution max (age fifty and up)

Benefits

- tax is deferred, which may lower your current tax bracket
- money grows tax-free until withdrawal
- Roth designations of plan may be available

Withdrawal (Distribution) Rules

- no-penalty withdrawals starting at age fifty-nine and a half
- special circumstances where money can be withdrawn early penalty-free
- must start taking withdrawals by age seventy-two (unless still at job)
- loans against 457(b) may be possible
- more flexible (penalty-free) withdrawal options if you leave your job

7. SEP IRA

Finally, a SEP IRA (simplified employee pension) is an **employer-based plan** that provides **business owners** with a simplified method to contribute **"pre-tax"** dollars toward their **employees'** retirement as well as **their own** retirement. Contributions **grow tax-free but** are **taxed upon withdrawal** in retirement. Only **employer contributions** are permitted toward all participants' retirement (both **employee** and **business owner**). While contributions are somewhat flexible in timing and amount, they must be uniform among all participants of the plan.

Here is a basic breakdown of the plan:

Contribution Details

- only employers contribute (not employees)
- contributions made at will (but usually once per year)
- cannot exceed the lesser of 25 percent of participant's pay or $61,000

Benefits

- contributions grow tax-free till withdrawn
- employer contributions to employees are like free money
- since employees do not have to make contributions to benefit from this plan, employees end up with more money in their pockets every pay period
- contribution amounts allowable are far greater than other plans

Withdrawal (Distribution) Rules

- No-penalty withdrawals starting at age fifty-nine and a half
- special circumstances where money can be withdrawn early, penalty free
- must start taking withdrawals by age seventy-two

BONUS: EIGHT MORE RETIREMENT PLANS

Congratulations! You've made it through our exhaustive list of retirement plans. Now that you have a general idea of how some of the more common retirement plans work, here's a very brief (rapid-fire) breakdown of another eight retirement plans that might be right for you. Again, we recommend that you speak to a CFP to determine what works best for your personal situation.

1. **Self-Directed IRA:** A personal plan that allows individuals to invest in things not allowed in a regular IRA (like precious metals, commodities, and real estate).
2. **Education IRA:** A personal plan that helps individuals save for their kids' education.
3. **Spousal IRA:** A personal plan that allows a working spouse to open up an additional IRA on behalf of a non-working spouse, so as to benefit from making twice the allowable contribution amounts.
4. **Roll-Over IRA:** A personal plan that helps individuals move retirement funds from a prior employer into an IRA to maintain the tax-deferred status of their money, and avoid early withdrawal penalties at the time of transfer.
5. **Solo 401(k):** A personal plan that helps self-employed "individuals" reap similar benefits of a 401(k) plan, which is normally an "employer-based" plan.

6. **Simple IRA:** An "employer-based" plan that helps employers and employees of small businesses (of less than one hundred persons) reap similar benefits to a traditional IRA plan, which is normally a "personal-based" plan.
7. **Annuity:** A personal investment issued by an insurance company that protects individuals from outliving their retirement income. An annuity provides guaranteed income on either an immediate or deferred basis. Most experts suggest that an immediate fixed (inflation adjusted) annuity is best. And finally . . .
8. **Health Savings Account:** Both an employer-based and personal-based account that helps employees and individuals (with high-deductible health plans) save for future medical expenses.

So, that's it, gang! You've survived our list of tax-advantaged retirement accounts. We provided lots of choices and you may feel overwhelmed, but know that self-employed musicians typically go with a traditional IRA and employed musicians go with their employer's 401(k). Despite this advice, we once again suggest you speak with a CFP who can look at your personal situation and guide you appropriately. Okay guys! Now, check out our summary of top retirement plans below (Fig 15.1) and start saving for your future. Good luck!

7 TOP RETIREMENT PLANS AT A GLANCE				
Plan	Type	Contributions	Withdrawals	Funded By
Traditional IRA	Personal	Pre-Tax Dollars	Taxed	Self
Roth IRA	Personal	After Tax Dollars	Not Taxed	Self
401K	Employer-based	Pre-Tax Dollas	Taxed	Employee & Employer
Roth 401K	Employer-based	After Tax Dollars	Not Taxed	Employee & Employer
403B	Employer-based (Non-profit)	Pre-Tax Dollars	Taxed	Employee & Employer
457B	Employer-based (Government)	Pre-Tax Dollars	Taxed	Employee & Employer
SEP-IRA	Employer/Self-employer-based	Pre-Tax Dollars	Taxed	Employer

8

INVESTING

If you want excitement then take up skydiving. Don't do it with your investment portfolio.

—William Bernstein, author of *The Four Pillars of Investing*

16

One Hundred Finance and Investment Terms Musicians Should Know

Just scrolling through finance and investment news on your smart phone is enough to make your eyes glaze over. All that lingo makes finance seem like another language—yikes!

But if you're thinking about investing your cash to secure your financial future, then you should know some basic finance terms.

What follows are one hundred finance and investment terms that musicians need to know. Upon completing this list, you'll be better equipped to read the financial news, speak with investment advisors, and even show off a little bit at the next cool party you attend.

Oh, and one more thing: to provide perspective, you'll find we organized the terms in contextual categories, rather than alphabetically. Sound cool? Good, now let's get to the terms.

GENERAL FINANCE

Basics terms you might hear in a general conversation about finance and investments include:

1. **Personal Finance:** The management of an individual's affairs related to income, expenses, debt, credit, investments, insurance, taxes, and estate issues.
2. **The Economy:** The employment rates, income levels, retail sales, and production outputs related to a country or region. When it's a "good economy," people are generally optimistic about making money and spending it on things like your tours,

merchandise, entertainment, and more. When it's a "bad economy," just the opposite.
3. **GDP (Gross Domestic Product):** A numeric snapshot (in trillions) that represents the total output of a country's production and economic growth during a specific time period.
4. **The Federal Reserve (The Feds):** The central bank of the United States that oversees the nation's financial systems such as setting long-term interest rates.
5. **The US Treasury:** The department of the US government that prints our money, issues treasury bonds, notes, bills, and more.
6. **Strong Dollar:** The value of the dollar related to other countries' currency. When the dollar is strong, you'll get more value for your dollar when touring outside of the United States.
7. **Weak Dollar:** The value of the dollar related to other countries' currency. When the dollar is weak, you'll get less value for your money when touring outside of the Unites States.
8. **Inflation:** A general increase in prices causing the buying power of money to decrease. The same item you bought in 2000 for $10 was $16.48 in 2022.
9. **Recession:** A period of contraction when a GDP declines (e.g., unemployment increases, people make less money, people spend less money, and production slows).
10. **Depression:** A more severe and longer-lasting period in time when a country's GDP drops (the Great Depression of 1929 lasted ten years and wiped out millions of investors).
11. **Wealth:** Assets (possessions, cash, investments) minus liabilities (or debt) equals wealth (or net worth). A decrease in debt and an increase in assets produces wealth.
12. **Rich:** The state of having and spending a lot of money. While often used interchangeably with the term wealth (which is built by increasing assets and decreasing liabilities), "rich" people might also carry loads of debt.

INVESTMENT CHOICES

Some of the investment choices a financial planner might mention to you include:

13. **Cash:** Refers to any short-term, low-risk, and liquid obligation that pays a low rate of interest (e.g., bank savings accounts,

certificates of deposit, and money market funds). *Note*: This is not to be confused with the cash in your wallet.

14. **Stocks:** An ownership share of a company held by an individual or group where the value is based primarily on an estimate of future growth. While stocks are known to provide the possibility of high rewards, they are volatile with no guarantee for success. The two types of stocks in the United States are: (1) common (the most common) and (2) preferred (less common, less risky, and less rewarding with regard to returns).
15. **Bonds:** Loan agreements to entities (typically corporate, governmental or state municipality) where you earn a fixed rate of interest over time and get your principal back at the end of the term (called maturity). In contrast to stocks, bonds tend to be a less volatile investment and have a low correlation to stocks (they tend to behave adversely and smooth out a stock's volatility), but they typically provide lower returns.
16. **Mutual Funds:** A professionally managed fund containing hundreds of securities that are mutually owned by many investors who pool their money into the fund. Investors own shares of the fund based on the amount of money that they invest.
17. **Index Funds:** A passively managed, low-cost mutual fund containing hundreds of securities in a portfolio uniquely constructed to match or track the components of a market index, such as the Standard and Poor's 500 index (S&P 500). An index mutual fund is said to provide broad market exposure, low operating expenses, and low portfolio turnover. It is a highly recommended fund by many pro investors.
18. **ETFs (Exchange Traded Funds):** A low-cost passively and actively managed mutual fund containing hundreds of securities that uniquely can be traded throughout the day like stocks (most other mutual funds can only trade at the end of the trading day).
19. **Precious Metals:** Investments in gold, silver, and platinum.
20. **Options:** Contracts that grant the "option, but not the obligation" to buy or sell an underlying asset at a set price on or before a certain date.
21. **Futures:** Financial contracts "obligating" the buyer to purchase an asset—or the seller to sell an asset (such as a physical commodity or a financial instrument)—at a predetermined future date and price.
22. **Cryptocurrency:** Digital money that generally cannot be subject to government interference. While many young musicians buy

into the hype of potentially making lots of money, cryptocurrency is also highly volatile and lacks regulation.

INSURANCE INVESTMENT VEHICLES

Now here's a short list of insurance vehicles that often get mentioned with investments:

23. **Annuities:** A form of income insurance, which guarantees you income in monthly payments or a lump sum.
24. **Life Insurance:** Insurance that pays out a sum of money either on the death of the insured person or after a set period of time.

RETIREMENT INVESTMENT ACCOUNTS

Here's a short list of common retirement accounts that you can use for long-term investing:

25. **IRA (Individual Retirement Account):** An account that you can personally set up (especially when you do not have an employer plan) to invest "pre-tax" dollars that are not taxed till they are withdrawn.
26. **Roth IRA:** An account that you can personally set up (especially when you do not have an employer plan) where you can invest "after-tax" dollars that grow in your investments—and can be withdrawn—tax-free.
27. **401(k):** A retirement plan offered by employers where you can invest "pre-tax" dollars that are not taxed till withdrawal.
28. **Roth 401(k):** A retirement plan offered by employers where you can invest "after-tax" dollars that grow in your investments—and can be withdrawn—tax-free.

TYPES OF ACCOUNTS

Here is another short list of various accounts you often hear financial people mention:

29. **Tax-advantaged Account:** A retirement account that allows you to invest pre-tax money on a tax-deferred basis, or to invest

after-tax money to grow tax-free. Yearly limits on the amounts you can invest apply. Examples of tax-advantaged accounts include IRA, Roth IRA, 401(k) and Roth 401(k).
30. **Taxable Accounts:** An account that allows you to invest after-tax money (only) and pay annual taxes on the earnings. No yearly limits apply to the amount you can invest and there are no withdrawal restrictions. While these accounts can be used for long-term retirement (particularly when you've maxed out your annual retirement account limits), they are mostly used for shorter-term goals like buying a house or car.

CAST OF CHARACTERS

Now this list defines some of the stakeholders you may hear about in the investment world:

31. **CFP (Certified Financial Planner):** A professional who helps individuals manage their finances by providing advice on money issues such as investments, insurance, mortgages, college savings, estate planning, taxes, and retirement.
32. **Fiduciary:** Someone who must put you before his or her own best interests at all times. Said another way, fiduciaries are not your typical salesperson out for the highest commisions on financial products you may not need. *Note*: CFPs are fiduciaries.
33. **Brokerage Firm:** A financial institution that facilitates the buying and selling of financial securities between a buyer and a seller. Said another way, if you want to buy and sell securities, you have to open an account with a brokerage firm. Examples of brokerage firms include: Charles Schwab, Fidelity, E*Trade, TD Ameritrade, Vanguard, Merrill Lynch, and Morgan Stanley.
34. **Broker:** A broker is a representative of a brokerage firm who executes buy and sell orders (on behalf of investors) for a fee or commission.
35. **Financial Analyst:** An expert who studies financial data (e.g., company income statements, balance sheets, and cash flow statements), looks for trends, and recommends appropriate business actions to investors and others.
36. **Day Trader:** An investor who attempts to profit by making rapid trades daily.
37. **Warren Buffett:** One of the most successful investors of all time (not to be confused with musician Jimmy Buffett, who wrote

"Margaritaville") noted for his thorough research of companies, long-term investment strategies, and love for index funds.

GENERAL INVESTMENT TERMS

General investment terms you'll hear folks in the financial world mention include:

38. **Assets:** Typically refers to your investments—stocks, bonds, mutual funds, and more.
39. **Equities:** Refers to investments like stocks that give you ownership in a company.
40. **Securities:** Refers to a broader range of investments like stocks that give you ownership in a company and bonds that are loan agreements to entities.
41. **Capital:** The money you have readily available for investing or starting a business.
42. **Principal:** The original sum of money put into an investment.
43. **Interest:** A regular percentage paid to investors or a fee charged by lenders.
44. **Interest Rate:** The rate of interest paid to an investor, or the percentage of interest charged by a lender (expressed typically as an annual percentage rate).
45. **Compound Interest:** Interest that is earned on both the principal and earned interest.
46. **Yield:** The net amount of interest received (on an investment like a bond) in a year—typically calculated by taking the interest or dividends earned and dividing that by the initial investment principal.
47. **Appreciation:** An increase in the value of stocks, bonds, real estate, and other investments.
48. **Return:** Refers to the profits you make from your investments.
49. **Maturity:** When the time frame of an investment (such as a bond) is over.
50. **Dividend:** A share of the profits that companies pay out to its shareholders of stocks, for instance, as a reward for investing with them.
51. **Portfolio**: A range of investments held by a person or organization.
52. **Sector:** A section of the investment world (e.g., health care, technology, steel).

53. **Capital Gains Tax:** A tax levied on profit from the sale of an investment held for a year or more (long-term capital gain) or less than a year (short-term capital gain).
54. **Expense Ratio:** One of the fees for owning a mutual fund.
55. **Load Fee:** A sales commission paid for entering into a managed mutual fund.
56. **Beneficiary:** A person who benefits from receiving monies from your investments, such as in the case when you pass away.
57. **Liquidity:** Refers to cash investments or any other type of investment that can be easily converted to cash without losing a lot of value.
58. **Volatility:** The level of fluctuation in the value of an investment.

INVESTMENT STRATEGY

Now here are a few terms associated with investment strategy:

59. **Risk Tolerance:** The level at which an investor can cope with investment loss.
60. **Asset Allocation:** Deciding how to divide up your money and where to park it.
61. **Diversification:** Spreading out your investments over many different investments.
62. **Time Horizon:** The duration of time associated with meeting an investment goal.
63. **Rebalancing:** The process of adjusting the allocation of stocks to bonds over time, to ensure the allocation matches your current risk tolerance. Rebalancing might occur every few years when your accounts get out of balance (up to 5 percent from where you want them), or when you are getting older and want to lower your risk ratio of stocks to bonds.
64. **Speculative Investing:** The process of engaging in high-risk (and potentially high gains) investing.
65. **Buying Long:** When you buy a stock with the intention of owning it for a long period of time.
66. **Selling Short:** When an investor borrows shares from a broker and immediately sells them, hoping he or she can scoop them back up at a lower price, return them to the lender, and pocket the difference. This is a riskier than normal stock investing.
67. **Buying on Margins:** Borrowing money from your broker with the intention of purchasing securities and then selling them at an

amount that far exceeds the loan. It's like borrowing money from your friend to bet on the horses, hoping you'll win more than your friend loaned you. This is also a high-risk type of investing.

MANAGEMENT OPTIONS

The various methods for managing your money include the following:

68. **Active Management:** An approach where investors rely on the regular support of financial professionals who frequently pick and sell securities, and monitor and adjust funds. Fees are associated with active management.
69. **Passive Management:** An approach where investors rely on investing in securities like index funds and ETFs that follow a stock market index and are infrequently traded on the market. Low to no fees are associated with passive management.
70. **Self-directed Management:** A DIY-style approach to investing.
71. **Robo-advisors:** A passive low-cost form of investing that relies on algorithms. A robo-advisor picks all of your investments and allocates them appropriately, based on a variety of questions you answer. This could be a great alternative for beginners.

MARKET TALK

Terms you might hear regarding the stock market as a whole include:

72. **Trade:** Buying and selling stocks, bonds, and other instruments on the open market.
73. **Market Order:** A buy (or sell) order to be executed immediately at current market prices.
74. **Market Stop Order:** A buy or sell order to be executed when the price of a security surpasses a particular point.
75. **Bull Market:** A market in which share prices are rising or are expected to rise, which encourages buying.
76. **Bear Market:** A market in which share prices are falling or are expected to fall, which discourages investors.
77. **Market Cap (Market Capitalization):** The value of a company that is traded on the stock market, calculated by multiplying the total number of shares of a company by the present share price. There are large-cap, small-cap, and mid-cap companies.

78. **Blue Chip Stock:** The stock of a large-cap, well-established, and financially sound company that has operated for many years.
79. **Market Crash:** A sudden dramatic decline of stock prices across a significant cross-section of a stock market, resulting in a significant loss of "paper wealth." Crashes are driven by panic as much as by underlying economic factors.
80. **Ticker Symbol:** An abbreviation used to uniquely identify publicly traded shares of a particular stock on a particular stock market (e.g., Apple's ticker symbol is AAPL).
81. **Prospectus:** A formal legal document that provides details of an investment.

INDUSTRY-RELATED INVESTMENT TERMS

Now looking at the investment world as an industry, here's another group of words:

82. **Stock Exchange (or Market):** A market in which securities are bought and sold.
83. **New York Stock Exchange (NYSE):** The world's largest market in which securities are bought and sold. Companies going public have to decide whether to list their shares on the NYSE or the NASDAQ.
84. **The NASDAQ (National Association of Securities Dealers Automated Quotations):** A global electronic marketplace for buying and selling securities. The majority of the North American equities trade is either on NASDAQ, or the New York Stock Exchange. Companies going public have to decide whether to list their shares on the NASDAQ or the NYSE.
85. **Public Company:** A company whose shares are traded freely on a stock exchange.
86. **IPO (initial public offering):** The first time that the stock of a private company is offered to the public. IPOs are often issued by smaller, younger companies seeking capital to expand, as well as large privately owned companies looking to become publicly traded.
87. **Securities and Exchange Commission (SEC):** An independent, federal government agency responsible for protecting investors, maintaining fair and orderly functioning of securities markets, and facilitating capital formation.

88. **FDIC (Federal Deposit Insurance Corporation):** Protects customers of a bank in the unlikely scenario that the bank fails (hey, it happened during the Great Depression).
89. **SIPC (Securities Investor Protection Corporation):** Protects customers of a brokerage firm in the unlikely scenario that the brokerage firm goes bankrupt.

STOCK MARKET MEASURES

Here are some of the ways that the overall investment industry is measured:

90. **Stock Index:** A list of securities whose performance serve as a benchmark of the value of a section of the stock market. The three major indexes are the S&P 500, the NASDAQ, and the Dow. There is also the Wilshire 5,000 and the Russel 3,000.
91. **NASDAQ Index:** A benchmark index for US technology stocks. It includes more than 3,700 US and foreign companies listed on the NASDAQ stock exchange.
92. **S&P 500 Index (Standard and Poor's 500 Index):** An index of 500 select companies seen as leading indicators of US equities and a reflection of the performance of the large-cap universe.
93. **Dow Jones Industrial Average:** The Dow is a stock market index made up of thirty US companies (representing different industries), which serve as indicators of the market's strength and whether the economy is doing well. When "the Dow is up," the economy is said to be doing well, when "the Dow is down," the economy is said to be doing poorly. But always remember, the Dow represents only thirty stocks, so whether the news says it is up and down, it is a rather narrow indicator of success.
94. **Fortune 500 Company:** The 500 largest companies in the United States as compiled by Fortune magazine (not to be confused with the S&P 500).

FINANCIAL RESOURCES

Finally, here are a few top financial resources regularly available:

95. ***Wall Street Journal:*** A daily newspaper based in NYC that covers financial news.

96. **Morning Star:** An investment research and management firm.
97. **Yahoo Finance:** A financial news website and investment research tool.
98. **Investopedia:** A great website for understanding the basics of the finance world.
99. **Nerd Wallet:** Easy-to-understand articles and advice on all things finance.
100. **Motley Fool:** Nothing to do with the fools in Mötley Crüe, but rather investment fools (LOL) who offer a lot of investment information and top stock picks. Personally, we don't care for them, but we mentioned them because they are all over the internet.

Wow, you did it—a bit exhaustive getting through all the terms. But again, they are really meant for skimming so you have a ball park understanding of buzzwords often heard on the news. There are more than three thousand terms we could have added to the list, but one hundred is good for starters. So that's it! Now go speak money!

Seven-Point Checklist to Investing and Building Wealth

Invest! Invest! Invest! It's time to make money and get rich quick. After all, the pandemic of 2020 has got everyone in a hole and nothing could be better than striking it big! Right?

Perhaps! But let's not get ahead of ourselves. The road to true wealth (measured in assets and liabilities) is a long process. It involves several steps you must check off before grabbing your mobile phone and the latest investment app to try your luck. *Read*: Investing is not a game!

What follows is our seven-point checklist to responsible investing and building wealth. We start at the beginning with creating a steady flow of income all the way to playing with funny money if you must. Have patience—at times the process might seem boring and include advice you've already heard, but investing was never meant to be fun or sexy when done right.

Note: The seven steps presented here are in a systematic order, but depending on your situation, feel free to skip straight to investing or tackle two or more steps simultaneously. Just be sure to speak with a financial planner to make sure that your path to success is right for you.

1. CREATE AND MAINTAIN A STEADY FLOW OF INCOME

The first step to investing and building wealth is creating and maintaining a flow of income.

If you are a musician earning zero income or just living from one gig to the next, you are never going to get anywhere unless you turn on the money faucet. This could mean getting more music gigs, utilizing freelance methods, or getting a "real" job! Let's consider these options:

1. **Get More Music Gigs:** Always attempt to use your musical talents for work first. For me (Bobby speaking), I offered drum lessons in the house that I was renting with roommates. With a little advertising, I had thirty students at $30 an hour. On top of that, I got a house gig with a soul band at $225 a week for three nights a week. Furthermore, I played weddings with the teachers at Berklee College of Music on the weekends at $300 a pop. If I could earn 5k out of school, so can you.
2. **Utilize "Regular" Freelance Methods:** If music gigs are not an option, go with all of the available "regular" freelance methods to make money. One musician we know drives for Uber, Postmates, and Instacart and brings in several thousands of dollars per week (all without missing a single band rehearsal or evening gig). This guy even showcases his music to his Uber customers to get feedback while he works! In one instance, he even picked up a famous record producer, which led to a studio session.
3. **Get a "Real" Job:** Finally, if none of the above situations work for you, go for a steady day or night gig. We suggest you find something that is connected in some way to your ultimate dream of music. One musician we know got a steady gig working as a salesperson at Guitar Center. Not only did he make steady money; he promoted his gigs to customers to increase his concert draw, and networked with equipment reps to secure endorsement deals. He killed two birds with one stone.

Look gang, whatever route you take, just remember that the road to investing and building wealth starts with your own ability to generate income. While this might sound like common sense, you'd be surprised at the number of musicians who still sleep on their friends' couches penniless waiting to get discovered on TikTok. While people do get lucky, don't bet everything on number seven. So, roll up your sleeves, be strong, and put your human capital to work.

2. CREATE AND LIVE BY A BUDGET

Okay, so now that you have a steady flow of money coming in, it's time to create and live by a budget. Remember, it's not how much you make, it's how you manage your money that counts.

Follow these three steps:

1. **Set a Savings Goal:** Create a monthly objective setting forth a percentage of your take-home pay that you'd like to save each month. To illustrate, if your take-home pay was 5k a month, your objective might be to save 10 percent (or $500).
2. **List Expenses:** Now list all of your expenses showing how you'll cleverly use that 5k to meet your savings goal of $500. Know that fixed expenses like rent will be easy, but other expenses like groceries will require you making an educated estimate based on what you spent in prior months. And finally . . .
3. **Track Expenditures:** Track all of your expenditures throughout the month by counting receipts. If you stay on budget, then bravo for you. If there are overages, then readjust your budget and try again. Eventually, you'll find a plan that works for you. And best yet, you'll have that 10 percent surplus of money you were shooting for.

While creating a budget might seem like a lot of work, remember that it really is the hallmark to getting your financial shit together. And like everything else in life, the more you use a budget, the easier it will get. So, take our word for it gang, live and die by a budget!

3. PAY OFF DEBT AND ESTABLISH STRONG CREDIT

Now that you have a surplus of monthly cash, put it to good use by knocking out your debt.

For most musicians, debt will probably be limited to credit cards, school loans, and an automobile. Whatever the case, just know that there are a number of strategies to get debt free.

Consider the following:

- **Use the Debt Avalanche:** Use the "debt avalanche" strategy to double-down consistently on your "highest interest loan" while at least paying all your minimum balances on your other loans. Once paid off, take the amount of money you allocated for the highest interest loan and add it to the minimum payments on the next highest interest loan, and so on, until you no longer have debt.
- **Use the Debt Snowball:** Alternately, you can use the "debt snowball" strategy to double-down on your "smallest balance

loan" while paying at least all your minimum balances on your other loans. Once paid off, take the amount of money you allocated for the smallest balance loan and add it to the minimum payments on the next smallest balance loan, until you no longer have debt.

Look peeps, the bottom line is that paying off debt means ridding yourself of wasteful interest payments. Furthermore, it means building your credit for important loans down the road, and saving a little money that you can use for a rainy day.

4. ESTABLISH AN EMERGENCY FUND

After digging yourself out of debt (congratulations), the next step in our seven-step process to investing and building wealth is using that surplus money to establish an emergency fund. This is money you amass for life's unexpected moments when all things go south.

Consider the following:

- **Save for Six Months to a Year:** Attempt to save at least six months' worth of living expenses. I (this is Bobby) personally feel more comfortable with one year of living expenses. I was injured in an accident (struck by a truck) and it took longer than a couple of months to heal. On top of that, it took a couple more months to reestablish work. So, whether it's six months or a year, just build up that freakin' fund y'all.
- **Keep It Liquid, But Let It Grow:** Keep your emergency fund in a safe place where it is liquid (immediately available) and growing in interest. Consider a savings account with an online bank, a money market account with a local bank, or a short-term bond fund via a brokerage company like Vanguard. Wherever you park your money, just remember you'll need access to your "cash in a flash" when the "shit hits the fan." So, never tie this money down in stocks or long-term CDs or bonds. And finally . . .
- **Keep it Fully Funded:** Remember that should you ever use your emergency fund, you need to refund it. Be clear that the plan is to be fully funded and ready for any emergency for the rest of your life. Okay? Good job! Now. let's move on!

5. START SAVING FOR RETIREMENT

Now that you have a job, a budget, no debt, and an emergency fund, we can begin thinking about shifting all your surplus money into retirement accounts. Make no mistake, retirement (or retirement planning) is not just for old folks; it starts as early as twenty years old and lasts a lifetime.

Be sure to consider the following:

- **Take Advantage of Employer-Based 401(k)s:** Start by taking advantage of "tax-advantaged" accounts such as a 401(k) offered by your employer. This allows a payroll administrator to direct a portion of your pre-tax income directly into an interest earning account to grow and be taxed upon withdrawal in retirement. You can contribute as much as $20,500 a year if you're younger than age fifty, and $27,000 annually if you're fifty or older. And if your boss is really cool, they'll even match additional funds up to a percentage of your contribution (yup, free bonus money). Hey, this is the best deal in town.
- **Open Up an Individual Retirement Account:** Now, if you don't have access to a 401(k), open up an individual retirement account (IRA) on your own. A traditional IRA allows you to personally invest "pre-tax" dollars to grow and be taxed upon withdrawal in retirement. You can contribute as much as $6,000 if you're younger than age fifty, and $7,000 when you're age fifty or above. There's also a Roth version of this plan (Roth IRA) where you can personally invest "after-tax" dollars to grow and be withdrawn tax-free at retirement. All good stuff!

Look, no matter which retirement accounts you use, just be clear that Uncle Sam makes it easy for you to save for your retirement and avoid thousands in taxes over your lifetime. While doing this, you can still utilize other non-retirement accounts (called "taxable accounts") for short-term objectives (like buying a house) or even long-term investments (like extra retirement income). But just be clear that maxing out your tax-advantaged retirement accounts first is always a good idea. Seriously! Retirement is an investor's biggest priority. And don't forget it!

6. INVEST RESPONSIBLY

After completing all six steps of our seven-step process to investing and building wealth, you can now consider yourself a financial rock star. So, go ahead, take a bow, you've come a long way.

But now you need to really focus on the principles of investing responsibly. After all, it's not enough to just throw your hard-earned money in tax-advantaged (and taxable accounts) and just hope for success. Hope is never a long-term and sustainable financial strategy. Believe that!

Consider the following nuggets of wisdom:

- **Always Set Investment Goals:** Setting goals, or more specifically, the time horizon of each goal, is critical to investing responsibly. You see, it's time that typically determines the type of investment vehicle that you will use. As a general rule, the longer the time horizon for your goals, the riskier and more rewarding the investment (such as stocks). The shorter the time horizon for your goals, the more conservative and less rewarding the investment (such as short-term bonds). This is generally because a long-term investment strategy can better hedge against the associated risks of market swings or downturns. To illustrate, a long-term goal of saving x dollars for retirement in fifty years would typically mean utilizing a large variety of stocks. A mid-term goal of saving x dollars for a modest house in ten years might mean utilizing a mix of stocks and bonds. And a short-term goal of saving x dollars for a modest car in three years might be to use short-term bonds, bank CDs, or money market funds. So always remember, goals and their time horizons heavily influence your investment decisions.
- **Know Your Risk Tolerance:** Knowing your risk tolerance and the amount of money that you are comfortable with potentially losing, is also important to investing responsibly. Or said another way, knowing your allocation of stocks to bonds is critical to your investment success. Remember that stocks (which are highly volatile) and bonds (which are less volatile) are not widely correlated and can help to balance out your portfolio over your lifetime. The legendary Jack Bogle (Vanguard's founder) says, "Put your age in bonds and the rest in stocks." So, if you are a twenty-year-old musician saving for retirement, you might put 80 percent into stocks and 20 percent into bonds. At age forty, your portfolio might hold 60 percent in stocks and 40 percent

in bonds. And at age seventy, your portfolio might hold 30 percent in stocks and 70 percent in bonds. You get the point—your investments become less risky as time progresses. So, knowing your risk tolerance and getting your stock to bond ratio right is important to both building and preserving your wealth. Take this tip very seriously.

- **Diversify Your Portfolio:** Diversifying your portfolio is yet another extremely important tip to investing responsibly. This essentially means that rather than trying to find a needle in the haystack (i.e., picking the winning stock), you buy the whole freakin' haystack. This means buying investments such as index mutual funds that cover a number of different companies, sectors, and geographical regions. To illustrate, a thirty-year-old investor might purchase a 70/30 (stock to bond) risk allocation including: Vanguard's Total Stock Market Index Fund (which contains 4,070 companies in technology, consumer discretionary products and financials all over the United States); Vanguard's Total International Stock Market Fund (which contains 7,754 companies in consumer cyclicals, financial services, and health care all over Europe, the Pacific, and emerging markets); and Vanguard's Total Bond Market Index (which contains 10,127 investment-grade bonds in US treasuries, and mortgage-backed securities all over the United States). As you can see, index funds are very diversified and can prevent you from putting all of your eggs in one basket. This way you win some and lose some, rather than lose everything on a one-horse bet.

- **Avoid Management Costs:** Keeping costs low is also extremely important to investing responsibly—and this is where the news is really going to get great. Not only are index funds (just mentioned above) a highly diversified investment, they can also be one of the lowest-cost investments. This is because index funds track a stock market index and do not require the more expensive "active management" associated with other types of mutual funds and individual stocks. Since the fund essentially mirrors a section of the stock market, tracking its performance is much easier and less time consuming. It does not require the daily management of numerous stock transactions attempting to beat the market returns. This is why time and time again, expert investors such as Warren Buffett have strongly recommended index funds. So, if you're smart, this just might be a great move for you too.

- **Aim to Beat Inflation:** Another super important tip to consider when talking about investing responsibly is the risk of inflation on your investments. Inflation (an increase in prices and decrease in the power of money), has averaged at about 3 percent over the last decade. This essentially means—in this example—that your investments must earn 3 percent in annual interest to keep up with the pace of inflation. If your money is sitting in the bank earning an annual interest rate of 0.01 percent, you're screwed. Thus, your best chance of beating inflation is probably going through an investment vehicle like our trusted Vanguard stock mutual index fund. While past performance is no guarantee of future results, stocks have historically provided higher returns than other asset classes. This, coupled with the low costs associated with passively managed index funds, will likely help you net the decent annual returns on your investments you need to succeed. Just remember, inflation is critical to watch.
- **Aim to Lower Taxes:** Dovetailing nicely with inflation costs, taxation also poses serious costs on investment returns. According to the Schwab Center for Financial Research, this is because you not only lose the money you pay in taxes, but you also lose the growth that money could have generated if it were invested. This is why it is so important that you employ as many tax-efficient investment strategies as possible. Here are just three to think about: (1) Max out your "tax-advantaged" retirement accounts (401(k)s, Roth IRAs, traditional IRAs, etc.) each year since these accounts are almost like free gifts the government provides to help you save on taxes. (2) Invest wisely in your other "taxable accounts" by using long-term buy-and-hold strategies that won't trigger regular short-term capital gains taxes (which are higher taxes incurred from selling your investments in under a year). And finally, (3) Delay a portion of any lump sum payment you might be owed (like a large publishing or merchandising advance) till next tax year. This way you might avoid falling into a higher tax bracket and paying more income tax in the current year. Sound good? Look gang, whatever strategies you use, just never pay more in taxes than you need to. Avoid taxes legally when you can.
- **Avoid the Noise and Stay the Course:** Finally getting to the end of our investment tips, know that avoiding all the financial noise in the media and just staying the course is hugely important to investing responsibly. There are so many experts filling you up with supposed opportunities and gloom and doom, it's

enough to make you jump ship on your financial plan in search of a better solution. But if you're constantly buying in and out of the market due to greed and fear, you are doing yourself a major disservice. You are allowing your emotions to get the best of you, costing yourself time and money, and creating a lot of stress and worry. So, stop looking at your investments every minute and have faith in long-term investing. Sure, the movements of the stock market are always going to fluctuate on the short term, but know that the market tends to rise steadily over the years. In fact, since 1928, the US stock market has averaged returns of 9.8 percent per year. So, go live your lives a little. Write that new hit song that brings in hundreds of thousands and go get that publishing deal. Have faith that you put together a killer financial plan, and stand by it. Know that staying the course is a sound piece of advice. It's also the famous slogan of Vanguard's founder Jack Bogle (who actually created the Index Fund). Wow! Godspeed!

7. PLAY WITH FUNNY MONEY (ONLY IF YOU MUST)

Finally, moving away from our perspective on investing responsibly, it's time to play with "funny money," if you must.

Funny money is money you can afford to lose. It's the money where you can be highly speculative, throw down on a crypto stock pick that some guru mentions in a Facebook group, or invest in a buddy's restaurant. Who knows, you might even get super rich and finally get that mansion, yacht, and lime green Lambo. It doesn't matter if you lose it because it's all about having a little fun. After all, you deserve it. You've busted your ass, followed our advice, and have the above six steps completely under your control. Hey, whatever makes you happy!

But before running off to the race track, it's important to look back on the past. Throughout history, people have always been trying to get rich quick. There was the gold rush of 1848 where everyone got greedy thinking they were going to strike gold (most didn't); there was the dot com craze in 2000, where everyone got greedy thinking they were going to strike it rich (most didn't); and now there is the crypto thing where people want to get a taste of the millionaire dream (and many have already lost their asses).

So, look, if you want to play with "extra" money, have fun! But always be realistic about the odds and never let "playing" get out of control. Adhere to our six steps above, and remember smart investing is not supposed to be fun. Take this advice seriously, folks. Okay? Peace!

So that's our seven-point checklist to investing and building wealth. This stuff is not revolutionary, but it is crucial to your personal financial education and your future.

Some of this stuff you've likely heard elsewhere, and some of it you've heard from us in other articles and chapters we've written. But maybe that is the point—what works is worth repeating. And what works is worth adapting to your own investment playbook.

So, on that note, give these seven points a try, and speak with a financial planner who can create a plan customized to your needs. One or two sessions can never hurt. Sound good? Peace!

Recommended Reading on Investing

Here are a few investment books and other resources that we highly recommend. After all, lifelong learning should be yet another smart step to every responsible investor. Happy reading!

Books

- *The Little Book of Common Sense Investing*, by Jack Bogle
- *The Little Book of Bulletproof Investing*, by Bill Stein and Phil DeMuth
- *How to Think About Money*, by Jonathan Clements
- *The Random Walk Guide to Investing*, by Burton G. Malkiel
- *Rescue Your Money*, by Ric Edelman
- *The Wealthy Barber*, by David Chilton
- *The Richest Man in Babylon*, by George Clason
- *The Index Card*, by Helaine Olen and Harold Pollack
- *The Coffee House Investor*, by Bill Schultheis
- *The Bogleheads Guide to the Three-Fund Portfolio*, by Taylor Larimore
- *The Bogleheads Guide to Retirement Planning*, by Taylor Larimore, Mel Lindawer, Richard Ferri, and Laura F. Dogu
- *Common Sense Investing*, by Rick Van Ness
- *Why Bother with Bonds*, by Rick Van Ness

- *Think, Act, and Invest like Warren Buffett*, by Larry E. Sweroe
- *Four Pillars of Investing*, by William Bernstein
- *The Only Investment Guide You'll Ever Need*, by Andrew Tobias
- *Get a Financial Life*, by Beth Kobliner

Websites

- Investopedia https://www.investopedia.com.
- Nerd Wallet https://www.nerdwallet.com.
- Bankrate https://www.bankrate.com/.
- The Finance Buff https://thefinancebuff.com/archive.
- Oblivious Investor https://obliviousinvestor.com.
- Forbes Advisor https://www.forbes.com/advisor/.
- Yahoo Finance https://finance.yahoo.com.
- Morningstar https://www.morningstar.com.

Nine Must-Know Quotes on Money, Investing, and More

There are so many brilliant authors who have written about the principles of money and investing. People like Jack Bogle, Warren Buffett, and Burton G. Malkiel are just a few.

Because these experts are so brilliant at delivering memorable tidbits of valuable advice, we wanted to turn you on to nine must-know quotes on money, investing, and more.

From risk tolerance, to asset allocation, to choosing the right investments, you're getting a combined seven hundred years of valuable financial wisdom from some of the best financial experts.

So, sit back, take in the nuggets, and grow.

1. CHRISTINE BENZ ON RISK TOLERANCE AND DIVERSIFICATION

Risk tolerance (how much money you are comfortable losing) and diversification (the investments, sectors, and regions in which you place your money) are important concepts for a discussion about money and investments. Here is what Christine Benz had to say about it all.

> As long as you have a risk tolerance you can handle, a well-diversified portfolio, and a sufficient emergency fund, you shouldn't need to worry about market fluctuations.
>
> —Christine Benz, author of
> *Morning Star's Guide to Mutual Funds*

This makes perfect sense, gang. Let's break down each portion of this quote.

- **Risk Tolerance:** Since stocks are a highly volatile, high return investment, and bonds are a less volatile, low return investment, it's necessary to have a comfortable balance (or ratio) between the two securities that you can live with no matter which direction the market goes. One rule of thumb is to "put your age in bonds" for long-term investments. To illustrate, a twenty-year-old saving for retirement forty years out would put 20 percent in bonds and 80 percent in stocks. Note a twenty-year-old can afford to be a little more aggressive since he/she has adequate time to recover from potential market losses. Bottom line, as long as you have a risk ratio you can handle, you're good!
- **Diversification:** While betting on one prized horse might earn you greater returns, you'll also suffer greater losses should your horse come in last. To offset this risk, you need to diversify your investments and spread out your bets among several horses (i.e., securities, companies, industries, and regions). Regardless of market swings, diversification will hedge against risk and improve the stability of your investment portfolio. Remember, "diversity reduces adversity." And don't forget it.
- **Emergency Fund:** Finally, building an emergency fund (up to six months of living expenses to get you through the downs) can really help to ease the panic involved when the markets are tanking. Without an emergency plan, you might do something stupid like sell all your investments well below what you paid for them. This is a surefire way to lose at investing.

So, as you can see, gang, investing is not rocket science; it's actually just common sense.

2. RIC EDELMAN ON STRATEGIC REBALANCING OF YOUR ACCOUNTS

You already learned above that you need to balance out your risk between stocks and bonds so that you can better tolerate market swings. But even when doing this, some of your investments will inevitably be winners and some losers, causing your account to get "out of balance." When this happens, you'll need to "strategically rebalance." Here is what Ric Edelman had to say.

> Keeping an eye on your accounts over time so as to maintain your appropriate level of risk through strategic rebalancing, is one of my secrets to successful investing and to selling high and buying low.
>
> —Ric Edelman, author of *Rescue Your Money*

Understand that if your stocks are outperforming your bonds, the difference between the value of stocks to bonds will be higher than you originally allocated. Thus, in order to rebalance your portfolio back to your desired risk ratio, you would need to sell some stocks and buy some bonds. While your instincts may be to hold on to your winning stocks while the winning is good, remember that rebalancing is actually a pretty sweet deal. You'll be selling your stocks when they're high and buying more bonds when they're low—all while maintaining your desired risk ratio!

There are no hard rules about how often you should rebalance. Some people do it yearly, some when their desired risk ratio is above a 5 percent deviation, and some as they age and approach retirement so as to keep their "age in bonds." Do as you like.

If your accounts are being managed by an administrator (like in your 401(k) retirement account), rebalancing back to your desired asset allocation usually happens automatically.

However, if your accounts are self-funded (such as your traditional IRA), you might have to rebalance yourself with the assistance of your broker. Or, more simply, you can just buy into a "target-dated index fund" where you can "set it and forget it." Yup, target dated funds automatically rebalance and are hassle free. We definitely recommend that you check them out.

3. WARREN BUFFETT ON CHOOSING THE RIGHT INVESTMENTS

Choosing investments can be quite overwhelming, whether they are stocks (ownership in companies), bonds (loans), or funds (consisting of numerous securities). This is because we all want to make the right choices and avoid dumb mistakes. But selecting your investments doesn't have to be so complicated. Here is what Warren Buffett had to say.

NINE MUST-KNOW QUOTES ON MONEY, INVESTING, AND MORE 159

> Most investors are better off putting their money in low-cost index funds ... I'd rather be certain of a good return than hopeful of a great one.
>
> —Warren Buffett, famed investor

Index funds mirror a market index. A market index, such as the S&P 500, benchmarks the performance of America's top five hundred companies as a whole, instead of one company individually.

Index funds tend to produce an average return of the market, but slightly less than average when factoring in expense ratios for maintaining the funds. This is actually a good thing! Trying to pick single stocks and hoping for above-average returns will likely end up costing you.

As proof, Warren Buffett *won* a million-dollar bet that index funds would *out-perform* a collection of managed hedge funds over a ten-year period. Yup, it's true! Index funds might be a very hands-off, passive, and boring investment, but investing was never meant to be a game.

4. JACK BOGLE ON THE SIMPLICITY OF INVESTING

Sometimes the simplest approach to investing your money is the absolute best approach. But don't just take it from us, here is what Jack Bogle had to say about simplicity.

> The beauty of owning the market in just three index funds [like a total stock market domestic fund, a total bond market domestic fund, and a total stock market international fund] is that you eliminate individual stock risk, you eliminate market sector risk, and you eliminate manager risk. . . . This helps ensure that you'll at least get your fair share of market returns.
>
> —Jack Bogle, founder of Vanguard, author of the *Little Book on Common Sense Investing*

When you have several choices, the simplest approach is often best. The odds of repeatedly outpacing the markets by trying to pick the right stock, sector, and manager is extremely low. So why bother when you can keep things simple and buy the entire market in three index funds? There will be ups and downs, but you'll have more time to live your life productively as opposed to spending all day trying to guess the market. After all, your mission is life is being a musician, not a stock analyst.

5. SPENCER JAKAB ON KEEPING INVESTMENT COSTS DOWN

Investment costs can take a significant bite out of your investment returns. A 5 percent return with costs can be more like a 3 percent return, which barely keeps up with inflation. This is not good at all! So, let's take a look at what Spencer Jakab had to say about keeping costs down.

> The typical investor spends as much as $170,000 in fees by the time they retire. Instead, they should keep their investing as low-cost as possible.
>
> —Spencer Jakab, *Wall Street Journal* investment columnist, and author of *Heads I Win, Tails I Win*

Investment costs can really hinder a portfolio's performance. The four most obvious costs include:

1. **An Active Money Manager:** The cost of professional management.
2. **Inflation:** The increase of prices over time.
3. **Taxes:** What Uncle Sam wants. And . . .
4. **Fund Fees:** The general costs of buying an investment.

For these reasons, Jakab recommends buying and holding index funds. Here's why:

- Index funds are passively managed funds (thus eliminating management and other fees).
- Index funds are known to beat inflation on average over the long term (earning about 13.95 percent if considering the S&P 500's performance over the last decade).
- Index funds are tax-efficient (since they do not buy into and out of the market in effort to get above market returns). And finally . . .
- Index funds have some of the lowest fees, called expense ratios, allowing investors to keep more of their hard-earned money in their pockets.

So always consider the effect of fees on your portfolio, because they can really cost you.

6. BARON ROTHSCHILD ON A DOWN MARKET

While most people freak out while the markets fall, the truth is that a down market is really the best time for the smart investor. This is because assets are now available at rock-bottom prices. Here is a quote from perhaps one of the most legendary billionaires of all time—Baron Rothschild.

> The time to buy is when there is blood in the streets.
>
> —Baron Rothschild, billionaire

We love this quote! But all things said, no one can ever predict with accuracy when the markets will be down (or up). So, really the best approach is to continually—through thick and thin—allocate a steady flow of funds into your investments and stay the course for the long term.

Sometimes you'll buy low and sometimes you'll buy high, but over time your dollar will average out. This is generally known as the concept of "dollar cost averaging," and it works.

So, why don't you give it a try?

7. JACK BRENNAN ON BEING A BUY-AND-HOLD INVESTOR

No one likes a down market (well, no one other than Baron Rothschild). It can keep investors up all night and cause them to make stupid decisions. But typically your best bet is to just stick with your plan over the long term. Now, here is what Jack Brennan had to say about the matter.

> If you're determined to succeed at investing, make it your first priority to become a buy-and-hold investor. You might time the market once, but the odds are it will only be once.
>
> —Jack Brennan, former Vanguard CEO and author of *Straight Talk on Investing*

Watching the markets rise and fall on a daily basis is enough to make you seasick. Trying to guess the best time to buy and sell is a crapshoot that even the gurus can't get correct.

But time and again, experts have proven that just buying and holding on to your investments over the long term is the real key to your success. Just look at a graph of the S&P 500 over a ten-year period and it looks more like walking up a hill with a yo-yo (lots of fluctuation on the short term, but a steady climb overall). You just have to be patient and have nerves of steel.

8. BURTON G. MALKIEL ON BEHAVIORAL FINANCE

Getting close to the end of our famous quotes on money and investing, we can't forget to say something about behavioral finance.

Behavioral finance is a field that studies how human behavior affects financial decisions. Because investing can be very emotional, listen carefully to what Burton G. Malkiel had to say.

> Don't be your own worst enemy. . . . An understanding of how vulnerable we are to our own psychology can help us to avoid the stupid investor delusions that can screw up our financial security.
>
> —Burton G. Malkiel, author of
> *A Random Walk Down Wall Street*

Investor delusions that cause stupid mistakes typically stem from three biases:

- **Overconfidence:** This is a person's ability to feel that they are more knowledgeable, lucky, skilled, researched, and destined for success than the next person. We see many of our young musician students using the Robinhood app on their phones believing they're going to pick the right stock and be driving Lambos by next year. It disgusts us how companies encourage this behavior, by making investing appear to be as easy as downloading an app. Make no mistake, overconfidence gets lots of people in big trouble.
- **Herd Mentality:** Another bias is the herd mentality—everyone has a fear of missing out on all that potential wealth. After all, there is so much happening in the cryptocurrency and NFT world that one may feel tempted to invest while the "getting is

good." But remember, the past success of one "random occurrence" is not a guarantee of future hits. So, chasing something because of a few lucky winners guarantees nothing. In other words, the chances for success when relying on emotion are extremely low. And finally . . .
- **Entertainment:** The last bias is a person's view of what's entertaining and what's not. And unfortunately, many young musicians view short-term gains from one of those sexy stocks far more entertaining than holding index funds for decades. And this is a damn shame. Because, you know what? Unless you get really lucky with that one stock, you are way more likely to win over the long term with the boring index funds. Make no mistake, entertainment should never be a factor in the investment world. This bias can just sink you.

9. TONY ROBBINS ON EXECUTION

Finally, to close out our piece on nine must-know quotes on money and investing, we leave you with a quote on execution—getting things done. After all, if you only think, read, and talk about building financial security, you'll never get anywhere. Here's what Tony Robbins had to say.

> Knowledge is not power, execution is. Just make a little bit of progress each day or each week, and before you know it, your path to financial freedom will be realized.
>
> —Tony Robbins, life coach and author of the book
> *Money: Mastering the Game*

Look peeps, financial freedom starts with taking baby steps. Your success depends on taking action—not by overthinking, making excuses, and blaming others for your current state of affairs.

Once you understand the basics, you need to roll up your sleeves and just get to work. Even by just saving a dollar here and there, your newfound attitude on finance will encourage you to improve other aspects of your financial life. Soon enough, you'll be on the road to financial freedom. The younger you start the better, but it's never too late to get moving.

So, that's it, guys, for our nine must-know quotes on money, investing, and more. There are so many more quotes we could have added, but we definitely left you with some of the best. Just always be sure to seek advice from credible people and avoid the tricksters. Use sound investment principles, make smart decisions, and kick serious ass. Investing is not a short-term game and you have to be in it for the long haul. We wish all of you the utmost success. Peace!

Finding Experts to Provide Smart Financial Guidance: Ten Tips

Finding financial guidance is not at all difficult to do these days—there are great books, websites, classes, and research tools readily available to anyone who wants to use them.

However, finding an expert who can sit down with you and handle your unique personal situation is a more challenging endeavor with many different options.

Options include (1) financial planners who provide overall advice about personal finance (for as little as one hour for a flat fee); (2) advisors who suggest actual investments as part of a longer-term relationship (for a fee or percentage); and (3) money managers who invest and manage your money for potentially several decades (for typically a percentage of your money under management).

While financial planners will most likely be your first option for all practical purposes, the information that follows really applies to any one of the experts we mentioned above.

So, broadly speaking, here are our ten tips on finding experts to provide financial advice.

1. CONSIDER YOUR FINANCIAL SITUATION AND OBJECTIVES

The first step in getting started in your search for a financial expert is to consider your own financial situation and why you are looking to hire someone.

Here are two things that you might consider:

1. **Do You Really "Need" an Expert?** Look in the mirror and decide if there's a little more that you can do for yourself first before paying others to tell you the obvious. You don't need to pay an expert hundreds (if not thousands) of dollars to tell you the very basics like "spend less money and make more." Unless you're already in serious debt, that's something that you can start doing on your own. So just do it!
2. **Do You Have Realistic Goals?** Think about what you ultimately want to achieve by meeting with a financial expert. If you want to get out of debt, pay off school, and put a down payment on a house within the next ten years, that's something legit that a financial planner can discuss with you in detail. But, if you're only interested in getting rich quick, throwing cool mansion parties, and driving lime green Porsches, then you are probably not ready to work with a certified financial planner.

2. GET RECOMMENDATIONS FROM SOMEONE YOU TRUST

Also look for approved recommendations from people you know and trust and avoid non-approved recommendations at all costs. Consider the following:

- **Approved Recommendations:** Consider asking the finance teacher at your college to see if they know someone. Ask the HR/payroll director at your place of work if there is someone they can refer. Or even ask good ol' Mom or Dad (or brother, sister, cousin, uncle) if they can refer someone. Anyone who seems to have their financial shit together is an approved recommendation in our book.
- **Non-Approved Recommendations:** Avoid recommendations from those who present an inflated image of success or seem to have an overopinionated and narrow view of wealth. A gentleman on Instagram who posts pictures flaunting his Ferraris and mansion parties doesn't automatically make him a credible reference for financial advice. Sorry, but we just do not approve of recommendations coming from people who seem to be too "showy" or risky with their money. In fact, we'd say, run.

3. CONSIDER IF HE/SHE IS PART OF A LARGER OR SMALLER FIRM

Also consider whether the expert is part of a large or small financial firm. Here are a few things to think about:

- **Larger Firms:** Larger firms might include Charles Schwab, Morgan Stanley, J. P. Morgan Chase, Vanguard, Fidelity, or Merrill Lynch. These companies are all well known and very credible and could certainly provide you with a strong level of comfort. On the other hand, these companies are so big that you might not feel you are getting the personalized attention that you really desire.
- **Smaller Firms:** Smaller firms might include Cheviot Value Management in Beverly Hills, California; Oppenheimer & Co in Princeton, New Jersey; Mill Creek Capital in Philadelphia, Pennsylvania; Concierge Wealth Management in Boston, Massachusetts; Edelman Financial Engines in Las Vegas, Nevada; or even the firm located right in your very own neighborhood. These companies can also be credible companies, but they might make you feel uncomfortable because you've never heard of them. On the other hand, they might give you the personal attention that you need.

Decide what works best for you. And remember that the two choices are not always exclusive of each other. If you look hard enough, you just might get the best of both worlds.

4. CONSIDER HOW LONG HE OR SHE HAS BEEN IN BUSINESS

Also consider how long the financial expert has been in practice as well as the number of years the firm (where they are employed) has been in business. This is not too difficult to do:

- **Evaluate Your Financial Expert:** Using Google, you'll be able to drum up all the info you need to determine whether a candidate is acceptable. What's acceptable, you ask? While answers will vary, we'd like to think that any financial expert should have at least three years of experience. Hey, this is not much different from the music business. I (this is Bobby) once got rejected from a huge audition with a classic rock band because they said

I didn't have enough years of experience—at that time—playing stadiums. Hey, people like proof, and so should you!
- **Evaluate Your Expert's Company:** And don't forget to research the company where your potential advisor has been employed. How long has the firm been in business? What's their story? You could have someone who has been working for years in the business, but just opened up their own establishment. We don't know about you, but we'd be concerned as to whether that firm is going to survive. Think we're making things up? I (this is Britt) once considered establishing a long-term relationship with a new financial planning firm in Palm Springs, California. Fortunately, I took a pass because the firm didn't make it past the two-year mark. Had I chosen them, I would have had to start my search all over again and become familiar with a whole new planner.

5. CONSIDER IF HE OR SHE HAS OTHER CLIENTS LIKE YOU

Also consider whether your financial expert understands and works with people just like you.

While most financial experts are true professionals and can handle it all, keep in mind that some experts do cater to a very specific clientele. And this can make a huge difference.

For instance, some financial persons specialize in working with folks who have "normal everyday jobs." But financial advice to a musician playing piano with Ariana Grande is going to be very different from the schoolteacher. The musician's gig and career could dry up tomorrow, while the teacher's job could last thirty-plus years. Two different beasts!

Think we're exaggerating? I (this is Bobby) had a financial expert who treated me as if I was going to work as a successful musician forever. I thought that his financial strategies were way too aggressive for someone in my profession, as he advised against having a chunk of money sit (unmanaged) in liquid emergency money market funds and short-term bonds. I don't think he understood the unstable nature of the music business, because I was his only entertainment client.

To be sure, find someone who is highly experienced working with people like you.

6. CHECK PROFESSIONAL CREDENTIALS

Also check the professional credentials (or designations) of the financial expert whom you are considering to hire. While there are many types of designations that exist in the financial world, some of the more common ones that we've seen are:

- certified financial planner (CFP)
- certified fund specialist (CFS)
- chartered financial analyst (CFA), and . . .
- certified investment management analyst (CIMA)

While all of these designations are admirable, the one that we'd like to draw the most attention to is the certified financial planner (CFP).

A CFP is someone who:

- graduated with an undergraduate degree,
- graduated from a college program in financial planning,
- passed rigorous financial exams,
- has at least three years of experience working in personal finance, and . . .
- abides by a certain code of ethics of the certified financial planner board.

To find a financial expert with a CFP designation, or to check the status of someone's CFP designation, we suggest that you check the CFP Board website. Also check FINRAs Broker Check to get a sense of your expert's professional background. Finally, be sure to check the SEC's Investment Adviser Public Disclosure databases to see if there are any disciplinary reports on your expert.

Here are the URLs:

- **CFP Board:** https://www.cfp.net
- **FINRAs Broker Check:** https://brokercheck.finra.org
- **SEC's Investment Adviser Public Disclosure:** https://adviserinfo.sec.gov

7. FIND OUT IF HE OR SHE IS A FIDUCIARY

While on the topic of checking professional credentials, also find out if the person you are considering to hire is a fiduciary.

A fiduciary is someone who must put your best interests first. Said another way, fiduciaries cannot make financial recommendations to you just because it will benefit them with a high sales commission. You see, many financial experts may also be salespersons for financial insurance products like annuities and life insurance, and you don't want these products being recommended to you if it's not really in your best interests.

So, find out if your expert is a fiduciary! Just ask them! You can also check the database of the National Association of Personal Financial Advisors and/or use the Securities and Exchange Commission's "Check Your Advisor" tool.

Oh, and good news, CFPs (mentioned above) are indeed fiduciaries, which is yet another reason we decided to elaborate on them. Okay?

Now here are the URLs:

- **National Association of Personal Financial Advisors:** https://www.napfa.org
- **Securities and Exchange Commission:** https://www.sec.gov/check-your-investment-professional

8. BE CLEAR ON HOW HE OR SHE GETS PAID

Also be clear on how your financial expert gets paid before you even decide to meet.

There are essentially three different ways that financial experts are compensated.

1. **Hourly Fee:** I (this is Bobby) was once quoted $300 per hour by a financial planner. This is normal. Rates can range from $100 to $500 and more.
2. **Flat Fee:** I (this is Britt) was once quoted $1,200 by a financial planner to write a financial plan. This is also normal. Rates can range from $1,000 to $3,000.
3. **Percentage:** I (this is Bobby again) was once charged 1 percent of the value of all of my assets by a private firm for active management (which is really the industry average). And another time,

I was charged only 0.30 percent by a very large company (Vanguard) for just passive advice. (Note that active management is where the financial expert makes investment transactions regularly, and passive advice is where they advise the client, but only when the client asks for specific advice.)

Of the three choices, we recommend a flat fee-based situation for the occasional advice you may need. And always ask about fees before meeting with a pro. You want to make sure that you are walking into something that you can ultimately afford and feels right. So, speak up!

9. MAKE SURE YOU REALLY LIKE THE PERSON

Getting close to the end of our ten tips, also make sure that you really like your financial expert. But, since the word "like" is so broad, let's talk about someone that we dislike.

I (Bobby here) once met with a financial expert who was part of a really big firm. Consider this:

- First, on the phone, I couldn't tell the difference between him being an employee of a huge reputable company, or some douchebag trying to sell me a gym membership. He was totally pushy.
- Then, at his office, this guy walks in sporting a flashy tight suit, a Rolex watch, and a BMW keychain that he slid across the table so I could see it (wow, double douchebag).
- Then he made sure to drop a few names by explaining that his friend's cousin lives down the street from Bon-Jovi (wow, who cares!).
- And finally, he told me how great he was at picking winning stocks and that he could make me rich (come on, no one knows "for sure" how the market will behave). This is definitely someone I disliked.

Look, a financial expert should be someone who commands your respect, who doesn't make huge promises or guarantees of how rich you are going to get, and who also represents himself or herself with dignity and composure.

Sorry if it sounds like we are being tough on financial experts. But hey, you're reading this because you want real advice, not candy-coated crap. Of course, not all financial experts act like used car salespeople, so take the time to find someone you really like.

10. ASK ABOUT COMMUNICATION

Finally, when looking for a financial expert, ask about communication! This is also huge! Communication deals with how often your expert is going to be open to answering your questions without getting annoyed. Seriously! This is especially important when working with a financial expert on more of a continuous basis, such as in an advisory or management situation.

Consider the following questions:

- Will they provide you with quarterly or biannual updates?
- Will they occasionally meet with you face to face to catch up? And finally . . .
- Will they be cool talking whenever you're freaking out about the markets?

On the latter note, the ups and downs of the financial markets can be quite overwhelming. Just listen to the news for two days straight and you can hear it for yourself—"The Dow is up two hundred points," and the next day, "The Dow is down five hundred points." It's an emotional roller coaster ride that may cause you to act irrationally and require a little hand holding. Many financial experts totally understand this (they take pride in protecting you from yourself), and others will be annoyed by it.

So, think about the type of communication you will want from a financial expert, and then pick someone who will provide it with total professionalism. Again, this is huge!

So, that's pretty much it, gang. Finding financial experts (whether a financial planner, advisor, or money manager) can be a difficult endeavor particularly because it involves your hard-earned money. You really have to like and trust the person, and feel confident that he or she understand your needs. It's gotta click! And most importantly, the person has to have the right credentials! So, take time with your search and don't be afraid to fire someone if he or she doesn't satisfy your needs. Okay? Good luck!

20

Seven Investment Apps You Might Consider

The world of investing has come a very long way.

Investing once seemed very complicated and only the experts had access to detailed research. Eventually, with online platforms and new developments in things like Index funds and robo-investing, the need for active managers and detailed advice became even more questioned.

Today, with the ease of mobile phones and apps—and with the ability to make fractional investments for very little money and nominal fees—younger folks are now joining the action. While there are a variety of different services out there all trying to get your business—and many of these services can seem quite similar despite a few competitive advantages here and there—what follows is a brief overview of seven investment apps you might consider.

Important note: Investing is not a video game. There is always risk of loss and it should be taken very seriously. Many experts agree that the best results often come from long-term strategies where you buy and hold. Nothing sexy and nothing exciting—that's what video games are for. Okay peeps? So, without further ado, let's get started with our overview.

1. ROBINHOOD (JOIN A NEW GENERATION OF INVESTORS)

Robinhood offers its twenty million plus users the opportunity to invest in stocks, EFTs, and cryptocurrency like Bitcoin and Ethereum without paying any fees on trades (though other small fees might apply). What's more, you can manage your own cash with the Robinhood cash card.

According to their website, Robinhood helps you to:

- Start building your portfolio to trade stocks, options, and EFTs for just $1.
- Dive into selling crypto for no commissions (note that other crypto exchanges are known to charge up to 4 percent).
- Earn weekly rewards for spending your cash with the Robinhood cash card.

In sum, Robinhood helps you to join a "new generation of investors." Be sure to check out their website at https://robinhood.com.

2. ACORNS (INVEST SPARE CHANGE, GROW, AND SPEND)

Acorns offers the opportunity to invest your spare change, bank smarter, and add Bitcoin to your portfolio—all for a small monthly subscription fee, ranging from $3 to $5 (depending on the services that you use). Acorns is known as being a great platform for beginners.

According to their website, Acorns allows you to:

- Invest your spare change in a number of diversified platforms created by experts, get your portfolio rebalanced, and learn helpful tips about personal finance.
- Add Bitcoin to your investment portfolio simply (note there are no extra apps, digital wallets, and vulnerable passwords needed as there is with other platforms).
- Bank smarter with the Acorns debit card (that saves and invests for you every time you spend) as well as set up direct deposits with Acorns's checking account where you can "get paid two days early."

As Acorns puts it, "From little acorns mighty oak trees can grow." Be sure to check out Acorns's website today at https://www.acorns.com.

3. FIDELITY (STOCKS BY THE SLICE)

Fidelity offers you the opportunity to buy fractional shares of stocks allowing you to buy what you want, at the price you want, for as little as $1 down. You might not get more than 0.038 shares of your favorite stock, but hey, it's a start.

According to their website, Fidelity allows you to:

- Open up a brokerage account with no minimum dollar balance needed, no account fees, and no commissions on trades for US stocks and EFTs.
- Choose from more than seven thousand US stocks and EFTs to trade fractionally.
- Trade with no dollar maximum and no commission.

Look gang, Fidelity makes it look so easy to get started, we'd be surprised if you weren't tempted to get your "stocks by the slice" today. Go to fidelity.com/slice.

4. BETTERMENT (ROBO-ADVISING AT ITS BEST)

Betterment offers investing with automated portfolio management at a fee of 0.25 percent of the value of your holdings, which is perfect for the hands-off investor with a low balance. It also offers a premium service with unlimited phone access to certified financial planners for a fee of 0.40 percent of the value of your holdings, which is perfect for more serious investors with higher balances and more needs. There's something for all.

According to their website, Betterment helps you to do the following:

- Open a brokerage account with as little as a $10 balance. Additionally, using their automated (robotic) platform, you can get invested in multiple portfolio options including socially responsible portfolios that can help you make the world a better place. Accounts are automatically rebalanced.
- Open up a variety of retirement accounts including IRAs, Roth IRAs, and SEP IRAs.
- Set up a savings or checking account and use their cash-back debit card.
- Talk to customer service agents by phone if you have any questions.

In sum, Betterment gives you the automated tools, inspiration, and support you need to become a better investor. Check out their website at https://www.betterment.com.

5. FUNDRISE (THE FUTURE OF REAL ESTATE INVESTING)

Fundrise offers the opportunity to invest in real estate stocks in the "palm of your hand." With as little as $10, you can join a community of more than 150,000 investors who are taking advantage of the rising world of real estate without actually having to buy a physical house or condo.

According to their website, you can:

- Get access to premium real estate across the country with lower fees to help you maximize your long-term return potential.
- Get the flexibility to invest the amount that best fits your goals, (unlike most private real estate investments that have minimum requirements).
- Track your performance and watch as new real estate properties are acquired, improved, and operated across the country.

In a nutshell, "Fundrise introduces you to the future of real estate investing." If you want to "join the movement," check out their website right here: https://fundrise.com.

6. MARKETSMITH (THE INVESTOR'S RESEARCH PLATFORM)

Stating at $149 monthly, MarketSmith allows you to get high-quality market research on the best stocks to buy and sell. Whether you are a beginner or a serious professional investor, you will get the most detailed investing advice to help you potentially beat market returns.

According to their website, MarketSmith helps you to:

- Leave behind your old stock research routine. Instead of spending hours reading dozens of websites, newsletters, and magazines, you can streamline your investing research into a single window.
- Find the best-performing stocks, use stock charts to conduct in-depth fundamental and technical research, and see—right on the charts—the optimal time to buy and sell.

- Get access to almost one hundred new webinars a year, including weekly "take on the market" updates and monthly market recaps. Personal coaching is also available.

Bottom line folks, MarketSmith introduces you to the world of stock picking, market timing, and potentially higher returns (higher risks too). If you don't mind the monthly fee of $149, be sure to check out their website today at https://marketsmith.investors.com.

7. COINBASE (THE LARGEST CRYPTO AND NFT EXCHANGE)

Last but not least, Coinbase offers the opportunity to buy, sell, and trade crypto on the most user-friendly and secure platform. By joining Coinbase, you join over eighty-nine million people and businesses who are taking advantage of the "future of money" in the palm of their hands.

According to their website, you can:

- Explore cryptocurrencies like Bitcoin, Ethereum, Dogecoin, Pluton, and hundreds of others.
- Store crypto in your own personal crypto wallet, explore decentralized finance, buy and sell NFTs, and more.
- Use the crypto rewards visa to buy anything—from your daily coffee to weekly groceries—and earn up to 4 percent back in a crypto reward of your choice.

In sum, Coinbase helps you dive into a new and exciting area that many people believe is the future. For a 0.5 percent commission on trades and additional fees for optional services, you can get started right now. Be sure to check out their website at https://www.coinbase.com.

So, that's all we've got for you, guys. Be sure to check out other big players on your own like TD Ameritrade, EquityBee, AcreTrader, E*Trade, Charles Schwab, and Firstrade.

Just exercise caution when investing your money. *Read*: investing is not a video game! While apps sell the dream of getting rich quick, more people statistically lose their ass daily.

So, use sound judgement. Be patient. Be wise. Be prosperous. And be awesome! Peace!

9

INSURANCE

The price of insurance isn't cheap, but it is relatively small in comparison to the potential total loss from a financial catastrophe.

—Eric Tyson, author of *Personal Finance for Dummies*

Ten Types of Insurance You May Need in Your Twenties

Insurance essentially ensures that during a paid policy term you are going to receive some level of outside financial assistance should any unforeseen calamity take place in your life.

Consider breaking your arm on tour, for instance: as long as you have been making your monthly payments (or premiums) and are within the policy term, the insurer will assume the responsibility for the costs, typically above a certain amount (or deductible).

While it may be tempting to go without insurance in order to save thousands of dollars, your life could suddenly come crashing down in the blink of an eye due to a severe mishap. This is why insurance is such an important part of your personal finance education.

Since there are so many details surrounding specific insurance plans and just as many factors that determine who should buy certain policies and when, what follows is simply a brief introduction to the ten types of insurance musicians will most likely need in their twenties. The purpose is to make you aware of the basics and inspire you to conduct your own research.

1. HEALTH INSURANCE

Health Insurance is something you should seriously consider purchasing, and—depending on your state, you might even "need" to purchase it—so check your local laws.

Heath insurance covers you when normal and unexpected medical expenses occur. Health insurance typically covers most doctor and hospital visits, prescription drugs, wellness care, and medical devices (like crutches and even hearing aids—say what?).

While most young musicians may think they are invincible and that nothing will ever happen to them, think again: I (this is Bobby) got slammed by a truck while out on tour and had a pulmonary embolism. I also got a large nerve cell tumor (benign) in my thumb (likely caused by drumming) and had to get it cut out (three different times). Yes, insurance covered it all!

If you are twenty-six or younger, you might be able to get coverage as a dependent on your parents' health plan. If you are working a "normal/regular" job, your employer might offer coverage. And if you are a freelance musician, you can search for an affordable plan online.

Plans will vary from HMOs (where you have one primary doctor) to PPOs (where you can choose from a network of doctors), so be sure to ask lots of questions to see what fits you.

Generally, an HMO is cheaper and should be fine for young and healthy musicians.

2. DENTAL INSURANCE

Dental insurance is another type of coverage that you should also consider.

Dental insurance typically covers you for basic dental care including x-rays, cleanings, fillings, crowns, and root canals (love em'—not). Braces, bridges, and teeth alignment may also be covered as long as they are deemed to be "medically necessary." Whenever in doubt, just ask!

But do musicians really need to worry about dental insurance? As long as you brush your teeth and floss, shouldn't you be pretty cool for a good portion of your young adult life?

Well, what happens if you're a vocalist and you chip your tooth on your microphone during a performance? Or, what happens when you're dancing in the mosh pit and you get your front tooth knocked out? These things are not uncommon, and they can be quite costly to fix!

So, now that we've got your attention, we know what you're thinking—"I'm gonna sign up for an HMO dental plan, get coverage, and do a whole lot of work on that Instagram smile of mine." Well, not so fast! Know that cosmetic procedures that are not "medically necessary," like teeth whitening, veneers, and grills are usually not covered by dental insurance! Sorry folks!

3. VISION INSURANCE

Vision insurance is often overlooked but nonetheless an important form of coverage—and it is even mandatory in certain states for persons eighteen and younger (yup, it's really true).

Vision insurance generally covers you for eye examinations, glasses, contact lenses, eye surgeries, treatments of various eye diseases, and more. The exact coverage you receive, however, will depend on your specific policy.

While many people don't think they need vision insurance, consider a likely scenario: you're performing on stage, the pyrotechnics blow up, and you suffer flash burn to your eyes. You're able to make it through the entire show, but you're in extreme pain and notice your eyes are sensitive to light. Sounds scary, right? Well, with vision insurance, you'll be able to see a vision specialist and get the proper treatment you need to get healthy.

Vision insurance can usually be obtained through your employer's health insurance. If not, or if you are self-employed, vision insurance can be purchased relatively inexpensively. You can easily search companies online and contact them for more details. Happy searching!

4. DISABILITY INSURANCE

Disability insurance is yet another important form of coverage you may really need.

Disability insurance provides some income when you are not able to work due to injury, illness, or disability. Coverage typically begins after a short waiting period and can last for as long as fifty-two weeks.

So, when I (this is Bobby) got slammed by that truck, I received state disability insurance for the six months that I was unable to work. The amount represented about 50 percent of my regular pay as a touring musician, which was enough to get by.

If you're an employee and live in California, Hawaii, New Jersey, New York, Rhode Island, or Puerto Rico, you'll have access to disability insurance through a state disability insurance (SDI) program.

However, if you are not from the above five states, or if you are self-employed, you'll have to purchase disability insurance on your own by searching online and finding a plan that best fits your needs. In California, self-employed performers can even take advantage of optional disability insurance elective coverage (DIEC) through the Employment Development Department (EDD). Be sure to check it out.

5. AUTO INSURANCE

Auto insurance is a form of coverage that drivers must purchase in most states (except Virginia and New Hampshire).

Auto insurance basically covers you for (1) bodily injury and (2) property damage in an unexpected auto incident.

Bodily injury includes:

- **Bodily Injury Liability:** This covers the medical expenses, legal fees, and loss of income suffered by the occupants of another vehicle who have been injured in a traffic accident caused by you.
- **Medical Expense Payments:** This covers the medical expenses you—and any occupants of your vehicle—suffer due to a traffic accident caused by you.
- **Uninsured and Underinsured Motorist Protection:** This covers the medical expenses you—and any occupants in your vehicle—suffer due to a traffic accident caused by another driver who is uninsured or underinsured. It also covers you and your occupants against drivers who may hit you and run.

And finally . . . property damage includes:

- **Property Damage Liability:** This covers the property damage suffered by the occupants of another vehicle in a traffic accident caused by you. It also covers the damage to street signs, light posts, and other property in an accident caused by you.
- **Collision:** This covers the property damage suffered to your own vehicle in a traffic accident caused by you. Note that this coverage is required by the lender for leased or financed cars. And finally . . .
- **Comprehensive Physical Damage:** This covers the property damage suffered to your own vehicle for anything other than a traffic accident. It covers you against theft, fire, flood, vandalism, glass breakage, and even damage to your car from hitting an animal. Note that this coverage is also required by the lender for leased or financed cars.

But what happens when you rent a van to go on tour and get into a wreck? No problem! Many auto insurance companies cover rentals, or you can purchase coverage from the rental company (the former being the better choice).

Auto insurance can be bought from reputable companies like State Farm, Geico, and Allstate, to name just a few. But there are many more that can provide coverage at a competitive price. A Google search is your best friend. And most times, you can get an online quote immediately.

6. RENTERS INSURANCE

Renters insurance is another form of coverage that many musicians don't think about, despite the fact they'll probably be renting for several years before buying a house.

Renters insurance typically covers "personal use" property inside and outside of your flat. It may also cover relocation expenses should your dwelling become damaged or unlivable due to a tragic event, such as a fire. Further, it can shield you from liability in the event someone is injured within your unit.

So, you don't think you need renter's insurance? Well, imagine your apartment goes up in smoke and your furniture is destroyed. Or, a water pipe bursts upstairs and drips water all over your flat-screen TV. Or some jackass steals that Rad Power Bike that you rode to school? These are real-life scenarios, and depending on your policy's terms, you should be covered.

Most policies will pay "actual cash value" (the current value of your items). But for a higher monthly fee, insurance companies will pay the "replacement cost" (the cost to rebuy the item today)—as long as your policy limit covers these items. (Note that replacement cost is always the best choice, otherwise you could get $400 for a bicycle that costs $1,500 to replace.)

Just be sure to video your items, list them in a spreadsheet with the serial numbers, and keep all your receipts in case the "shit really does hit the fan." This will help when filing a claim.

Renters insurance can be bundled with your auto insurance or bought separately.

7. INSTRUMENT INSURANCE

Since renter's insurance only covers "personal use" property (not "business use" property like your guitars), instrument insurance is another type of coverage that you need to consider.

Instrument insurance covers your professional business gear worldwide from the threat of fire, theft, vandalism, water damage, earthquakes, and accidental damage. So, if you are on tour and accidentally drop your guitar, or you are at home and find your studio gear has been stolen, you should be good.

Policy coverages can range from $10,000 into the millions of dollars. According to one representative from Music Pro Insurance, "We have clients with $5 million dollar policies covering all types of gear from PAs, to microphones, to lighting rigs, to vintage guitars."

If you think instrument insurance is right for you, then consider a company like Music Pro Insurance, among others. You may also receive insurance as a benefit via your relationship with the American Federation of Musicians (AFM), assuming that you are affiliated.

Look gang, wherever you get your policy, be sure to get the terms of your coverage in writing! And also keep good records of your gear should you ever have to file a claim.

8. PET INSURANCE

Pet insurance is a special type of coverage that you should consider if you're a beloved pet owner. When deciding on the type of policy you want to purchase, know that insurers generally offer three main coverage options:

1. **Accident and Illness Coverage:** This covers the costs of treating injuries from accidents and complications from diagnosed illnesses including hospitalization, surgery costs, and prescription medications.
2. **Accident Only:** This covers the cost of treating injuries from accidents (only) including examinations, hospitalization, surgery costs, and prescription medications.
3. **Wellness Coverage:** Finally, this covers the costs of routine procedures including vaccinations, microchipping, neutering surgery, and flea/tick preventatives.

Don't think you need pet insurance? Well, imagine if your beloved pet needs an emergency treatment that costs anywhere between $800 and $1,500. Yikes! This would be hard for most up-and-coming artists to cover.

So, it's time to get your best friend the care he or she needs.

9. TUITION REFUND INSURANCE

Getting close to the end of our ten types of insurance you may need in your twenties, tuition refund insurance is a type of coverage you might purchase if you're currently a student.

In the event of a health-related emergency, tuition insurance covers you for non-refunded tuition money, room and board expenses, and any additional fees you may be charged.

So, imagine if you are attending a very expensive private music school (that doesn't have a medical withdrawal policy) and you become ill and have to leave. Without tuition insurance, you risk the chance of losing all of that tuition you paid to the school. Not good . . . especially when things like pandemics are very possible (whoever saw COVID-19 coming?).

Tuition insurance can usually be purchased from your school before the first day of classes. However, it may already be included with your actual tuition costs, so be sure to check with your school before purchasing a third-party policy.

10. IDENTITY THEFT INSURANCE

Finally, identity theft insurance is a form of coverage that we all should consider, especially in today's digital world.

Identity theft insurance covers you for restoring your financial identity including:

1. The cost of obtaining extra copies of credit reports;
2. Lost wages when taking time off to file police reports and other bullshit; and . . .
3. Legal costs.

Identity theft insurance can be obtained through places like Life-Lock, Aura, Identity Guard, and more. A simple online search will provide you with many options. So, get searching!

BONUS: FUTURE INSURANCE POLICIES YOU SHOULD KNOW ABOUT

Congratulations! You made it through our list of insurance that you might need in your twenties. Just for fun (NOT!), here's a real "quick" look at various types of coverages you may need in the future. What follows is only an introduction, so conduct extra research if needed. Let's do it!

1. **Life Insurance:** Covers your loved ones when you bite the big one. It ensures that your wife or husband and kids will be taken care of when you're gone. Policies include: term life (which could expire before you die) and whole life (which lasts your full life). Whole life is the most popular and has many sub-varieties. However, term life is way more affordable.
2. **Property Insurance:** Covers property damage caused by fire, flooding, theft, weather, and more, and is typically purchased by homeowners and renters. It provides financial reimbursement of a "structure" and its "contents," as well as to any individual (non-owner/renter) who is injured on the property.
3. **Earthquake Insurance:** Covers loss from damage caused by earthquakes to your home and belongings. Legally, you do not have to carry earthquake insurance, but it is recommended in earthquake-prone areas like California. There are some limitations on this kind of coverage, as it won't replace everything, but will help restore your home to a livable condition.
4. **Umbrella Insurance:** Covers damages beyond the limits of your regular insurance coverage. Typically, it will provide additional coverage for injuries, property damage, various lawsuits, and personal liability situations. It may also cover claims (beyond your current liability policy) like false arrest, libel, and slander. Essentially, it covers what your other policies do not.
5. **Annuity Insurance:** Covers you with a guaranteed stream of income should you ever outlive your retirement funds. Policies generally include: immediate (where you pay a lump sum and receive immediate lifetime payments), or deferred (where you pay a lump sum and receive payments at a later time, till death). Advisors we know suggest immediate fixed annuities that adjust with inflation. But see what's right for you.
6. **Long-Term Care Insurance:** Covers some medical costs beyond regular health insurance policies and Medicare. It is usually for chronic medical conditions that may be related to a disability or disorder such as dementia. Most policies will reimburse you for care provided at your home, an assisted community organization, or other facility.
7. **Body Part Insurance:** Covers the asset(s) that make you money. Drummers might insure their hands, and singers might insure

their vocal chords. On the latter note, Bruce Springsteen took out a $6 million policy on his voice. This really isn't necessary for up-and-coming musicians like you. But the option is available for you when you hit it big. And finally . . .

8. **Accidental Death and Dismemberment Insurance:** Covers you for accidental death or dismemberment. Accidental deaths include car crashes, drowning, and any other situation that can't be controlled. Dismemberment includes the loss—or loss of function—of a body part (leg, arm, eyesight, hearing, and voice). Think shit won't happen to you? The drummer in Def Leppard lost his arm in an automobile accident. The guitarist in Black Sabbath lost the tips of two fingers when working in a sheet metal factory. Shit really does happen! God forbid this happens to you!

Well, that is pretty much it, gang! So sorry to end on a deadly note, but maybe that will hammer the point home that "shit really can hit the fan." And when your butt is not covered with insurance, you could easily find yourself up shit creek. So, insure to ensure! Okay? Peace!

10

TAXES

You must pay taxes. But there's no law that says you gotta leave a tip.

—Morgan Stanley advertisement

22

Eleven Frequently Asked Questions about Filing Income Taxes

Each year millions of Americans must pay income taxes and file income tax returns. The average person pays about 34 percent of their income (or $530,000) over the course of his or her lifetime.

Because filing taxes can be very confusing for many musicians, and there can be severe penalties for those who file incorrectly, it is particularly important to review a few tax basics.

What follows are eleven frequently asked tax questions by our music students and clients. Due to the complexity of taxes, we strongly recommend that you also consult with a tax accountant regarding your particular set of circumstances. Okay? Cool! Now, let's do this.

1. WHO HAS TO PAY INCOME TAXES AND FILE A TAX RETURN?

This is a perfect first question. Many young musicians are confused about who pays and files.

Here's a quick breakdown:

- **Who Pays:** All working residents and citizens of the United States are generally subject to paying federal income taxes. Some may even be subject to state and city taxes depending on the territory. Check your local area for specific information.
- **Who Files:** Not all persons have to file an annual tax return. Whether you file or not will be determined by your age, marital status, and annual gross income. For instance, if you are

twenty-one years old, single, and earned less than $12,550 working a six-month side gig at Guitar Center, then you probably won't have to file.

2. ARE THERE DIFFERENT TYPES OF INCOME TAXES I HAVE TO PAY?

There are essentially three types of income taxes you may have to pay (depending on whether you are an employee or self-employed worker). These include:

1. **Income Taxes:** This is to help fund our great nation (fix highways, pay for our military, fund the police, etc.). Both employees and self-employed workers pay this tax from their wages.
2. **Social Security and Medicare Taxes:** This is to help fund our nation's retirement and health care program. Both employees and self-employed workers pay this tax from their from wages. However, note that employees split this payment with employers (7.65 percent each), and self-employed workers pay the full amount (15.3 percent).
3. **State Disability Insurance:** This helps support injured or ill employees in certain states who are unable to work (California, Hawaii, New Jersey, New York, and Rhode Island). Only employees—not self-employed workers—pay this tax from their wages.

3. SO, AM I AN EMPLOYEE, SELF-EMPLOYED WORKER, OR BOTH?

Since this affects the way you pay income taxes, this is a great follow-up question to number 2.
Here's a brief description:

- **Employee:** This is a person who: (1) works on a continued basis with an employer, (2) receives instruction and guidance with regard to how to complete the job, and (3) accepts pay on a regular schedule (typically every two weeks). Therefore, you're likely an employee when touring nationwide with Pink, receiving instruction from a musical director on stage, and accepting pay every two weeks.

- **Self-Employed Worker:** This is a person who: (1) hires out their services to one or more people on a short-term basis, (2) works without regular supervision or control, and (3) accepts pay after each gig. Therefore, you're likely a self-employed worker when teaching guitar lessons to ten different students in the morning, recording a track on your friend's album that afternoon, and performing a live show and selling merch at a club that evening.
- **Both Employee and Self-employed Worker:** This is obviously a person who falls under both worker classifications. Therefore, you are likely an employee and self-employed worker if you go on tour and return home to freelance, or simultaneously work a steady day gig and do a bunch of self-employed gigs at night.

4. HOW OFTEN DO I HAVE TO PAY INCOME TAXES?

The US tax system works on a pay-as-you-go system. This is an arrangement whereby tax estimates are paid throughout the year, rather than in one lump sum at the end of the year.

Employees and self-employed workers use this system differently as follows:

- **Weekly Payroll Withholdings:** Employees have their employer deduct estimates from every paycheck.
- **Quarterly Tax Estimates:** Self-employed workers deduct their own estimates from their pay on a quarterly basis: April 15, June 15, September 15, and January 15.

5. HOW ARE INCOME TAX ESTIMATES GENERALLY DETERMINED?

To help estimate taxes you pay throughout the year, there are generally two different tax forms—each depending on whether you are an employee or self-employed worker. These include:

- **W4 Forms:** Provided by the employer to the employee at the time of employment. This form helps the employee estimate their tax withholdings from their pay. The amount withheld is based on the following information provided by the employee: (1) personal information, (2) multiple jobs or if your spouse works, (3) number of dependents, and (4) other adjustments

(like investment income, deductions, and extra withholdings). The form must be filled out correctly to ensure that enough taxes are withheld. While there are no legal limits on estimates, it is highly recommended to overestimate to avoid underpayments and potential penalties. A sample W4 form with instructions can be found here: https://www.irs.gov/pub/irs-pdf/fw4.pdf.
- **1040 ESO:** Obtained by the self-employed worker from the IRS. This worksheet helps self-employed workers estimate their tax withholdings. Questions to help determine tax estimates might include: (1) the income you expect to earn that year, (2) whether you plan to itemize deductions, (3) whether you'll have dividend earnings or capital gains from investments, (4) the amount of self-employment taxes you think you will pay, and so much more. While there are no legal limits on estimates, it is highly recommended to overestimate to avoid underpayments and potential penalties. A sample 1040 ESO can be found here: https://www.irs.gov/pub/irs-pdf/f1040es.pdf.

6. WHAT OTHER TAX FORMS ARE IMPORTANT TO KNOW ABOUT?

Other tax forms you need to know about—depending on whether you are an employee and/or self-employed worker—are W2 and 1099 forms for filing taxes. Here's a brief description:

- **W2 Forms:** Provided by the employer to the employee at the end of the tax year (no later than February 1). This form states the employee's annual earned income and taxes withheld from their pay. W2 forms are needed when filing annual tax returns, so be sure to keep them in a safe place.
- **1099 Forms:** Provided by the contractor to the self-employed worker at the end of the tax year (no later than February 1). This form only states the income of the self-employed worker, as contractors do not withhold taxes. 1099 forms are needed when filing annual tax returns, so be sure to keep them all in a safe place. (*Note:* you may not receive a 1099 form if your annual income from a single contractor was $600 or less.)

7. ARE THERE ANY OPPORTUNITIES TO REDUCE THE TAXES I PAY?

Yes! The government provides deductions and itemizations to help you reduce the amount in taxes you have to pay when you file your annual tax return.

These deductions and itemizations can save you thousands, and include the following:

- **Business Expenses:** The US tax system allows self-employed workers only (not employees) to deduct business expenses that are "standard and ordinary" related to their trade and business. This can include a host of things like advertising costs (TikTok, YouTube, and Facebook ads), equipment purchases and repairs (for guitars, drums, and keyboards), and business use of your home (for your home studio, office use, etc.). Just be sure to keep all your receipts and records so that you can back up these costs. Also be sure to see the longer list of deductions we have below.
- **Standard Deductions:** The US tax system also allows a standard deduction to employees and self-employed workers to help reduce their tax liability. The amount for single filers is currently $12,550. But the standard deduction amount is adjusted regularly to keep up with inflation, so be sure to check for the latest rate.
- **Itemized Deductions:** The US tax system also allows employees and self-employed workers to itemize qualified expenses above the standard deduction. *Note*: between itemizations and the standard deduction, the larger figure can be used to reduce one's tax liability. However, be aware that qualified Schedule A expenses are limited to things like medical and dental expenses, charitable deductions, state and local taxes, casualty and theft losses, and home loan interest.

8. GOT EVEN MORE BUSINESS EXPENSE DEDUCTIONS?

There are several more business expense deductions that specifically "self-employed" performers may be entitled to. Here are just a few:

- **Union Dues:** The cost of joining the AFM or SAG-AFTRA.
- **Service Fees:** For joining professional services like Taxi, ASCAP, and DistroKid.

- **Mailing:** Mail costs for résumés and promotional kits.
- **Dry Cleaning:** Dry cleaning costs for stage clothes, etc.
- **Conventions:** Music conferences such as NAMM and SXSW.
- **Business Gifts:** Greeting cards, a fine bottle of wine for the boss, etc.
- **Attorney Fees:** The cost of hiring an attorney to review a contract, etc.
- **Accountants:** The cost of hiring a tax accountant (which we recommend).
- **Education:** Educational expenses for school, music lessons, and seminars.
- **Telephone Calls for Business:** The portion of your bill that was specifically used for business calls (*note:* for practical purposes, this might require making an estimate).
- **Promotion:** Website hosting, Internet service providers, and Google adverts.
- **Stage Clothing:** For stage clothing that would not normally be worn on the street.
- **Entertainment Meals:** Lunch and business meals with a colleague to discuss business.
- **Research Tools:** The cost of vinyl, streaming subscriptions, and movie tickets to study how music is used in various media.
- **Related Work Tools:** Instrument fees, repairs, and maintenance.
- **Subscriptions:** Magazines such as *Billboard*, *Guitar Player*, and *Rolling Stone*.
- **Home Office Expenses:** The cost of office space in your home or apartment used exclusively for business, such as home studios, rehearsal rooms, and soundproof booths for music lessons (*note*: deductions may include a portion of your rent, utilities, cable, phone, and the like).
- **Recording Expenses**: The cost of recording and distributing your music.
- **Travel Expenses:** The cost of airline tickets, passport photos, passport application fees, lodging, taxis, limousines, food, personal grooming related to work (shampoos and conditioners, etc.), tips (for meals, baggage handlers, etc.), and travel costs for an associate (if for a bona fide business reason). And finally . . .
- **Car Expenses or Standard Mileage:** The cost of leasing fees, insurance, gas, tolls, parking, car washes, depreciation of your vehicle, and trailers to haul extra gear. Or, you can deduct the miles you put on your car for commuting to a temporary, but not a regular, place of business.

9. WHAT'S ALL THE RACKET ABOUT THAT THING CALLED A TAX BRACKET?

Good question! The phrase "tax bracket" is regularly used on the news, yet many people are unaware of what it really means. Simply put, tax brackets help determine the various rates at which your money will be taxed. There are seven tax brackets: 10 percent, 12 percent, 22 percent, 24 percent, 32 percent, 35 percent, and 37 percent. These rates are subject to change each tax year.

The more income you make, the higher the rate your money will be taxed. The less income you make, the lower the rate your money will be taxed.

So, the racket with the bracket is simply finding creative but legal ways to stay in the lowest bracket through tax planning and avoidance methods.

10. WHAT ARE A FEW TAXES PLANNING AND AVOIDANCE METHODS?

In addition to claiming the many deductions we've already mentioned earlier, here are a few more options you may consider to lower your taxable income and tax bracket:

- **Delay Income:** If you make a lot more money than usual in one year and it moves you into a higher tax bracket, you might ask your employer if a payment could be delayed into the next year. This way you balance your taxes out.
- **Get On Your Employer's 401(k) Plan:** If you are an employee, ask your employer if they offer a retirement plan like a 401(k). This will allow you to contribute "pre-tax" money from your earnings on a tax-deferred basis. Said another way, depending on your age, you can shield anywhere from 20k to 27k of pre-tax income per year, and pay taxes on it much later in life when you retire. This could place you into a lower tax bracket and thus lower your current taxable income. Sometimes employers will match the contributions you make (up to a certain amount), so you are completely insane if you ignore this opportunity and don't get onboard with a 401(k).
- **Open up a Traditional IRA:** If you are an employee or self-employed worker, you can also invest "pre-tax" money on a tax-deferred basis, by opening up your own individual retirement

account (IRA). The amount you can shield—depending on your age—ranges from $6,000 to $7,000 per year. Again, you pay taxes on this much later, but the upside is that you can drop into a lower tax bracket for the current tax year. Pretty smart, right?
- **Get Married and File Jointly:** Finally, if you are married and file your taxes jointly, you may qualify for some important tax advantages that could drop you into a lower tax bracket. But don't get married just for that. Ha! Remember that 50 percent of all marriages fail, and the last thing you want to do is lose 50 percent of all your stuff.

11. WHAT HAPPENS IF YOU DON'T FILE YOUR TAXES CORRECTLY?

This is the perfect question to end on. When filing taxes incorrectly, here's what usually happens:

1. **Letter:** You receive a letter from the IRS asking you to pay more or to submit a reasonable explanation as to why you paid the amount that you did.
2. **Audit:** You receive an audit request by the IRS, which could happen in two different ways: (1) A paper audit where you have to send in really meticulous receipts backing up everything that you deducted or itemized in your tax returns; or (2) An in-person audit where a tax representative visits with you (or your tax accountant) and looks through your receipts and records. The in-person audit is far easier and less of a pain.
3. **Court:** You are asked to appear in court for tax evasion. Would you believe that Rapper NAS found himself in a debt of $6.5 million in taxes to the IRS. Don't let this happen to you when you become a big star—because this is just flat-out dumb!

So that's it for taxes, gang. Be sure to check out the graphic below (see figure 22.1), which essentially lays out the entire tax process for you. We know taxes can be a little dry, but they are not going away any time soon and thus they are necessary to your personal finance education.

And just to be absolutely sure, unless your tax situation is extremely simple and you can file your own tax return, we highly suggest that you hire a certified public accountant (CPA) to assist you. A CPA understands tax law, and can provide service specific to your situation. Okay? Cool! Good Luck!

FILING YOUR TAXES: COMPUTING WHAT YOU OWE
This chart offers a very basic breakdown of how you might arrive at your taxes due.

	Gross Income	All "employee Income," Self-employed profits or losses (difference of income and allowable biz expenses), Investment interest and dividends, etc.
less	Adjustments	Retirement fund deductions (401K, IRA, etc.) Student loan interest deductions, self-employed health insurance deductions, and more
is	AGI (Adjusted Gross Income)	
less	Standard Deductions *or* Itemized Deductions (whichever is greater)	Standard = Set amount of money on which no taxes are paid. *Or* Itemized = job-related/mis-expenses, donations, moving expenses for job, casualty & theft, med and dental expenses, state/local taxes, certain interest, and much more that is above the standard deduction.
is	Taxable Income	
x	Tax Rates (the various percentages in which your money is charged till the last dollar)	Rates are progressive. Meaning, for example, the first $10K is charged at one rate, the next $30K, at another rate and so on). The last/highest level is called your marginal rate or bracket. Fortunately, a new/simpler "Tax Table" calculates all this for you.
less	Tax Credits (additional special reductions)	Education credits, retirement savings credits, foreign tax credits, home improvements such as solar panels, hybrid cars (if you are paying taxes in other countries). Note: Tax credits change regularly...
is	Tax Due Subtotal	
less	Tax Already Paid	Estimated withholdings from employer made on the "pay as you go" system or payments you have made as an independent contractor on quarterly basis
is	Total Tax Due / Tax Refund	

Speak to your accountant for specific and up to date adjustments, credits, and more. Check http://www.irs.gov

23

Six Steps to Organizing Your Tax Expense Receipts (and More)

Taxes pay for the roads you travel on tour, the unemployment benefits you collect between gigs, and the police you call when a crazy fan stalks you (no joking).

Taxes can be quite costly—even for musicians. But fortunately, Uncle Sam allows for certain expenses to be deducted or "written off" as a way to reduce your annual tax bill.

The problem is, you'll need well-preserved receipts to back up most of your costs. And by "well-preserved" we don't mean crumpled up, mildewed, faded receipts stuffed into a desk drawer for a full year. We mean something far more organized.

While there are numerous methods and tools available for organizing your tax receipts, below are six simple (IRS-approved) steps that will simplify your already taxed life. Oh, and just to be sure, IRS stands for Internal Revenue Service—a federal agency that may come after you via audit if you don't do your taxes right. So, pay close attention to everything we say herein!

1. CREATE EXPENSE CATEGORIES USING ENVELOPES

Grab a handful of white, legal-size envelopes and categorize them according to different expense deductions allowable by the IRS.

If you're an employee (i.e., you work one job for a continued period, such as a sales gig at Guitar Center), the deductions you may be entitled to include:

- medical and dental expenses

- gifts to charity
- casualty and theft losses
- home mortgage and home insurance interest (if you have a home)

If you're a self-employed worker (i.e., you work several freelance jobs such as studio sessions, private lessons, and weddings), the deductions you may be entitled to include:

- equipment (e.g., computers, guitars, recording gear)
- recording studio costs, distribution, and promotion fees
- business use of your home (including rent, utilities, phone, internet)
- office supplies (including printer ink, printer paper, and more)
- business mailing (including any fan materials or press kits you might send)
- promotion (including website hosting, distribution charges, advertisements)
- research and subscriptions (including Amazon, Spotify, and Netflix)
- car and truck expenses (including standard mileage, or actual expenses such as gas, oil, repairs, insurance, registration, and even washing)
- education (e.g., courses you might take to improve your music skills)
- parking fees (business related)
- travel (including airlines, hotels, taxis, meals)
- business entertainment expenses (including entertainment-related meals)
- legal and professional services (e.g., accountants, attorneys, producers)

If you're both an employee and a self-employed worker, you may be entitled to deductions from both lists above. Therefore, to determine which expense categories to create, visit the IRS's website (irs.gov) and speak with a certified public accountant (CPA). Everyone's tax situation is different, so it is important to do your research.

2. NUMBER EACH RECEIPT AND INCLUDE A SHORT EXPLANATION

Now that you've created all of your expense categories and obtained envelopes, get into the daily habit of separating your expense receipts and categorizing them appropriately (gas, legal, office supplies, and professional services, etc.).

Number each receipt (starting with #1 for each category), write a short description at the top, and then place the receipt in the appropriate expense envelope for temporary storage.

To illustrate, a business meal receipt might be labeled number one, marked with the description, "Had dinner with Michael Eames of Pen Music Group to discuss music licensing," and then placed into the envelope marked "Entertainment-related meals." All this attention to detail will really matter should the IRS ever decide to question you.

3. LAY OUT YOUR RECEIPTS ON 8.5 X 11 SHEETS OF WHITE PAPER

Approximately a month after labeling and placing your receipts into categorized envelopes, you will then want to transfer them into a more permanent storage format.

Take the receipts from each envelope organize them side-by-side onto 8.5 x 11 sheets of white, three-hole paper, and affix them with adhesive tape to keep them in place. Use the front and back of each page to fit as many receipts as possible from the same category.

For instance, if you have ten "gas" receipts, you might place five of them side-by-side on both sides of the page, preferably in chronological order.

Not only will this keep your receipts from getting wrinkled, it will also make it easy to store and access them later. Additionally, should you ever receive a mail audit request from the IRS, you'll be able to easily make yourself photocopies of each sheet and provide them the originals.

4. INSERT YOUR RECEIPT SHEETS INTO A THREE-RING BINDER

Now that your receipt sheets are nicely laid out, insert them into a heavy-duty three-ring binder with colored divider tabs for better organization and protection from damage.

Organize the divider tabs alphabetically (gas, legal, office supplies, professional services, etc.) and then clip your receipt sheets into the binder within the appropriate colored tab.

As a finishing touch, label the spine of the binder with something like "Tax Receipts for the Year 20XX," and store it in a place that's easily accessible. Remember, each month you'll be inserting new pages as your expense envelopes fill up with receipts.

5. TAKE A PICTURE OF EACH RECEIPT TO STORE ELECTRONICALLY

After creating your beautifully organized receipt binder, it's time to create digital backups. This serves as an extra precaution should some unfortunate accident lead to "receipt Armageddon!"

Using your phone's camera, focus in on each page (or even each receipt) and snap the photograph. Next, download the pictures to your computer and drag them into appropriately labeled folders you create (gas, legal, office supplies, professional services, etc.).

I (this is Bobby) store all of my tax receipt photos in the Photos application on my Apple Macbook. Additionally, I copy everything to a spare thumb drive for a back-up, just in case.

6. RECORD RECEIPT DATA INTO AN EXCEL WORKBOOK FILE

As a final step in organizing your tax receipts, take one last precaution by typing all your expense data into a Microsoft Excel workbook file under the same categories we've been using throughout this piece (gas, legal, office supplies, professional services, etc.)

Be sure to include all of the receipt numbers, transaction dates, descriptions, methods of payment, and the payment amounts. For instance, under the category "entertainment-related meals," your entry in Excel might read something like: R#1—January 28—Had dinner with Michael Eames of Pen Music Group at Chin Chins to discuss music licensing—Visa credit card—$78.84.

Creating an Excel file provides a written digital summary of all your expense receipts in one place, and also acts as supporting documentation should you ever get audited. While this might seem like overkill, know that the IRS scrutinizes everything when conducting an audit. So, you want to be more than prepared.

Additionally, listing all your expenses in an Excel workbook file makes it far easier to tally up each expense category for your tax accountant. For the sake of absolute clarity, your tax accountant only needs your totals—not the three-ring binder, pictures, or Excel spreadsheet. Those items are to be kept in your records for three to seven years in case of audit. Okay gang! That's it! Good luck!

BONUS TIP #1: TRY QUICKEN

Now that you've learned our six steps to managing your tax receipts, you might be wondering whether there are any alternative methods for getting the job done. Yes, there are—well, sort of. You can try a software tool called Quicken.

Quicken is the gold standard software in home financial management. For a yearly subscription fee of about $35, Quicken allows you to set up multiple accounts for your savings, checking, and investments that can be managed either manually or via a link to your bank.

Quicken also allows you to set up a number of income and expense categories including Social Security and Medicare deductions, retirement fund allocations, and so much more.

Quicken will also help you generate expense reports, by category, when doing your taxes. And if you want to get a real complete picture of your financial health, you can also view your total net worth (what you owe, versus what you own). Quicken essentially does it all.

However, the downside is the steep learning curve in using the software. It's not the most user-friendly software, and it could take you several months before you get the hang of it. Yuck!

Another problem is that while Quicken does help get all your numbers in order, you still have to organize those darn receipts too! Boo!

So, in closing, Quicken is probably not the best choice for the young musician who is more interested in hunting down new gigs and writing songs than doing finances. Oh well!

BONUS TIP #2: USE NEATRECEIPTS

Our second bonus tip for organizing your tax receipts is NeatReceipts. Pretty cool name, right?

NeatReceipts is an economical portable USB scanner with software that helps you to scan your tax receipts and store them digitally on your computer, in the cloud, or on a remote hard drive. The data automatically populates into certain fields (such as date, amount, method of payment), which can come in handy when you need to generate expense reports for doing your taxes.

Neat company makes a variety of NeatReceipt models ranging from $150 upward to $600. The reviews of this device are good, so on the surface it's not a bad value for an alternative method. But there are also some downsides.

First, you can only scan one receipt at a time. This could take forever if you have a pile of receipts. Second, the data does not always populate correctly (i.e., you have to check each scan for accuracy). And finally, third, you still must organize all those original receipts. Yikes! Seems like we can never get past those darn physical receipts. On well!

BONUS TIP #3: CHECK OUT SHOEBOXED

For our third bonus tip on organizing tax receipts, we'd like to introduce to the concert stage . . . Shoeboxed.

Shoeboxed claims they can "save you time and money by managing all of your paper clutter for you." That's right, they do it all for you.

After starting an account, Shoeboxed will send you "magic envelopes" that you are required to stuff with your most recent receipts. They will then start an account for you, scan all your documents on their high-tech scanners, check the scans for accuracy, and organize the data into customized categories. They will then return all of your original receipts and send you another magic envelope to repeat the process.

If you'd prefer, Shoeboxed also has a mobile application. This allows you to take pictures of your receipts and email them to your special Shoeboxed email address for processing. With all of your data in one convenient place, you can run reports of your various expense categories during tax season.

Shoeboxed charges a monthly fee of $9.95 for up to fifty scans, $29.95 for up to 150 scans, and $500 a month for five hundred scans. The only problem, once again, is that you still need to keep and organize your original receipts. Yes, even with digital scans, the IRS may still want the originals.

BONUS TIP #4: USE AUTOMILES

Finally, for our fourth bonus tip, you might be wondering how to track potential deductions for things like business mileage when there are no physical receipts. Well, one answer is to keep a journal in your car listing the date, destination, and miles of every business trip that you take. Another solution might be to use an app like Automile.

Automile is the automatic auto tracking application for your smartphone.

While other tracking applications require you to enter starting and ending points and clicking start, Automile literally senses when you are driving and starts tracking your miles automatically. Best yet, at tax time, you can print out a report of all your business miles and give it to your accountant, who may get you a mileage deduction that reduces the amount of taxes you owe. The application is free for the first one hundred miles and then costs about $5. Not bad!

However, the only problem is that Automile does not always start tracking when you are driving—so you have to keep your eye on it. Furthermore, it tracks "all" of your miles—both personal and business, which means that you'll have to go through every trip and determine what mileage was business-related and personal-related. This could be quite tedious. Oh well!

Be sure to check out other mileage applications including Mileage Log Plus and MileIQ.

So, that concludes our discussion on organizing your tax receipts and basically getting your tax shit in order! While we know that it all sounds like a pain in the ass, the process eventually becomes as habitual as brushing your teeth. And the best part is that you'll have a running total of all of your potential tax deductions that you can forward to an accountant. You'll also have physical receipts and digital copies for backups. And just think, no more mildewed, crumpled receipts overflowing from your desk drawer that you have to organize at tax time. So, do the best you can with this stuff. Anything is better than nothing. Have fun!

24

How to Find a Tax Accountant to Do Your Returns: Ten Tips

Depending on your personal work and life situation as a musician, filing a tax return each year with Uncle Sam can range in complexity from fairly straightforward to extremely confusing.

Because mistakes on tax returns can lead to fines and penalties (and even worse if the mistakes are found to be intentional or fraudulent), hiring an experienced tax accountant to get your returns done properly may be one of the smartest choices that you make this year. (Just ask rapper Fat Joe, who was recently charged with tax evasion and sentenced to jail time. Yikes!)

What follows are ten tips to finding a tax accountant. From getting referrals from people you trust to utilizing free services by the IRS and more, what you're about to read will save you time, money, and loads of frustration. So, grab a yellow highlighter, and let's do this!

1. GET SEVERAL REFERRALS FROM PEOPLE YOU TRUST

The tip, above all, to getting a great tax accountant is asking for referrals from people you trust.

Trusted sources might include a professor at your school, a music teacher with whom you study, and/or a professional musician you know in your own community.

As the proverb states, "The proof is in the pudding" (i.e., the success of something can only be judged by putting it to its intended use). So, if a few close friends or associates can offer some solid referrals, then you are off to a really good start.

2. MAKE SURE YOUR TAX ACCOUNTANT HAS OTHER MUSIC CLIENTS

Even if your music teacher or local professional musician provides you with some good referrals, make sure the accountant you choose has other music clients.

Tax accountants who work with musicians understand musicians' needs and the exact deductions they might be entitled to. For instance, SXSW convention fees, DistroKid charges, SoundBetter session fees, TikTok advertising costs, and AFM union member dues.

Bottom line, you want your tax accountant to understand the nuances of your industry. Someone who knows taxes is good. But someone who speaks fluent "musician" is the best.

3. LOOK FOR THEIR CPA CREDENTIAL

In addition to getting an accountant who speaks "musician," be sure to look for an accountant with the acronym "CPA" (certified public accountant) at the end of their name.

Know that anyone, without much difficulty or expense, can obtain an IRS Preparer Tax Identification Number (PTIN) and become a paid tax return preparer.

But being a CPA ensures that an individual graduates from an accredited university, passes the Uniform CPA Examination, and regularly satisfies continuing education requirements.

So, what else do you need us to say? Just go out and find yourself a music CPA!

4. CONSIDER THE ACCOUNTANT'S EXPERIENCE

Experience is another important factor to consider when looking for a tax accountant. We'd say this should be a major deal breaker.

Would you hire a guitar player with no or little recording experience to help you record your next single? Of course not! Well, doing taxes is even more critical.

Most accountants will list their experience on their websites. But if not, you can check the "board of accountancy" in the state the accountant works to get his or her license issuance date.

5. UNDERSTAND YOUR ACCOUNTANT'S FEE STRUCTURE

Another tip that will serve you well in your search for a tax accountant is to understand his or her fee structure. But before simply picking up the phone and inquiring, be sure to evaluate the various methods that exist so that you're prepared to discuss them on the call.

There are generally six legitimate methods used (and one illegitimate method to avoid):

- **Flat Fee:** A guaranteed amount (usually from $300 to $800 for a return).
- **Hourly Rate:** A rate with incremental billing rounded to ten minutes (e.g., a two-minute call can be rounded up to ten minutes—at $300 an hour, that's $50. Crap!).
- **Base Rate Plus:** A minimum payment plus an hourly rate on top.
- **Type of Tax Form:** Based on the forms and the complexity of your situation.
- **Value-Based:** How valuable they feel their information was to you.
- **Referral Rate:** The same rate as a client who referred you. And finally . . .
- **Percentage of Your Return:** An amount based on your annual income. Yikes! Run for the hills on this one. Accountants are not permitted to do this.

Of all of the methods above, we prefer a flat fee for the job (get it in writing, if possible). This way you'll find no surprises when you receive your bill.

Just don't be afraid to negotiate the accountant's fee by explaining that you're "easy" to work with—you're organized, won't be calling a lot, and just need him or her to file a straightforward tax return. Believe it or not, this could knock a hundred or more bucks off your bill. So, be sure to remember this tip!

6. ASK IF HE OR SHE WILL REPRESENT YOU IN AN AUDIT

While on the topic of fee structures, another crucial question to ask your tax accountant is whether he or she will represent you in an IRS audit at no additional cost. An audit is when the IRS wants to review all of your records to validate the information on your tax return. Scary!

So, will your accountant meet with the IRS field agent? And more importantly, will you be charged more money for that service? This is an extremely important question to ask, because otherwise, you could end up paying the accountant hundreds.

Many accountants we know take the responsibility for handling the matter, because after all, they filed the return (and reviewed and certified it too). Other accountants might feel they have the right to tack on additional fees. And some may just refer you elsewhere. So always ask!

7. ASK IF THEY WILL BE DOING ALL THE WORK

Asking your accountant "if they'll be doing all the work" is yet another crucial factor in your search for a tax accountant.

You see, some accountants will use their name and reputation to draw in new clients, only to have lower-level or starter accountants prepare tax returns.

This is actually happened to me (this is Britt). I was referred to an experienced accountant who was charging me $300 per hour. I liked him, but I quickly realized that he wasn't even doing my taxes (all correspondence from his office was with some junior-level dude I'd never even met). Needless to say, I took my business elsewhere the following tax year.

Look peeps, there's nothing wrong with confirming who will be working on your taxes. Just ask who will be doing the work! It could save you a lot of time and frustration.

8. DOES HE OR SHE PROVIDE ADDITIONAL BUSINESS ADVICE?

Another question you might ask is whether your accountant provides business and financial advice—in addition to doing your taxes.

For instance, will he or she be able to advise you about business entities and the benefits of forming a corporation or an LLC (Limited Liability Company)?

Furthermore, will the accountant break down the benefits of starting an IRA (individual retirement account) or Roth IRA (a special type of retirement accountant)?

All of these things are related to the world of taxes, so it's not a bad idea to ask. But also know that this advice will most likely cost extra. So, find out about fees as well.

9. CONSIDER USING VITA IF YOU CAN'T AFFORD A CPA

If money is an issue and you are unable to afford a tax accountant, you might consider using VITA (Volunteer Income Tax Assistance) offered by the IRS.

VITA is a program that will assist you with preparing your tax returns at no cost (yup, that's right—you get advice for *free*).

All VITA personnel must meet the strict standards established by the IRS. In addition, the IRS guarantees a quality review check of every return prepared at a VITA location.

To qualify for VITA, you must meet at least one of these requirements: (1) you make $58,000 or less per year, (2) you have a disability, or (3) you have limited English language skills.

For more information on this program or to find a VITA location, use this link: https://www.irs.gov/individuals/free-tax-return-preparation-for-qualifying-taxpayers.

10. CONSIDER WHETHER YOU CAN DO IT YOURSELF

Finally, if your tax situation is rather straightforward, you might consider doing your own taxes using tax software like TurboTax or the step-by-step guides found on the IRS website (irs.gov).

However, if you're tax situation is rather complex, then doing it yourself is a bad idea. Don't even try! It's probably best to use a tax accountant you trust. Good luck, gang!

BONUS: EXTRA "ANAL" TIPS WHEN LOOKING FOR AN ACCOUNTANT

Now that we've covered ten important tips for finding a tax accountant, let's check out a few extra points to aid you in your search. These are a bit nit-picky, but hey, we thought we'd share.

- **Verify Your Accountant's CPA Credentials:** Double check whether your CPA is really legit. While it's hard to believe that an individual would actually try to fake their CPA credential, accountants are not above the possibility of being tricksters. Check out the Directory of Federal Tax Return Preparers at https://irs.treasury.gov/rpo/rpo.jsf.

- **Consider the Prestige of the Accountant's Alma Mater:** Evaluate the university from which your accountant graduated. Someone with a degree from USC or UCLA makes a statement over someone with a degree from a lesser-known school—particularly because the standards to get into elite schools are so much higher.
- **Check to See If They've Worked for the IRS:** Know that it's not often that an accountant will have IRS work experience, but if they do, it can be a big plus. It proves they really understand the ins and outs of taxes from the perspective of the people who scrutinize millions of returns yearly.
- **Consider Their Speed in Returning Your Calls:** Realize that it's not a good sign if your accountant takes several days or weeks before they get back to you (unless you're calling at the busiest tax time of the year—typically mid-April). This could be a sign that they are too busy, understaffed, or unenthusiastic about working with you.
- **Decide If You Like Their Demeanor or Vibe:** Understand that you're not looking for a best buddy to hang out with (like if you were looking for a new singer for your band). But remember, you should definitely pay attention to the vibes you get from the person. Because as the old adage puts it, "First impressions matter."
- **Ask for a Price Quote in Advance:** Consider your accountant's willingness (or lack thereof) to give you a price quote in writing. If he or she doesn't want to provide you with a quote, it just might be a sign that you can expect a surprise on your bill.
- **Ask If They'll Take a Few Quick Questions during the Year:** Remember that accountants have a way of charging for every minute—even when they give you a flat rate. So, avoid getting that extra $50 charge for a five-minute call by asking up-front.
- **Ask If They File Electronically:** Know that accountants who file more than 250 returns per year must file electronically. So, electronic filing makes an extra statement about the accountant's experience. Also, in order to be accepted to the electronic filing program with the IRS, the accountant must pass extensive reviews by the IRS, including FBI background checks. So, this is yet another mark of the accountant's credibility.
- **Ask If They Have Financial Credentials:** Finally, inquire if they possess a personal financial specialist (PFS) or a certified financial planner (CFP) certification in addition to their CPA. Hey, if you're going to be asking them financial questions and getting charged for it, it doesn't hurt to ask.

So, there you have it, guys! You now have all the ammunition needed to find an experienced, well-trusted accountant who can get your tax returns done right.

Just take your time with this. It's not easy to find a good tax accountant. Happy searching!

11

ESTATE PLANNING

Death is not the end. There remains the litigation over the estate.

—Ambrose Bierce, American writer

25

Eight Ways to Prepare for the End (Depressing but Important)

Estate planning is simply the process of planning how you, your property, and family will be taken care of when you become incapacitated or pass away. While we know this is the farthest thing from your mind, remember that shit happens (God forbid), and you want to be prepared for the end. This is especially necessary after you acquire a lot of assets as a famous musician.

While estate planning can be very complex, the good news is that we are keeping it simple. Our objective is to just introduce basic concepts of estate planning and give you a few things that you can do to prepare right now. Sound good?

What follows is eight ways to prepare for the end. These points are to die for.

1. KEEP A LIST OF YOUR ASSETS AND LIABILITIES

Keeping a list of your assets and liabilities is the process of itemizing everything you owe and own, respectively. Should anything ever happen to you, having this organized list will help an appointed representative (such as a spouse or child) liquidate your estate more efficiently.

Using an Excel document, categorize your assets in any way you wish. For instance:

- **Investments:** Taxable accounts, retirement accounts, and bank accounts.
- **Hard Assets:** Collectible art, expensive furniture, and instruments.

- **Larger Properties:** Real estate, boats, and automobiles.

Now categorize all of your liabilities as you wish. For instance:

- **Secured Debt:** Home mortgage loans, home equity lines of credit, and car loans.
- **Unsecured Debt:** Credit cards, student loans, and personal loans.

Once your list is complete, be sure to date it, share it with a trustworthy representative, and update it periodically. Remember, this list will help ensure that your assets are included in the liquidation of your estate and that your debts are cleared in a timely manner. After all, the last thing you want to do after your death is leave your loved ones with a huge mess to clean up.

2. DESIGNATE BENEFICIARIES ON YOUR FINANCIAL ACCOUNTS

Naming beneficiaries on your financial accounts (investment, retirement, and bank accounts) ensures that your loved ones will get your cash after your death without delays and long legal proceedings. Naming beneficiaries is not at all difficult to do. Just consider the following:

- **Investment and Retirement Accounts:** When opening an investment or retirement account, you will be asked to name your beneficiaries by filling out a simple form. Just be careful to update your beneficiaries as things change in your life (divorce, death, disownment of a child) or your money might go to an undesired ex-spouse.
- **Checking and Savings Accounts:** When opening a bank account, you will typically not be required to list beneficiaries. Thus, you will have to transfer your account to a payable on death (POD) account and then designate your beneficiaries. The process is relatively simple and can be updated anytime.

Bottom line, gang, whether it be your investment and retirement accounts, or just your checking and savings accounts, name your beneficiaries. This way, your loved ones can get to your cash in a dash without major holdups.

3. CONSIDER THE VALUE OF LIFE INSURANCE FOR YOUR LOVED ONES

Consider the value of making small regular monthly payments to a reputable insurance company that will pay your loved ones (spouse, kids) a sum of money after you kick the big one.

While no one ever thinks they need life insurance when they're young and healthy, remember shit happens, especially in the life of a touring rock star.

Here are just a few more valuable reasons why you might consider life insurance:

- To help your family cover your burial expenses, which can be anywhere from $3,000 to $10,000.
- To help your family pay for any outstanding debts or medical expenses resulting from your final shit show. And . . .
- To replace lost income to your family now that you're gone.

Setting up a life insurance policy is simple. But since there are so many different types of policies you can get, you should speak to a personal financial advisor who can recommend a plan that fits your personal needs. And while on this note, your planner will also advise when you can discontinue (or exclude) a life insurance policy from your estate. If you don't have loved ones who depend on you, there's no point in having a policy.

4. KNOW THE BASICS OF ESTATE AND INHERITANCE TAXES

Knowing the basics of estate and inheritance taxes involves understanding how your death could impact the value of your estate and the money that you're leaving beneficiaries. If you're blessed with an amazing career, your loved ones could be cursed with a steep tax bill upon your death.

Here's a real brief tax breakdown:

- **Estate Taxes (Federal and State):** Estate taxes may be levied against the beneficiaries at your death should your estate be valued at $12.8 million or more in assets (which is possible if you make it as a huge pop star). First, at the federal level, your beneficiaries could be taxed up to 40 percent. Next, at the state level (only thirteen states impose estate taxes), your beneficiaries

could be taxed at an additional 10 to 20 percent. Together, your beneficiaries may have to give up half of your estate. Yikes!
- **Inheritance Taxes (State Level Only):** Inheritance taxes may also be levied against the beneficiaries at your death should you become a super wealthy pop star ($12.8 million or more in assets). But, unlike estate taxes, your beneficiaries will be happy to know that inheritance taxes only exist at the state level in six states. The amount they could pay, depending on the state, ranges from 10 to 18 percent with a variety of different thresholds. Jeez, it seems that death can be more expensive than life.

Look, gang, if you believe the value of your estate is going to break the $12.8 million tax thresholds, then you may want to speak to an estate attorney about tax avoidance measures. After all, who wants to pay Uncle Sam more than necessary? Right? Right! Now, let's move on.

5. PREPARE A WILL

Preparing a will, one of the more important parts of the estate planning process, involves outlining your last intentions in the event of a sudden and unexpected tragedy. Just remember that life gets crazy out on the road, and accidents are not uncommon. Thus, preparing a will is really something that everyone—even young musicians like you—can and should do today.

Here are a few things that you might include in a will:

- **The Executor:** Name the person who will execute the closing of your estate, handle all of your personal matters, and prove your will as "valid" in probate courts.
- **Who Gets Your Stuff:** List the beneficiaries (like your spouse, kids, or friends) who will inherit your valuable assets (like your house, cars, and collectible guitars).
- **The Guardian:** Name the person who will assume responsibility for providing care to any young children you might have, including those from a current or past marriage.
- **Pet Care:** List the person who will be responsible for watching after Fido. After all, Fido is your best friend and he or she will be missing you greatly.

- **Charities:** List charitable organizations you'd like to donate cash (including music schools, churches, or certain special causes).
- **Online Accounts:** List the person you'd like to monitor your online accounts (like TikTok, YouTube, and Instagram), and don't forget to include your passwords too.
- **Specific Funeral Wishes:** List important information that your heirs should know regarding specific funeral wishes (like if you want to be cremated and your ashes snorted by Keith Richards of the Rolling Stones . . . true story). And finally . . .
- **Love Letters:** Share a brief note to your surviving loved ones about how they touched your life. That's always a nice way to end.

So, what happens if you die without a will? Good question! Typically, your estate will first go to your spouse. If you have no spouse, your estate will pass to your children. If you have no children, it will then pass to your closest relatives. And if no have relatives, your estate goes to the state.

An attorney is not needed to establish a will, as long as your estate is simple—you can write your own will by using online forms offered by LegalZoom, Nolo, or Ramsey Solutions.

However, if your estate is more complex, due to the millions in assets you acquired from being a major rock star, then an attorney is highly advised to assist you.

So, what are you waiting for? Get that will drafted today so that you can have peace of mind for tomorrow. And be sure to keep it in a safe place. Sound good? Okay, then let's move on.

6. CREATE A HEALTH CARE DIRECTIVE

Creating a health care directive is the process of directing others how to handle your health care needs should you no longer be able to make these decisions yourself. This could happen if you are in a coma from a serious accident or if you go completely insane from doing bad drugs.

Since no one can ever predict when health-related tragedies might occur, it's a good idea to create a health care directive today. Speak with your doctor, attorney, or just use online forms.

While health care directives can differ from one state to the next, they generally include:

- **An Appointed Person:** The person who will carry out your directions.
- **Special Care Desired:** Pain management, bathing, or hospice care that you desire.
- **Type of Treatment:** Whether you have any religious requests (prayers by a priest, etc.).
- **Medical Directions:** Whether you want to be put on life support if needed or unplugged (no, were' not talking about your acoustic set).
- **Do Not Resuscitate Notice:** Whether you want to be resuscitated should you suffer a heart attack or you stop breathing for some other reason. And finally . . .
- **Organ Donation:** Whether you want any of your organs to be donated to someone who needs them or to be donated for medical research.

Be clear that your health care directive becomes effective when you experience an emergency and can no longer communicate, and it stays in effect only for that duration.

You can update your health care directive anytime you'd like. In fact, it is highly recommended that you review your directive regularly to make needed adjustments.

Finally, be sure to keep your directive in a safe place. Give a copy to your primary doctor and the person who will carry out your directions. Okay, gang? That's all for now.

7. CREATE A FINANCIAL POWER OF ATTORNEY

Similar to creating a health care directive, creating a financial power of attorney (FPA) is the process of giving a person authority to handle important decisions should you no longer be able to make those decisions yourself—only with an FPA, you are specifically giving a person financial authority. This is another document you might want to consider setting up today.

Typically, FPAs include the following responsibilities:

- **Paying Bills:** Mortgage loans, auto loans, and credit card bills.
- **Paying Medical Expenses:** Costs related to your calamity.
- **Paying Taxes:** Home property and income taxes.
- **Managing Real Estate:** Repairs, expenses, rent collection. And finally . . .
- **Running a Business:** Employee and client issues.

Remember that unless otherwise directed, your FPA only becomes effective when you become incapacitated and cannot make decisions for yourself, and stays in effect only for as long as you cannot communicate.

Also remember that you can change your FPA at any time, but you want to make sure that your appointed representative receives your latest version or at least knows where to find it.

To create an FPA today, simply contact an attorney—or consider online legal forms.

8. ESTABLISH A TRUST

Finally, establishing a trust typically involves meeting with an estate-planning attorney to create a "legal container" upon which your estate (cars, houses, investments, etc.) are placed.

The container becomes the property of the trust (no longer you) and it is managed by a "trustee" that you appoint to ensure that your property is dispersed in the manner that you decide.

Decisions can include:

- providing funds for your grandkids' education or retirement.
- funding an annual scholarship in your name at your alma mater, and . . .
- giving money to an important cause you believe in.

Understand that a trust can be in effect while you are still alive (managed by you or a representative), and it remains in effect after you die. After your death, an appointed trustee, like a financial institution or attorney, will begin (or continue) to manage the trust on your behalf.

While there are many different kinds of trusts (living trusts, revocable trusts, irrevocable trusts, and more)—which can all be pretty complex and involve an estate planning attorney—know that the general advantages (and disadvantages) of a trust include:

- **No Probate Process:** Remember that wills must first be "validated" by state probate courts before most of the assets of the estate can be disbursed to the heirs (this can take time). With a trust, a trustee can immediately utilize funds for funerals, sell homes and other property, and give money to the beneficiaries.

- **Protection from Claims:** Know that since a trust is far more complicated to create than just a simple will, it is far more difficult for someone to contest. So, no crazy ex-spouses trying to get your dough. And finally . . .
- **Potential Estate Tax Benefits:** Remember that if you become a really successful musician and your assets are valued at 12.8 million or more, a trust may also help reduce—if not eliminate—certain taxes. Remember, estate taxes can account for almost half of everything you own. Yikes!

Now here are the general disadvantages of trusts:

- **Costly Attorney Fees:** Remember that trusts can be quite complex and will require the assistance of a seasoned estate attorney to help you decide on the type of trust, how to set it up, and how to appoint a trustee. This is gonna cost money, and if you ever want to make changes to your trust, you'll have to spend even more dough.
- **Takes Work to Fund the Trust:** Keep in mind that a trust is not in full effect unless you fund it (i.e., transfer all of your assets). This includes retitling your house in the name of the trust, retitling automobiles, and so much more. This takes a lot of time and it is certainly no walk in the park. And finally . . .
- **Creates Hassles While You're Still Alive:** Remember that since you no longer own your property (the trustee does), you are going to have to go through some major hurdles every time you want to make some changes (such as sell your home). This is true even when you are the appointed trustee.

So, folks, those are the very basics of trusts. While you might be wondering whether you need one, know that the majority of people get by just fine by writing a will. Okay? Cool!

So, to wrap up this complete piece on estate planning, remember that while this stuff is a long way off (we hope), it is still an important part of your personal financial education.

As always, we suggest that you get a personal financial planner or estate attorney to iron out all of the details. No rush, you have time, but we recommend you at least draft a will, health care directive, and financial power of attorney. Okay? So, be safe out there. Peace and love!

12

WRAP PARTY

The End is just the beginning.

—author Kelsey Macke

26

Twelve Key Takeaways of Personal Finance for Musicians

Personal finance is the continual process of managing your income and expenses, setting goals, and using the right investment vehicles to make your money grow. It's also about insuring yourself against personal liability, minimizing taxes, understanding inflation, and so much more!

If this all sounds like work, it is—and this is precisely why so many musicians (and other folks too) go about their lives living far above their means, hoping that everything is going to miraculously work itself out. After all, you could be one of the lucky ones who blows up on TikTok or picks the winning lotto ticket at the 7-Eleven. But even then, know that 70 percent of those who come into "sudden wealth" go broke due to bad financial planning.

What follows are twelve lasting thoughts about how to think about personal finance. This is not just a motivational listing to get you fired up for a few days, but rather a new lifestyle that may require your everyday attention. The good news is that it's never too late to start. So, let's jump in.

1. THINK PRACTICALLY ABOUT INCOME AND HUMAN CAPITAL

Remember that for most twenty-year-olds, the ability to generate a paycheck for fifty years at a stable job, invest it, and earn interest (on top of interest) will serve as one of the biggest factors toward achieving financial success than any one single investment. This is a concept known as human capital—the economic value of an individual's abilities to earn money.

But for musicians, who can easily risk twelve to fifteen years of their best income-generating years before making any substantial money (if they ever make any money at all), establishing alternate revenue streams while working toward "the big dream" is the needed course of action.

Whether it's writing for film and TV, recording other artists, or taking on other side hustles, you'll not only be more equipped to go the long haul, but able to pay your bills, build savings, and invest a little money too. It's not about falling back but, rather, hedging the risk of fame more wisely to ensure that you don't end up becoming a broke, couch-surfing thirty-five-year-old.

So, don't forget it, personal finance really does start with thinking practically about income and human capital. As Kanye West said, "Money isn't everything, but not having it is."

2. TREAT YOUR MONEY LIKE IT'S THE LAST DOLLAR YOU'LL EARN

Remember, there are valid reasons in the music business for the existence of phrases like "one hit wonder" and "where are they now files." Stars burn out just as fast as they shoot to stardom. Changing trends, label expectations, and fierce competition are all to blame.

So should you ever make money with your music, treat each dollar like it's the last you'll ever earn. While there might be a tendency to buy the $100,000 car with your first $100,000, be smart and take the frugal road instead. Consider putting some of it toward a short-term savings goal, some into your future retirement savings, and the rest toward your bills.

Bottom line, gang, the last thing you want is to live like a king for a few years and end up broke—that's just tragic.

3. BEWARE OF THE VERY SLIPPERY SLOPE OF CREDIT

Remember that credit, particularly a credit card, can be both an angel and devil in disguise.

When used wisely (i.e., charging items and paying off monthly balances on time), a credit card is an angel in that it helps build your credibility. The more credibility you have, the easier it is to qualify for important loans, apartment rentals, and lower quotes on automobile insurance, to name just a few.

On the other hand, when used unwisely (i.e., leaving large balances on your accounts and paying bills late), a credit card is a devil in that it can easily put you in debt, destroy your ability to obtain important loans, and land you in bankruptcy court.

If this all sounds melodramatic, know that the Federal Reserve estimates that the total outstanding US consumer debt is $3.4 trillion, with $9.29 billion attributed to revolving credit (i.e., credit cards). You should also know that the average American carries about $5,000 in credit card debt and can only afford to make the monthly minimum payment. So, be careful!

While obtaining a credit card is easy to do and necessary to building strong credit, know that there is a fine line between your stairway to heaven and highway to hell.

4. SHOP FOR THE BEST LOANS AND KNOCK OUT DEBT QUICKLY

Remember that taking out loans for most people is an inevitable part of everyday life. There are loans for schools, cars, houses, and even opening up a small business. While loans do build credibility and provide the convenience of being able to get something today and pay for it tomorrow, remember that you are just renting other people's money. And rent is very costly.

Shop diligently for the best loans, utilizing institutions like banks and credit unions. Thanks to the "truth in lenders law," most lenders must disclose the total cost of the loan, including all interest and fees and the various payback schedules. The level of transparency and amount of information available to consumers makes shopping for loans very easy.

And remember, the goal of managing any debt is to pay it off quickly. While making lower monthly payments over more years might sound attractive, you'll end up paying far more interest. Case in point, a $15,000 car with an 8 percent loan could easily cost $20,000 over seven years. That's $5,000 in interest charges you could have saved by paying the loan off sooner.

Read: paying off your debts quickly is one of your best investments ever!

Yup, so shop for the best loans and knock them out quickly. You'll be really glad you did.

5. START YOUNG AND EMBRACE THE POWER OF COMPOUNDING

Remember, the earlier you start investing your hard-earned money, the more likely you'll benefit from the power of compounding interest. Compounding interest is simply interest on interest.

To demonstrate, if you invest $100 in a bank CD that earns 2 percent interest annually, your $100 will grow to $101.02 in one year. Better yet, in the second year, the interest will accrue on the $1.02, and your money will grow to $104.04, and so on. Clearly, the more years of compounding you have, the better off you will be.

Not impressed? Then take a look at this example!

Take that same $100 from above, but contribute an extra $100 per month, and invest it into something more aggressive earning 9 percent interest annually over a fifty-year period (from age twenty to seventy). At age seventy, you'll end up with $1,073,565.04. However, if you wait till age forty to get started, you'll only have $179,617.03. Yikes! That's a significant difference.

Look, it's never too late to get started, but the earlier you get your shit together, the more you'll benefit from the power of compounding interest. So, stop wasting time!

6. REMEMBER THAT TIME-BASED GOALS ARE THE KEY TO INVESTING

Remember that setting goals, or more specifically setting time-based goals, is the foundation of all smart investing. You see, it's time (or the time horizon) that typically determines the type of investment vehicle that you will use to support your financial objectives.

Typically, the following advice holds true:

- **Short-term Goals:** Require fewer volatile investments (like CDs or money market funds) to preserve capital and earn a little interest.
- **Mid-term Goals:** Require more volatile investments (like stocks balanced with bonds) to beat inflation and get modest growth. And . . .
- **Long-term Goals:** Require even more volatility (leaning heavily toward stocks with some bonds) to beat inflation and achieve the maximum growth potential.

In sum, the shorter the time horizon for your goals, the more conservative and less rewarding the investment. The longer the time horizon for your goals, the riskier and more rewarding the investment. This is generally because a long-term investment strategy can better hedge against the associated risks of market swings or downturns.

So, look gang, whether you are saving for a car in five years, or retirement in fifty years, remember that setting goals, or more specifically the time horizon of each goal, is the cornerstone of investing and building wealth. So, set your time-based goals today!

7. UNDERSTAND HOW MUCH RISK YOU CAN "REALLY" TOLERATE

Remember that constant market fluctuations lead to stupid investor mistakes. Thus, one of the most important components to smart investing is to understand just how much volatility (or risk) you can truly stomach.

Risk tolerance quizzes are available online and ask things like your age, time horizon, current financial situation, and how you'd react to a market crash. Or, you can just use a useful "rule of thumb" by "putting your age in bonds" and adjusting your risk accordingly. The latter approach particularly works well for long-term investment goals.

To illustrate, a twenty-year-old saving for retirement fifty years out might use an asset allocation of 80 percent stocks to 20 percent bonds. As time passes, say at age thirty, the same investor might use an asset allocation of 70 percent stocks to 30 percent bonds. And at age fifty, the investor would use an asset allocation of 50 percent stocks to 50 percent bonds.

Typically, investors become more risk averse as they get older and approach retirement. This is due to the shorter time horizon before retirement and the lower probability of recovering from potential market losses.

So, remember, a huge part of smart investing is understanding and managing your risk tolerance. This is huge! Otherwise, in the words of the legendary value investor Benjamin Graham, "Your chief problem—and even your worst enemy—is likely to be yourself."

8. UNDERSTAND THE BENEFITS OF INVESTMENT DIVERSIFICATION

Remember that another important element to responsible investing is portfolio diversification.

Diversification involves spreading out your money across different investments, sectors, and geographical regions rather than "putting all of your eggs into one basket." By doing this, you're more likely to offset the losses with the wins and maintain a steadier rate of return.

To demonstrate what a diversified portfolio might contain, a thirty-year-old investor saving for retirement might purchase a number of index funds allocated to a 70/30 risk tolerance level.

Here's what it might look like:

- Vanguard's Total Stock Market Index Fund (which contains 4,070 companies in technology, consumer discretionary products and financials all over the United States),
- Vanguard's Total International Stock Market Fund (which contains 7,754 companies in consumer cyclicals, financial services, and health care all over Europe, the Pacific, and emerging markets), and . . .
- Vanguard's Total Bond Market Index (which contains 10,127 investment-grade bonds in US treasuries, and mortgage-backed securities all over the United States).

As you can see above, index funds are a great way to achieve market diversification. Rather than trying to pick a few winners in the stock market, index funds contain hundreds of securities in a portfolio adhering to the "win some-lose some" theory.

Said another way, rather than trying to find the needle in the haystack, you are investing in the entire haystack, thus increasing your odds of getting "your fair share of market returns" (as Jack Bogle, Vanguard's founder, would say).

Look, whether you use index funds or not, the whole point is that diversification is a super important concept for investors to understand. *Remember*: diversity deceases adversity!

9. TRY TO AVOID INVESTMENT COSTS

Remember that minimizing investment costs is another important component of responsible investing. Fees, commissions, and more can really eat away at your portfolio and potentially cost you several thousands of dollars over time.

Let's take the cost of active-management, for instance. Most managers charge you 1 percent of your assets under management in an effort to move your money around and beat the market returns. While 1 percent might not sound like a lot, it's $1,000 on every $100,000. This could amount to at least $50,000 over a fifty-year period and so much more if you consider what you might have earned if you invested that $50,000 in a compound interest investment.

Look, not to oversell our love for index funds (mentioned above), but know that they are a passively managed, low-cost investment that arguably gets you better market returns. Warren Buffett (a famed investor) bet that an S&P 500 index fund would outperform a hand-picked portfolio of more expensive actively managed hedge funds over a ten-year period. He won!

So, always consider the fees associated with all of your investments and ask yourself whether there is a way to streamline your costs so that you end up with more in your pockets. Make no mistake, people, your future self will probably thank you dearly.

10. PRACTICE TAX AVOIDANCE STRATEGIES

Remember that another smart investment strategy is to practice smart tax avoidance strategies. Be very clear that Uncle Sam can really take a big bite out of your money if you're not careful.

Here are just a few of the smart things you can do:

- If you receive a large lump sum of money (say a large publishing or merchandising advance), consider delaying a portion of that payment till next tax year to avoid a higher tax bracket and paying more income tax in the current year.
- Before selling certain investments, understand the difference between a short-term capital gain and a long-term capital gain. A short-term capital gain is an investment held shorter than a year and taxed at a higher rate. A long-term capital gain is an investment that is held longer than one year and one day and taxed at a lower rate. Meaning, it's probably better to hang on to your investments for the long term.
- Finally, when saving for your retirement, you should always max out tax-advantaged accounts like an IRA (pre-tax money to grow and be taxed at withdrawal), or a Roth IRA (after-tax

money to grow and withdraw tax-free). The government is purposely giving you a tax break to entice you to save for your golden years, so you're a complete fool if you're dragging your feet on this.

Look, gang, just remember: practicing tax avoidance strategies is crucial to building your wealth. Why give more money to Uncle Sam when you can keep it and invest in yourself! You'll end up with more money and be in a far better position to meet your goals. So, just do it!

11. BE SURE TO PROTECT YOURSELF AGAINST THE UNEXPECTED

Moving away from investment advice and building future wealth, also remember that another big part of personal finance is protecting your assets by insuring yourself against the unexpected.

If there is one thing that can put your finances into complete disorder, it's suffering a major calamity while uninsured or underinsured. But believe it or not, despite clearly stated laws that make certain types of insurance mandatory, there are still millions of people who take their chances. In the United States, thirty million automobile operators are uninsured, and many of those who are insured are "underinsured—meaning they only have the minimum protection.

So, make no mistake, shifting the responsibility of risk to someone else (i.e., an insurance company) who will pay most of your bills in the face of a serious crisis—could very well end up being one of the best investments that you ever make. Oh, and always go for the higher deductible insurance when appropriate. You'll pay less per month, and it will give you the protection you really need.

12. PROTECT YOUR ESTATE WITH PROPER PLANNING

Finally, while no one likes to discuss morbid and depressing issues, remember that you must also protect your personal estate with proper planning should you die or become incapacitated.

Of the many sophisticated things that you can do to create an effective estate plan (like buying a life insurance policy or starting a trust), the one simple thing that everyone can do right now—even if you don't have a lot of assets—is to create a will.

A will should indicate the following:

- an executor who will be responsible for distributing the assets of your estate,
- beneficiaries of your assets and the percentages they will receive,
- funds that will be used for paying certain taxes and outstanding debts,
- a guardian to take responsibility for any children or pets, and . . .
- instructions for how you would like certain burial wishes to be carried out.

Just know that without a will, you die intestate. This means the state in which you live may have to decide what to do with your property, how your money will be split among family members, and how the rights to your hit songs should be divided. This is something you definitely do not want!

Look, gang, no one likes to think about their demise, but shit does happen! With proper estate planning, even just a will, you can help ensure that everything will be in order.

So that's it for our twelve key takeaways of personal finance for musicians. We offered nothing overly sexy or exciting but, rather, the most practical personal financial tips for success.

But just remember, these tips do no good unless they are put into effect. Think of them as a way of life and not just a motivational hype list. It's never too late to start, so roll up your sleeves and get going. Remember, your future is purchased with the present! Peace and rock on!

A Few More Key Points at a Glance

In addition to our twelve points above, we just had to leave you with a few more rapid-fire nuggets for the road. We could literally leave hundreds, but here are some of our favorites. Enjoy.

- **Wealth:** Remember that the "true" road to wealth is making more money and spending less.
- **Budgeting:** Don't think of budgeting as suffering today but, rather, paying dues for a brighter tomorrow.

- **Savings:** Shoot for 10 percent of your monthly income, no matter how you have to do it.
- **Retirement:** Remember, retirement is about freedom, not about getting old.
- **Retirement Funds:** Think of retirement funds as legal tax shelters that can save you thousands of dollars.
- **The Investment Process:** Remember responsible investing is a seven-point process: (1) earn money, (2) budget, (3) pay off debt, (4) establish an emergency fund, (5) save for retirement, (6) invest responsibly, and (7) play with funny money (only if you must).
- **Investment Apps:** Never treat investing like it's a video game. Remember, you're playing with real money!
- **Investing and Fun:** Know that these two words should never be spoken in the same sentence. Smart investing is typically boring!
- **Investment Hype:** Avoid the noise, sexy stock picks, and gurus. They only lead to irrational behavior and the possibility of losing your hard-earned money.
- **Beating the Market:** Know that an entire industry is built around everyone's greed and the notion they can beat the market and get rich quick. Statistically speaking, very few investors can repeatedly do it.
- **Long-term Investing:** Long-term investing beats short-term trading almost every time.
- **Market Timing:** Remember, no one knows for sure when the markets will be up or down. It's entirely unpredictable and random no matter what anyone says.
- **Investment Returns:** What you see is not what you always get—don't forget about factoring in taxes, inflation, and other investment fees.
- **Market Declines:** Remember the market always bounces back.
- **Stock Market Losses:** It's never a loss until you sell.
- **The Biggest Danger to Your Portfolio:** Look in the mirror. Your fear and greed will kill you.
- **Monitoring Investments:** The less you look at your accounts, the better off you'll be.
- **Paying for Insurance:** See it as paying a little now, to save a shitload later.
- **Estate Planning:** Your demise is not the end. Rather, it's the beginning of a lot of work for your loved ones.

- **Wills:** Would you rather have an undesirable relative or the state get all your dough?
- **Certified Financial Planners:** Remember, an investment in knowledge pays the best returns.
- **Personal Finance:** Remember, it's not just about investing but also about covering your assets with insurance, budgeting, building credit, getting out of debt, understanding banks, keeping organized records, dealing with taxation, and planning your estate. Learn it and live it. Peace!

Index

Ableton, 39
accidental death and dismemberment insurance, 188
Accident and Illness Coverage, pet insurance for, 185
Accident Only, pet insurance for, 185
account alerts, from banks, 75
accountants, 16; spreadsheet used by, 203; tax deductions for, 195; for taxes, 46, 190, 206–12. *See also* certified public accountant (CPA)
account numbers: organization of, 54; security for, 96
accounts: beneficiaries for, 215; checking, 68, 76–77, 85–86; money market, 73, 168; Quicken to track, 203; retirement, 6, 117–19, 121, 122, 125–32, 137–38, 149, 152, 175, 196–97, 230–31; savings, 76–77, 105, 215
accounts receivables, organization of, 49
account statements: from banks, 68; organization of, 50
Acorns app, 174
active management, 141
advice, financial, 73, 154, 164, 165–72, 209; for CDs, 74; from

CFP, 114, 124, 125, 131, 138; Marketsmith for, 176–77
AFCC. *See* American Fair Credit Council
AFM. *See* American Federation of Musicians
Airbit, beats sold on, 31
AirGigs, as side hustle, 31
airline tickets, 45
Ally Bank, 78
alma mater, of accountant, 211
American Fair Credit Council (AFCC), 109
American Federation of Musicians (AFM), 25, 185, 194
American Idol, 29
Amoeba Records, 21
analyst, financial, 138
AnnualCreditReport.com, 91, 101
annual income, receipts to track, 48
annuity insurance, 124, 132, 137, 187
anti-spyware software, 99
antivirus software, 99
anxiety, 105; behavioral finance relation to, 12
Apple Macbook, Photos application, 202
apps: for budgets, 63; to check FICO Score, 95; for investments, 162,

235

173–77, 233; for mileage tracking, 205; for receipt storage, 202, 204
asset allocation, 140
assets, 139, 145; in estate planning, 214–15; on net worth statement, 57, 58–59
ATMs, 80; bank access to, 78; cash accessibility via, 69; fees from, 45, 77; identity theft at, 98
attorney: estate, 217, 218, 220–21; tax deductions for, 195
audience, sponsorship relation to, 41
audit, from IRS, 50, 197, 199, 202; accountant for, 208–9
Aura, 104, 186
authorized user, on credit cards, 86
auto insurance, 183–84
Automile, 205
avoidance methods, for taxes, 196–97, 230–31
Axos Bank, 78

bands: cover, 29–30; split costs in, 40
Bank of America, 74, 78
bankruptcy, 143; credit card debt relation to, 12; for debt relief, 109
banks: commercial, 4–5, 50, 74, 78; as community, 66; convenience from, 69–71; customer service of, 75; for direct deposit, 86; fees from, 45; loans from, 72–73; money tracking from, 68; protection by, 67
banks, online: brand recognition of, 78–79; cash challenges of, 79–80; interest rates of, 76–77; service interruptions of, 81–82
Bay, Mel, 33
bear market, 142
beats, websites to sell, 31
BeatStars, beats sold on, 31
behavioral finance, 12, 162–63
beneficiary, 140; in estate planning, 215, 232; in will, 217
Benz, Christine, 156
Bernstein, William, 133

BestMark. *See* secret shopper, as side hustle
Betterment, 175–76
Bierce, Ambrose, 213
Bigger Hammer, production work at, 33
bills, 44; creditor relation to, 84–85; credit reports relation to, 51; FICO score relation to, 94; payment of, 70–71, 87–88; spreadsheet to track, 49
birth certificate, organization of, 53
Bitcoin, 174
Bitdefender, as antivirus protection, 99
Black Sabbath, 188
blue chip stock, 142
"board of accountancy," 207
bodily injury liability, auto insurance for, 183
body part insurance, 187–88
Bogle, Jack, 150, 153, 159, 229
Bogleheads, 11
bonds, 74, 136, 140, 150–51, 158, 229; in retirement accounts, 120; as securities, 139
books, music: print royalties from, 20; transcription for, 33
Borg, Bobby, 27
bracket, tax, 196, 230
branded company: recording session fees from, 25; sponsorship monies from, 23–24, 41
brand recognition, of banks, 78–79
Brennan, Jack, 161
broker, 138
brokerage firm, 138; bank access to, 74; SIPC relation to, 143
budget, 4, 11, 62–63, 64, 146–47, 232; receipts for, 13, 44, 147; after retirement, 122; spreadsheets for, 43, 63
Buffett, Warren, 46, 138–39, 151, 158–59, 230
Bulletproof Investing (Stein and DeMuth), 113

bull market, 141
Business Basics for Musicians (Borg), 27
business expenses, as tax deduction, 194
busking, as side hustle, 30

California, insurance in, 182, 187
capital, 139
capital gains tax, 140, 193, 230
career: expensive lifestyle relation to, 15–16; investment in, 39
car insurance, 45
CarMax, 42
cash, 45, 79–80, 135–36; ATM for, 69; bank to protect, 67
cash advances, on credit cards, 110–11
Cash Crate. *See* survey companies, as side hustle
cash flow analysis, 4, 59–61, *61*
cashier checks, certified checks compared to, 71
CDs. *See* certificate of deposits
celebrity appearance fees, 24
certificate of deposits (CDs), 73, 74, 227
certified checks, cashier checks compared to, 71
certified financial planner (CFP), 138, 165, 169, 211, 234; for retirement plan, 114, 124, 125, 131
certified fund specialist (CFS), 169
certified investment management analyst (CIMA), 169
certified public accountant (CPA), 197–98, 200, 207, 210, 211
CFA. *See* chartered financial analyst
CFP. *See* certified financial planner
CFS. *See* certified fund specialist
charities, in will, 218
chartered financial analyst (CFA), 169
Chase Bank, 74, 78
check cashing services, from bank, 68

checking account: beneficiary for, 215; credit relation to, 85–86; interest from, 68, 76–77
Cher, 32
church gigs, as side hustle, 29
CIMA. *See* certified investment management analyst
Citibank, 78
citizenship certificates, organization of, 52
Clements, Jonathan, 17
clubs, celebrity appearance fees from, 24
Coinbase, 177
collision, auto insurance for, 183
communication, with financial experts, 172, 211
community, banks as, 66
compounding interest, 14, 116, 139, 227
comprehensive physical damage, auto insurance for, 183
confidence, 162; from cash flow analysis, 60
Consumer Credit Reporting Agency, 102
Consumer Financial Protection Bureau, 108
contacts, side hustles to make, 32
contribution limits, retirement, 121, 125–26
cosmetic procedures, 181
cost avoidance, in investments, 7, 151, 160, 229–30
cover bands, as side hustle, 29–30
CPA. *See* certified public accountant
credibility, 5, 225–26; debt effect on, 105, 111; of financial expert, 169, 211; survival job to build, 84–85
credit, 52, 70, 95, 225–26; checking account relation to, 85–86; as credibility, 5, 84, 225–26; late bill payment effect on, 87–88; reports for, 51, 89–94, 186

credit bureaus, 90, 102; errors corrected by, 92; identity theft report to, 93
credit cards, 45, 102, 225–26; from bank, 5, 69–70; bankruptcy relation to, 12; cash advances on, 110–11; interest on, 87, 105; secured, 86–87; security for, 96, 97–98; spending habits relation to, 88–89
"credit counselor" approach, for debt, 108
credit freeze, 102
credit history, 90–91; bankruptcy effect on, 109; effect on loans, 89; fraud signs in, 101
Credit Karma, for FICO score, 95
Credit One Platinum Secured, as secured credit card, 87
creditors, 92, 109; bills relation to, 84–85; credit report checked by, 90–91; debt consolidation through, 106; identity theft report to, 93
credit reports, 51, 89, 101, 186; creditors checking, 90–91; errors on, 91–92; FICO score on, 93–94
Credit Sesame, for FICO score, 95
credit unions, 66, 226
cruise ship, side hustles on, 29–30
cryptocurrency, 136–37, 162–63, 177; as funny money, 153; on Robinhood, 174
customer service, 35; of commercial banks, 75; of online banks, 80–81; as side hustle, 34

Dashlane, to organize passwords, 54
day trader, 138
Dean Markley Guitar Strings, sponsorship monies from, 24
debit cards: investment app, 174, 175; overdraft protection on, 69
debt, 4, 5, 58, 225–26; bankruptcy for relief of, 109; consolidation of, 106; credit card, 12; effect on credibility, 105, 111; in estate planning, 215; frugal lifestyle to pay off, 38, 110; retirement payments compared to, 116–17; strategies for, 107–8, 147–48
"debt avalanche" strategy, for debt, 106, 147
"debt settlement" method, 109
"debt snowball" strategy, for debt, 106–7, 147–48
debt-to-asset ratio, 58–59
deductions, tax, 194–95, 199–205
"deferment" strategy, for debt, 108
deficit, in cash flow analysis, 60
Def Leppard, 188
DeMuth, Phil, 113
denial, effect on debt, 111
dental insurance, 181
Department of Motor Vehicles (DMV), documents related to, 51
depression, 135
DIEC. *See* disability insurance elective coverage
Digital Performance Right in Sound Recordings Act (1995), 22
digital service providers: master money from, 21; mechanical royalties from, 18–19
digital storage, physical compared to, 54
Digital Underground, Tupac as roadie for, 32
direct deposit, banks for, 69, 86
Direct Marketing Association, 102
Directory of Federal Tax Return Preparers, 210
disability, effect on retirement, 115
disability insurance elective coverage (DIEC), 182
disbursements, in budget, 62–63
Discover Bank, 78
Disney Cruise Line, 29
Disneyland, 30
diversification, of investments, 7, 140, 156–57, 229
dividend, 139
DMAchoice, 102

DMV. *See* Department of Motor Vehicles
documents: estate planning, 56; investment, 51; invoice, 49; LLC, 54; net-worth statement, 57–59, 59; warranty, 55
dog walker, as side hustle, 35
dollar, strong or weak, 135
"dollar cost averaging," 161
Do Not Resuscitate Notice, in health care directive, 219
DoorDash. *See* food delivery
Dow Jones Industrial Average (DOW), 143
down market, 161–62
dreams, 15, 95; bank loans to achieve, 73; frugal lifestyle relation to, 38, 43
drum programmer, as side hustle, 33–34

Eames, Michael, 27
earthquake insurance, 187
economy, 134–35
EDD. *See* Employment Development Department, California
Edelman, Ric, 157–58
education, 56; investment, 144; IRA to save for, 131; music, 39; personal finance, 10–11; tax deductions for, 195, 200
Education IRA, 131
electronics, disposal of, 101
emergency fund, 148, 156–57, 168
emotions, effect on investments, 12, 133, 153, 162–63
employer: insurance through, 181, 182; retirement plans through, 119, 121, 127, 128–29, 130–32, 149; taxes through, 191, 192–93
Employment Development Department, California (EDD), 182
engagement, on social media, 40
entertainment: as investment bias, 163; money saved on, 42–43

Equifax, credit reports from, 51, 90, 101
equipment tech, as side hustle, 32
equities, 139
errors, on credit report, 91–92
estate attorney, 217, 218, 220–21
estate planning, 213, 221, 231–32, 233; assets in, 214–15; FPA in, 56, 219–20; health care directive in, 218–19; taxes in, 216–17; will for, 8, 217–18, 234
ETFs. *See* exchange traded funds
Excel, Microsoft. *See* spreadsheets
exchange traded funds (ETFs), 136, 141
execution, as power, 163
executor, of will, 217, 232
Expedia, airline tickets from, 45
expense ratio, 140
expenses, 3, 43, 49, 63; in budget, 147; in cash flow analysis, 60; in emergency fund, 148; medical, 180–81; tax deductions for, 195
Experian, 51, 90, 95, 101
expert, financial, 167–72, 211

Facebook, music education on, 39
failure, financial, 9, 115
Fair Isaac Corporation. *See* FICO score
"fake it till you make it" philosophy, 12, 111
family, effect on personal finance, 14
Fat Joe (rapper), 206
Federal Deposit Insurance Corporation (FDIC), 5
The Federal Reserve (The Feds), 135, 226
Federal Student Aid, 108
Federal Trade Commission (FTC), 92–93
fees: of accountants, 208; from commercial banks, 45; of financial experts, 170–71; load, 140; from online banks, 77; synch, 19, 20, 21–22; union reuse, 26

240   INDEX

FICO score, 93–94; apps to check, 95
Fidelity, 174–75
fiduciary, 138, 170
financial inventory, on net worth statement, 57–58
financial power of attorney (FPA), for estate planning, 56, 219–20
FINRAs Broker Check, 169
first impression, for side hustles, 36
Fiverr. *See* freelance platforms
Florida, state income tax in, 123
food, money saving tips for, 44
food delivery, 34, 85, 110, 146
Forbes, top-rated online banks by, 79
Fortune 500 Company, 143
457(b), 117, 129–30
401(k), 117, 118, 119, 127–28, 137, 149; contribution limits for, 121; for tax avoidance, 196; withdrawal from, 122
403(b), 117, 128–29
The Four Pillars of Investing (Bernstein), 133
FPA. *See* financial power of attorney, for estate planning
Franklin, Benjamin, 8, 9, 60, 73
fraudulent activity, 5; account alerts for, 75; in credit history, 101; on credit reports, 51, 91–93; identity theft as, 92–93, 96, 104
freedom, 163; retirement as, 6, 113, 114–15
freelance platforms, 33–34, 146
Freese, Josh, 30
frequent flyer statements, organization of, 55
frugal lifestyle, 41, 225; dreams relation to, 38, 43; effect on debt, 110
FTC. *See* Federal Trade Commission
Fundrise, 176
funeral arrangements, in estate planning, 8, 218, 220
"funny money," 153–54
futures, 136

GDP. *See* Gross Domestic Product
gear, music: document organization for, 55; money saved on, 38–39
gigs, music, 146
goals, 166; budget for, 62; investment for, 6, 227–28; for investments, 150; savings relation to, 67, 147
GoBankingRatesSurvey, on banking fees, 77
Google Sheets. *See* spreadsheets
Graham, Benjamin, 228
Grande, Ariana, 168
graphic design, as side hustle, 33–34
gratitude, for side hustles, 36
grocery delivery, as side hustle, 34
Gross Domestic Product (GDP), 135
Guitar Center, 33, 34, 85, 146

habits, spending, 4, 15–16, 43; credit card relation to, 88–89
Heads I Win, Tails I Win (Jacob), 160
health, 124; effect on retirement, 115; insurance, 180–81
health care directive, for estate planning, 56, 218–19
Health Savings Account, for retirement, 132
herd mentality, in investments, 162–63
Hilton, Paris, 24
HMO, health insurance, 181
home recording, as side hustle, 31
Hudson, Jenifer, 29
human capital, 2–3, 17; investments relation to, 146, 224–26

Identity Defense, as security monitoring service, 104
Identity Guard, 186; as security monitoring service, 104
identity theft, 96, 104; at ATMs, 98; insurance for, 186; through mail theft, 103; resolution of, 92–93; social security card relation to, 53
image, 12; money saved on, 40–41

INDEX 241

income, 20, 48; budget to monitor, 43; effect on "deferment" strategy, 108; investments relation to, 56, 145–46; invoices to track, 49; master-use fees as, 21–22; mechanical royalties as, 18–19; from NFTs, 26–27; personal finance relation to, 2–3; retirement distributions as, 123; sponsorship monies as, 23–24; tax bracket relation to, 196, 230; unions relation to, 25–26
income taxes, 123, 190–93, 230
index funds, 136, 151–52, 159, 160, 229, 230; passive management in, 141
individual retirement account (IRA), 117, 137, 149
inflation, 135; effect on deductions, 194; effect on investments, 152, 160; effect on retirement, 115
inflows: on budget, 62; on cash flow analysis, 60; outflows balanced with, 63
information, personal: phishing scams for, 100; security for, 96–97; spyware to obtain, 99
inheritance taxes, 217
initial public offering (IPO), 142
Instacart. *See* grocery delivery, as side hustle
"insta-famous" artists, 15
Instagram, buying followers on, 40
instrument insurance, 184–85
insurance, 7, 179, 188, 233; annuity, 124, 132, 187; auto, 183–84; car, 45; through employer, 181, 182; FDIC, 67; health, 180–81; interest on home, 200; life, 56, 137, 187, 216, 231; Medicare as, 123; pet, 185; records for, 53–54; through security monitoring services, 104; tuition refund, 186
IntelliShop. *See* secret shopper, as side hustle

interest, 135–36, 225–26; from banks, 67–68, 76–77; of CDs, 74; compounding, 14, 116, 139, 227; on credit cards, 87, 105; on home insurance, 200; of loans, 106, 148
interest rate, 139
Internal Revenue Service (IRS): accountant history with, 211; audit by, 50, 197, 199, 202, 208–9; retirement contribution limits of, 121; VITA of, 210
Internet radio, master performances on, 22
Introduction to Music Publishing (Borg & Eames), 27
Investment Adviser Public Disclosure, SEC, 169
investments, 2, 154, 164, 214, 227; apps for, 162, 173–77, 233; assets as, 139; beneficiary for, 215; brokerage firms for, 74; in career, 39; cash flow analysis relation to, 60; disbursements for, 62–63; diversification of, 7, 140, 156–57, 229; documents related to, 51; in down market, 161–62; emotions effect on, 12, 133, 153, 162–63; frugal lifestyle for, 38; human capital relation to, 224–26; income relation to, 56, 145–46; index funds as, 136, 141, 151–52, 159, 160, 229, 230; in knowledge, 73; management of, 141, 151, 158, 160, 165; real-estate, 176; retirement, 6, 119–20, 150, 228; of side hustle money, 35; taxable accounts for, 138, 193; terms for, 142–43
Investopedia, 11, 144
invoices, organization of, 49
IPO. *See* initial public offering
IRA. *See* individual retirement account
IRS. *See* Internal Revenue Service
itemized deductions, to taxes, 194

Jacob, Spencer, 160
Jay-Z, 3, 83
job, survival, 146; to build credibility, 84–85; for debt relief, 110
J. P. Morgan Wealth Management, Chase Bank relation to, 74

King, BB, 30
knowledge, investments in, 73

Lamar, Kendrick, 6
late payments, on bills, 87–88
lessons, music: as side hustle, 28–29; as survival job, 85, 110
liabilities, 145; in estate planning, 215; on net worth statement, 57, 58
life insurance, 56, 137, 187, 231; in estate planning, 216
LifeLock, 186; as security monitoring service, 104
lifestyle: budget relation to, 63; career relation to, 15–16; frugal, 38, 41, 43, 110, 225; health of, 124; after retirement, 122
Likierman, Andrew, 65
Lil' Kim (rapper), 16
Lil Nas X, 15
limited liability company (LLC), 209; document organization for, 54
liquidity, 140
Little Book on Common Sense Investing (Bogle), 159
live events: monies from, 22–24; sound engineering at, 32
live performance monies, 22–23
LLC. *See* limited liability company
load fee, 140
loans, 226; from bank, 5, 72–73; bonds as, 136; for buying on margins, 140–41; credit effect on, 89; interest of, 106, 148; as outflow, 60; payday, 110; student, 108; worthiness for, 58
Logic, 39

long-term care insurance, 124, 187
love letters, in will, 218
"lump sum" strategy, for debt, 107
Lyft. *See* ride share companies

Macke, Kelsey, 223
Madonna, 23
mail theft, security from, 103
Malkiel, Burton G., 162
management, 68; of debt, 5; investment, 141, 151, 158, 160, 165, 230; Quicken for financial, 203
manager, business, 16
market capitalization, 141
market crash, 142
Market Force. *See* secret shopper, as side hustle
market order, 141
Marketsmith, 176–77
market stop order, 141
Mastercard credit card, 88
master money, 21
master performances, on Internet radio, 22
master-use fees, synch fee compared to, 21–22
maturity, 139
McAfee, as antivirus protection, 99
mechanical royalties, from interactive digital service providers, 18–19
medical expense payments, auto insurance for, 183
Medicare, 123, 191
merchandising monies, 23
Merrill Edge, 74
mileage deductions, 205
Mileage Log Plus, 205
MileIQ, 205
military discharge papers, organization of, 53
millionaires, 14
minimum balance, for checking account, 86
minimum pay scale, of unions, 25

Mint, 63
MMAs. *See* money market accounts
mobile banking, 71
mobile DJ, as side hustle, 30
mobile notary, as side hustle, 35
money. *See specific topics*
Money (Robbins), 163
money market accounts (MMAs), 73, 168
money orders, 72
Monster energy drinks, 24
Morgan Stanley, 189
Morning Star, 144
Morning Star's Guide to Mutual Funds (Benz), 156
Motley Fool, 144
music business convention, celebrity appearance fees from, 24
music festivals, money saved on, 3, 43
Music Pro Insurance, 185
music stores, 20, 33, 34, 85
music transcription, as side hustle, 33
music video: money saved on, 39; synch fee from, 20
mutual funds, 136; from brokerage firm access, 74; load fee of, 140
myFICO, 95

NAS (rapper), 8, 16, 197
NASDAQ. *See* National Association of Securities Dealers Automated Quotations
NASDAQ index, 143
National Association of Personal Financial Advisors, 170
National Association of Securities Dealers Automated Quotations (NASDAQ), 142
National Foundation for Credit Counseling, 108
naturalization papers, organization of, 52
NBKC, 78
NeatReceipts, 203–4

needs, difference between wants and, 11, 42
NerdWallet, 11, 144; budgeting tips on, 43
net worth statement, 57–59, 203; for accounting, 4
Nevada, state income tax in, 123
New York Stock Exchange (NYSE), 142
NFT. *See* non-fungible token
NFT monies, 26–27
non-fungible token (NFT), 26–27, 177
Norton, as antivirus protection, 99
NYSE. *See* New York Stock Exchange

online accounts, in will, 218
options, 136
organization: of account numbers, 54; of documents, 48, 49, 50–56
outflow: on budget, 43, 63; on cash flow analysis, 60
outgoing mail, post office for, 103
Outsourcely. *See* freelance platforms
overconfidence, 162
overdraft protection, on debit cards, 69

paid in full (PIF), 49
Pandora. *See* Internet radio
paper shredder, for security, 104
passion, in side hustles, 36
passive management, 141
passports: birth certificate relation to, 53; organization of, 51–52
passwords: organization of, 54; security of, 98–99
patience: investment relation to, 7; in side hustles, 36
pawn shop loans, 110
payable on death account (POD), 215
payday loans, 110
"pay down the principle" approach, for debt, 107
peace-of-mind, budget for, 62

A Perfect Circle, 30
performance royalties, 19; synch fee relation to, 20
personal finance. *See specific topics*
Personal Finance for Dummies (Tyson), 179
personal financial specialist (PFS), 211
personal trainer, as side hustle, 35
pet care, in will, 217
PFS. *See* personal financial specialist
phishing scams, security from, 100
Photos application, Apple Macbook, 202
physical storage, digital storage compared to, 54
piano, tuning as side hustle, 33
PIF. *See* paid in full
Pimp My Ride (TV show), 15
Platinum Select Mastercard, as secured credit card, 87
PNC, 78
POD. *See* payable on death account
police report, for identity theft, 92
positive attitude, in side hustles, 36
Postmates. *See* food delivery
post office, for outgoing mail, 103
poverty: effect on retirement, 115; millionaires from, 14
power, execution as, 163
PPO, health insurance, 181
precious metals, 136
Preparer Tax Identification Number (PTIN), 207
price quote, from accountant, 211
Prince, 9
principal, 139
production work, as side hustle, 33
promotion, music: money saved on, 39–40; tax deductions for, 195, 200
property damage liability, auto insurance for, 183
property insurance, 187
prospectus, 142
Pro Tools, 39; as side hustle, 33–34

PTIN. *See* Preparer Tax Identification Number
public company, 142
public computers, security on, 99–100

Quarterly Tax Estimates, 192
Quicken, for financial management, 203
Quontic Bank, 78

A Random Walk Down Wall Street (Malkiel), 162
real-estate investments, 176
rebalancing, 140
receipts, 50; for budget, 13, 44, 147; to prevent identity theft, 98; for tax deductions, 48, 199–205
recession, 135
recording session fees, 25
referrals, for accountants, 206–7, 208
rehearsal complex, side hustles at, 32
rentals, auto insurance for, 183
renters insurance, 184
reputation, of banks, 4–5
Rescue Your Money (Edelman), 158
residence: creditor relation to, 85; money saved on, 41–42, 110
respect: for financial expert, 171–72; for money, 62; for side hustles, 36
restaurants: celebrity appearance fees from, 24; money saved on, 110
retirement, 123, *132*, 233; accounts for, 6, 117–19, 121, 122, 125–32, 137–38, 149, 152, 175, 196–97, 230–31; annuity insurance after, 124, 132, 187; as freedom, 113, 114–15; investments for, 6, 119–20, 150, 228; savings for, 116–17
revenue streams, alternate, 2–3, 225
Richards, Keith, 124
The Richest Man in Babylon, 13
ride share companies, 146; as side hustle, 34; as survival job, 85, 110

risk: insurance relation to, 7; of investments, 74, 159; in stock market, 120
risk tolerance, 156–57, 228–29; investment relation to, 6, 141, 150–51
roadie, as side hustle, 32
Robbins, Tony, 163
Robinhood app, 162, 173–74
robo-advisors, 141, 175
robots, for customer service, 80–81
Rocket Money, subscription services relation to, 44
Roll-Over IRA, 131
Rothchild, Baron, 161
Roth 401(k), 117, 128, 137
Roth IRA, 118, 126–27, 137, 148; withdrawal from, 122
royalties, 18–21

sacrifices, for savings, 3
SAG/AFTRA. *See* Screen Actors Guild/American Federation of Television and Radio Artists
Sam Ash music stores: music books at, 20, 33; side hustle at, 34
savings, 3, 62–63, 225, 233; budget for, 11; in cash flow analysis, 60; goals relation to, 67, 147; for retirement, 116–17
savings account: beneficiary for, 215; interest from, 76–77, 105
savings ratio, in cash flow analysis, 60
schedule, personal, personal finance in, 13
Schwab Center for Financial Research, 152
Screen Actors Guild/American Federation of Television and Radio Artists (SAG/AFTRA), 194; minimum pay scale of, 25
SDI. *See* state disability insurance program
SEC. *See* Securities and Exchange Commission

secret shopper, as side hustle, 35
sector, 139
secured credit card, 86–87
Secured Visa OpenSky, as secured credit card, 87
securities, 139; brokerage firm to sell, 138
Securities and Exchange Commission (SEC), 142, 170; Investment Adviser Public Disclosure of, 169
Securities Investor Protection Corporation (SIPC), 143
security, 103–4; of online banks, 81; for personal information, 96–97, 98–99; on public computers, 99–100; of websites, 101
security monitoring services, 104
Self-Directed IRA, 131
self-directed management, 141
self-employed worker: deductions for, 200; insurance for, 181, 182; taxes for, 191, 192, 193–95
SEP IRA, 117, 130–31
service interruptions, of online banks, 81–82
7-Eleven store, money orders from, 72
Sheeran, Ed, 30
sheet music, print royalties from, 20
Shoeboxed, 204
short term bond fund, via Vanguard, 148
Sibelius, music transcription on, 33
side hustle, 28–30, 36, 225; non-music related, 34–35; studio work as, 31; tech jobs as, 32–33
Simple IRA, 132
SIPC. *See* Securities Investor Protection Corporation
SiriusXM. *See* Internet radio
SIR studios, as side hustle, 32
smile, for side hustles, 36
Snoop Dogg, 3, 47
social media, buying success on, 40

social security, 122; retirement compared to, 116; taxes for, 191
social security card: organization of, 52–53; security for, 96
Solo 401(k), 131
SoundBetter, as side hustle, 31
SoundClick, beats sold on, 31
sound engineering, as side hustle, 32
Sound Recording Special Payments Fund, of unions, 25–26
S&P 500. *See* Standard & Poor's 500 index
speculative investing, 140
SPF. *See* union special fund monies
split costs, in band, 40
sponsorship monies, 23–24, 41
Spotify. *See* digital service providers
Spousal IRA, 131
spreadsheets, 49–50; accounting documents on, 57; budget using, 43, 63; to track receipts, 202–3
Springsteen, Bruce, 188
spyware, personal information obtained by, 99
Stage Ops, production work at, 33
standard deductions, to taxes, 194
Standard & Poor's 500 index (S&P 500), 136, 143, 159, 230
Starbucks, 35, 43
state disability insurance program (SDI), 182, 191
Stein, Ben, 113
Stewart, Rod, 30
stock index, 143
stock market, 153, 157–59, 172; from brokerage firm access, 74; risk in, 120; terms for, 141–42; time effect on, 14
stocks, 136, 150–51, 158; through Fidelity, 174–75; rebalancing of, 140; in retirement accounts, 120; as securities, 139
Straight Talk on Investing (Brennan), 161
student loans, "deferment" strategy for, 108

studio work, as side hustle, 31
subscription services, Rocket Money relation to, 44
success, financial: alternate revenue streams relation to, 2–3, 225; frugal lifestyle for, 41; personal finance for, 9
Superior Staging, production work at, 33
surplus, in cash flow analysis, 60
survey companies, as side hustle, 35
Survey Monkey. *See* survey companies, as side hustle
Swagbucks. *See* survey companies, as side hustle
synchronization fees (synch fee), 19; master-use fees compared to, 21–22; from user-generated content, 20

"target-dated fund," for retirement, 120
tax-advantaged retirement accounts, 6, 125, 137–38, 149, 152, 230–31; contribution limits for, 121; Roth IRA as, 118
taxes, 8, 11, 15–16, 48, 189, *198*; accountant for, 46, 190, 206–12; avoidance methods for, 196–97; capital gains, 140, 193, 230; deductions to, 194–95, 199–200; estate, 216–17, 221; income, 123, 190–93; on investments, 152, 160; for LLC, 54; retirement account advantages for, 6, 118, 125–32, 137–38, 149, 152, 230–31; spreadsheets to prepare for, 49–50
tax return, 190
teachers, music: music transcription for, 33; as side hustle, 28–29
tech jobs, as side hustle, 32–33
telemarketer, as side hustle, 35
television show: live performance monies from, 22; synch fee from, 20
1040 ESO, tax form, 193

1099, tax form, 50, 193
terms: general finance, 134–35; investment, 135–37, 138–41, 142–43; stock market, 141–42
theft: bank protecting from, 67; identity, 53, 92–93, 96, 98, 103, 104, 186
theme park performance, as side hustle, 30
therapy, retail, 45
ticker symbol, 142
ticket agency, as side hustle, 34
TikTok, 224; buying followers on, 40
time, as personal finance barrier, 14–15
time horizon, 140; investment relation to, 6, 150, 227
tips: for budget, 43; for cost-cutting, 44–46; for side hustles, 36
Toro, car rental on, 42
Total Bond Market Index, Vanguard, 151, 229
Total International Stock Market Fund, Vanguard, 151, 229
Total Stock Market Index Fund, Vanguard, 151, 229
trade, 141
Traditional IRA, 117, 118, 119, 125–26, 196–97; employer based retirement plan transferred to, 121; withdrawal from, 122
transportation costs, money saved on, 42
TransUnion, 95; credit reports from, 51, 90, 101
trust: brand recognition relation to, 78–79; of financial advice, 166
trustee, in estate planning, 8, 56, 220–21, 231
tuition refund insurance, 186
Tupac, 32
TurboTax, 210
Twain, Mark, 1
two-factor authentication (2FA), 99
Tyson, Eric, 179

Uber. *See* ride share companies
Uber Eats. *See* food delivery
UCLA Extension, personal finance classes at, 10–11
umbrella insurance, 187
uninsured and underinsured motorist protection, auto insurance for, 183
union reuse fees, 26
union special fund monies (SPF), 25–26
United States Department of Justice, 108
Upwork. *See* freelance platforms
user-generated content: master-use fees from, 21–22; synch fee from, 20
The US Treasury, 135
utilities, saving money on, 45

Vanguard, 151, 229; mutual index fund of, 152; short term bond fund via, 148
The Vanguard Target Retirement 2060 Fund, 120
variances, in budget, 63
VIP package monies, live performance monies relation to, 22–23
Visa credit card, 88
visas, organization of, 52
vision insurance, 182
visual media, master-use fees from, 21
Volunteer Income Tax Assistance (VITA), 210

W2, tax form, 193
W4, tax form, 50, 192–93
wallet, organization of, 55
WalletHub, 95
Wall Street Journal, 143
wants, difference between needs and, 11, 42
warranty documents, 55

wealth, 135, 232; assets and liabilities relation to, 145; tax avoidance strategies for, 231
wealth assessment, on net worth statement, 57–58
The Wealthy Barber, 13
websites: print royalties from, 20; security of, 101
Weekly Payroll Withholdings, as taxes, 192
Wellness Coverage, pet insurance for, 185
Wells Fargo, 78
West, Kanye, 3, 225
what-if analysis, in cash flow analysis, 61
Wiley, 63
will, for estate planning, 8, 56, 217–18, 231–32, 234; trust compared to, 221

Wired, online bank security article by, 81
wire transfer services, from banks, 70
withdrawals, from retirement accounts, 122, 127–29; 457(b), 130; SEP IRA, 131; Traditional IRA, 126

Xzibit (rapper), 15

Yahoo Finance, 144
yield, 139
YouTube: master-use fees from, 21–22; music education on, 39; user-generated content on, 20

Zelle, 72

About the Authors

Bobby Borg, MCM, is a former major label, independent, and DIY recording/touring artist with more than thirty years of experience working alongside the most respected musicians, songwriters, managers, producers, and A&R executives in the music industry. Currently, Borg is an adjunct professor at the famed USC Thornton School of Music, where he teaches music industry communications and DIY music marketing. He is also the author of several widely used books about the music industry including *Business Basics for Musicians*, *Music Marketing for the DIY Musician*, and *Introduction to Music Publishing for Musicians* published by Rowman & Littlefield. Borg also runs a YouTube channel where he educates musicians about music marketing, business, and finance and writes numerous articles for several music industry blogs. A lifelong learner, Borg holds a BA in professional music from Berklee College of Music, certificates in marketing management, project management, and instructor development from UCLA, and a master's degree in communications management (Phi kappa Phi) from the University of Southern California. Borg also completed numerous finance courses at UCLA, including personal finance, security analysis, financial analysis, behavioral finance, and investing, and has also taught his own class on personal finance at Musicians Institute. Walking the walk, Borg is debt-free, has a fully funded emergency fund, and a modest net worth. He lives in Los Angeles, California.

Britt Hastey, MBA, is the department chair of the Business Administration Department at Los Angeles City College. He began his career at LACC in 2001 as a full-time faculty member and took over as department chair in 2011. Britt is also an adjunct professor at UCLA, University of Massachusetts, and Chapman University (where he was awarded Faculty of the Year in 2004). He both teaches and develops curriculum for numerous business disciplines, including economics, management, marketing, and personal finance. Britt also serves as an advisory board member for the Highako Academy and the UCLA Financial Programs Council. Prior to his career in education, he was a financial analyst for Collectech Systems in Thousand Oaks, California, and marketing manager for the law offices of Hamilton and Samuels in Newport Beach, California. Britt holds an MBA from Chapman University and a BA in corporate finance from California State University, Fullerton. Britt also attended Cal Western School of Law, completing coursework in constitutional law, contracts, corporate law, criminal law, and property. When not teaching, Britt enjoys volunteering time in his community. His hobbies include modifying cars, watching sports, working out, cooking, and head-banging to his favorite 1980s rock bands. Britt currently lives in Los Angeles with no wife, no kids, and no debt.

www.ingramcontent.com/pod-product-compliance
Lightning Source LLC
Chambersburg PA
CBHW032021230426
43671CB00005B/159